T0345924

Strategy

Management: Mastering Complexity
Volume 3

Fredmund Malik

Strategy

Navigating the Complexity of the New World

Translated from German by Jutta Scherer,
js textworks (Munich, Germany)

Campus Verlag
Frankfurt/New York

The original edition was published in 2011 by Campus Verlag with the title
Strategie. Navigieren in der Komplexität der Neuen Welt.
All rights reserved.

ISBN 978-3-593-50611-1 Print
ISBN 978-3-593-43536-7 E-Book (PDF)
ISBN 978-3-593-43535-0 E-Book (EPUB)

Cover design: Hißmann, Heilmann, Hamburg
Typesetting: Campus Verlag GmbH, Frankfurt-on-Main
Printing office and bookbinder: Beltz Bad Langensalza
Printed in Germany

www.campus.de

*For the early thinkers on accurate navigation
and reliable strategies for the
Great Transformation21:
Aloys Gälweiler, Cesare Marchetti und Sidney Schoeffler*

How I Look at Management

Management is the driving force wherever a number of people pursue common goals they can only achieve by sharing the work and the knowledge.

Management is also the governing body in any institution of society—whether it is a business enterprise, a university, a hospital, a public authority, or any other kind of organization.

It is management's duty to give direction to those managed. This includes thinking through the organization's mission, determining its objectives, and organizing its resources for the results to be achieved.

Management is the organ of society which makes everything function properly.

Right and Good Management, in My Definition, Is...

... the function of society which enables its organizations and systems to function properly

This also includes responsible leadership and governance.

It takes right management to effectively transform a society's resources into meaningful results and value. Under this comprehensive concept, management also includes enabling people to make their contribution to the proper functioning of their organizations. As such, management provides purpose, orientation, structure, and performance, thus implementing political and societal responsibility and ethics.

Management—Mastering Complexity

One of the greatest challenges for management is presented by the exponentially growing complexity and dynamic change of today's globally interlinked systems. These profound changes are what I refer to as "The Great Transformation21"[1].

Management, in my mind, is *mastering complexity*, which is why I chose this title for my six-volume book series. It is the perspective that provides the most effective access to management in all its aspects and enables us to find the best solutions.

As far as the scientific foundation is concerned, my management systems are rooted in three sciences of complexity: systemics, cybernetics, and

---

1 How and why I use the term "Great Transformation21" is explained in the glossary section in the appendix to this volume.

bionics. I see systemics as the theory of the coherent whole, cybernetics as the theory of functioning, and bionics—at least the way I use it—as enabling managers to transfer nature's evolutionary solutions to their organizations in order to maximize performance.

This is what makes my management theory so very different from conventional approaches: It provides clarity where there is currently confusion, contradiction, arbitrariness, and the indiscriminate adoption of management fashions. Above all, I have long taken the subject far beyond the teachings of business theory and business administration, which has led to fundamental management innovations and provided new solutions to a number of management problems.

Management—Operating System for Organizations

In terms of its significance and impact, management is comparable to the operating systems in computers. Just like the proper function of a computer is enabled by its operating system, the proper functioning of organizations is enabled by the "operating system called management." In my view, right management is the operating system for organizations of any size and kind—a system that is capable of evolving.

Management—Profession of Effectiveness.

Managers are the people who fulfill this function and pursue it as a profession. This includes doing what is right for the organization, and doing it well. That is why consider management to be the *profession of effectiveness* in complex systems.

For people in the 21st century, it is just as important to master the basic skills of right management and self-management as reading and writing have been ever since the 18th century. Today, management is the key competence that makes people employable and effective in organizations. In any organization, accomplishments on the job are predominantly owed to what I call "right and good management". It is the key prerequisite to ensure that, in addition to economic resources, also things like talent, intelligence, creativity, information, knowledge, and insights are transformed into results.

Management *for people* and management *for organizations* are the dimensions of applying my wholistic management systems. They help create the conditions in which people can transform their strengths into performance, and thus to be successful and to find meaning and fulfillment in their work.

St. Gallen, 2013
Fredmund Malik

Contents

Part IV
Following the Change: Success Factors for Your Current Business

Preface

Strategic Solutions for ᴿEvolutions

This book describes my strategic solutions for the ᴿEvolutions of the New World, which—although already under way—have yet to be recognized for what they are. That is why most of the measures taken so far are ineffective, with some even having a destructive impact on society.

What I call the New World will be the result of one of the largest global transformations of business and society that has ever taken place. I call it "The Great Transformation21".[2]

The New Challenges

This transformation involves the danger of a social meltdown. At the same time, it also offers a chance for a new economic miracle to bring about a better and more humane social order where organizations function reliably.

What particular course this development will take depends, among other things, on the solutions, methods and tools that leadership elites worldwide can resort to in facing these challenges. It depends on which of the solutions at hand they can identify as genuine solutions, and which they ultimately opt for. One thing is certain: conventional means will not suffice to master the complexity of this transformation, as they have caused much of the current global crisis.

---

2 Why and how I have been using this name since 1997 is explained in the glossary section of this book.

A strong driving force arises from the strategic solutions themselves that I am presenting here. They contribute their share so the upcoming revolutions will happen quickly, while—contrary to previous revolutions—manifesting itself as an innovative breakthrough rather than a violent upheaval.

They liberate us from both, long outdated forms of management and organization and the grotesque limitations of todays's social and political problem-solving processes.

Since 2011 my *"Manifesto for Corporate ᴿEvolution"* has been laid down in my book *Corporate Policy and Governance*, the second volume in my series *Management: Mastering Complexity*. Many of the developments outlined there—and even before—have meanwhile materialized, first and foremost the beginning collapse of the financial system. Further profound changes, such as in technology and the sciences as well as in people's social value structures—in particular those of the younger generation—, in their perspective on and perception of the world, have progressed to a point where they cannot be stopped anymore, so they should be accelerated instead and directed along more constructive paths wherever possible.

So, what most people believed impossible at the time of the above publications became a reality just a few years later. In 2008 I wrote that knowledge would outrank money and information would outrank power. The ongoing self-destruction of the financial system proves my first point; the ever-increasing global impact of the social media proves the second. Ruling and leading will never be the same again.

The financial crisis itself, however, will not be a central topic in this book. I have published everything that needed to be said in this respect in the course of the past 15 years; now I let the facts speak for themselves. The scenarios I have presented—some of them as early as in the 1990s—have come true. The basic pattern of this development is "deflationary depression", accompanied by social impoverishment and revolution—that is, unless economists and politicians do a radical rethink and change their course of action. That is why this book is dominated not so much by analyses as it is by solutions and the tools required for implementation.

The Right Knowledge

The knowledge society in the stricter sense is another topic I will not elaborate on here. I have addressed it in my book *Corporate Policy*.

Rather, what I make available here is the strategic knowledge that enables top managers in all kinds of organizations to tackle the challenges of the Great Transformation21 reliably, quickly, and effectively. The means to do that are my Management Systems® and the navigation, information, and control systems they include, as well as my strategy concepts and about a dozen new and greatly improved methods and tools.

Many of the pioneers among the top managers applying my management systems are left speechless by the power and speed at which problems are solved and more and more often resolved. Particularly effective are the high-performance processes of the social technology of Syntegration which helps master even huge and highly complex challenges better than ever before.

Just like in earlier phases of epoch-making transformation, almost everything is going to change fundamentally and radically. But while past revolutions were driven by machines, the imminent revolution will be driven by a new functioning of societal organizations, of their management at all levels, of their strategies and methods—including the levers of cybernetic self-organization and self-control.

My cordial thanks go to Mag. Tamara Bechter and Dr. Sonja Böni for their enormously professional support with the new edition of what are so far three volumes of this series. Without their help I could have hardly accomplished the task.

St. Gallen, 2013
Fredmund Malik

The Right Strategy for the Great Transformation21

The Great Transformation21—as I have been referring to the transition from the Old to the New World—will be larger than any other social transformation we have seen so far, as it will span the entire globe.

The more intensely I studied the effective but also explosive power of the Great Transformation and the relevant strategic solutions, the tighter became the limits of language. Describing the complexity of globally interconnected systems and finding words for the simultaneousness of their change dynamics is just as difficult a task as putting a Beethoven symphony in words. Wherever I turn there is a lack of terms to describe the new, its many forms and dimensions, and above all the enormous speed of change as well as the unknowable that comes with it.

The usual superlatives—all the "super" and "mega" terms—, even if they were not as trite as they are, would never suffice to capture the scope of the Great Transformation. Apart from that, these terms originated in the Old World, so they can hardly convey any more than the Old World's limited power of imagination. Still, occasionally I have to use these terms for lack of better ones (at least to date).

If, for instance, the new methods introduced in this book enable even the most complex decisions to be taken and implemented 100 times faster, to increase team efficiency by more than 80 times, and to find solutions based on maximum consensus in just three days where even the smallest compromise was previously blocked by social gaps, and if this power of solution has led to success in hundreds of applications, without exception—what terms could be considered adequate for such achievements, when the aim is to describe the new dimensions of effectiveness but avoid both grandiloquence and advertising slang?

Historically, previous transformation of a similar kind—in particular in technology and science—have always spawned a new language because the new could not be put in old words. In the social and political sphere, however, new terms will often gain ground when the change itself progresses, or even later than that. For instance, people in the Renaissance age did not know they were experiencing the Renaissance—a term coined as late as in the 19th century. And it was more than 10 years after Columbus had landed in "India" (1492), in 1503, that someone else realized that a "mundus novus", something completely new, had been discovered—a fact that never occurred to the discoverer Columbus himself in his lifetime. Amerigo Vespucci had never set foot on the continent called "America"—which, however, was rightfully named after him, for he was the one who ultimately identified it.

The Revolution in the Great Transformation21

The Great Transformation from the Old to the New World will fundamentally—and almost completely—change *what* people do, *why* they do it and *how* they do it. It will also change *who* we are and what concept of the world we have.

It will revolutionize the way society and its organizations function. Functioning twice as well at half the money is just one of many challenges that most people consider impossible to solve—although its solution is already being practiced.

In just a few years' time it will be with incomprehension and pity that we think back of the sluggish political decision-making processes we have today, of coalitions getting in their own way, of corporate management bodies paralyzing themselves, of slowly moldering change processes, of lethargy and resignation in so many organizations, of monstrous mega conferences that had no impact, and of the cluelessness of global organizations.

With the challenges we are currently facing and which seem to have appeared out of the blue—such as the complete turnaround in energy policy, the rotten financial system, the global debt mountain, and the increasing decay of the social fabric—the limitations of our present problem-solving approaches have become more obvious than ever.

The leaders of these organizations will be pitied and admired at the same time for having given their best and having tried to do their duties even under such inhumane conditions—although their efforts have increasingly failed, as even the most outstanding driver cannot win a race if he is given an outdated car.

Innovative, Intelligent and Right Solutions

At the same time, people will wonder why the new solutions were not made available to those leaders much earlier, in particular as they had long been published by us and applied successfully in hundreds of cases. Anyone who knows these solutions will immediately see how they offer new ways to end crises, and even to use these crises to make inroads into the New World.

For me, the ethical mission resulting from all that is to ensure with all my might that the necessary information about these new, global, society-saving solutions will be spread.

The funds to be freed up by the new solutions—and which are presently and pointlessly tied up in old structures and processes—will be used to create the innovations of the New World, instead of continuing to finance outdated approaches from the previous century.

For instance, one key task will be to establish the new type of high-performance educational institution—preferably outside the current educational system, as this will be the fastest way—and teach the new generation right from the outset of their student careers the leadership skills that, had they been in place, would have had the potential to prevent the current calamity. They include wholistic and networked thinking, familiarity with systemics as the science of entities, practical application of cybernetics as the science of functioning, and the ability to leverage bionics by using evolution's best solutions to innovate societal organizations.

This would strengthen our social solution intelligence by several orders of magnitude, because all of the above can be accomplished in less than half the time and in one integrated and in itself fully compatible study course.

The present book—just like the other volumes of the series *Management: Mastering Complexity*—presents the knowledge and approaches required to prevent the imminent social disaster and bring about new prosperity as well as a well-functioning social order well beyond the current political categories of left-wing and right-wing.

Strategy: Navigating Effectively Through the Complexity of the Great Transformation21

In the six parts of this book, we will first look at the dynamics of the Great Transformation21, its inherent risks of crisis and its opportunities, as well as the labor pains of the New World.

After that, we will deal with the astonishingly effective cybernetic systems for strategic navigation, the strategy maps required, and the empirical quantification of existing and new businesses from where the new territory of innovation will be explored.

Finally, I will show the invariant patterns in the tidal currents of great transformations, as well as the resulting economic dynamics and the strategies to deal with them.

In the last part of the book I will describe the most revolutionary tools for social change known to date: the social methodology of Syntegration, which enables us to master ground-breaking strategic change with great precision and "at the speed of light," compared to conventional approaches, The Syntegration technology helps to manage the growth and size of companies with ease and even turn them into strengths, specifically in cases where conventional approaches have proven to be futile and to paralyze rather than strengthen organizational performance.

The almost magic efficacy of these methods is based on cybernetic communication processes which, to an extent previously unimaginable, enhance collective intelligence and generate social energies. The simultaneous use of innovative system design tools creates highly effective intelligence and power centers for successfully mastering the challenges of even hypercomplex systems as well as their control and regulation. "Mega Change of Mega Systems at Mega Speed" will then turn out to be more than just a pretentious advertising slogan, instead denominating a program to open a bright future in a New World.

The topic threaded throughout the entire book series is how to master the Great Transformation21 and its unprecedented complexity. In the following graph, this complexity is depicted by means of the double S-Curve, indicating the substitution of something new for something old. The Old World is replaced by a New World.

This replacement generates the revolutionary socio-political and economic distortions and crises we are faced with today. They represent the labor pains of a New World.

This third volume of the series *Management: Mastering Complexity*, I describe how the right strategy contributes to the development of an effective solution.

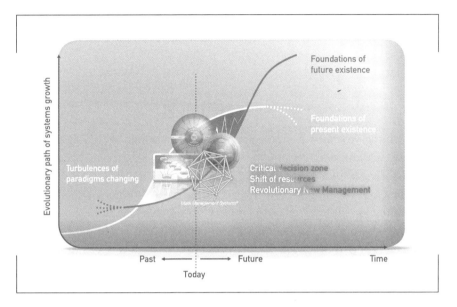

Figure 1: The Great Transformation21

Key Propositions

1. Both the world of business and society as a whole are going through one of the most fundamental transformations that ever occurred in history. An Old World ends as a New World is born.
2. The global economic crisis is part of the New World's labor pains.
3. Main causes of the global economic crisis were the wrong corporate strategies pursued in the Old World, as well as its traditional management and corporate governance concepts. They were less and less able to cope with the present complexity and dynamics of globally interconnected systems. Misguided economic policies were of minor importance.
4. The self-destructing corporate strategies became visible almost over night when leading financial institutions collapsed and their management systems failed.
5. The wrong strategies previously pursued were based on misleading success criteria. They encouraged management behaviors that were harmful to the system and affected large parts of it. This caused a historically unprecedented global misallocation of resources as well as the greatest debt load of all times and across all segments of society.
6. Therefore, effective solutions for the global economic crisis have to comprise much more than government-level programs: they have to encompass a new way of functioning for societal organizations as well as a profound change in the currently dysfunctional control loops which can be accomplished through new management systems. Solutions meeting these criteria are the cybernetic-wholistic management systems and the strategy concept described in this book.
7. The best model for the new functioning and the new management required for it is provided by natural organisms with their communication and control systems, their sensory and neuronal systems. Their

cybernetic laws of function have been integrated in my Wholistic Management Systems and the associated strategy concept.

8. Strategies for complexity have a very different logic and very different points of reference compared to the Old World's traditional strategies. They leverage the logic of evolution, and are thus set up to successfully deal with the unknown and the unknowable.

9. My strategy concept focuses on two areas:
   a. At the operational level of companies, it indicates the right direction with utmost precision and at maximum speed
   b. At the management level, it brings about the new functioning through flexibility, adaptability, and coherence, while at the same time ensuring viability through self-regulation and self-organization. The control principle is real-time control

10. Its foundation is a new kind of knowledge and new methods for enhancing intelligence and innovation in information, communication and management processes, based on insights from bionics and cybernetics which are now applicable to management.

11. Under this new strategy concept, navigation parameters that have proved useful are kept on board but are integrated in a more comprehensive, wholistic management and navigation system. In that system, they are reconfigured to obtain new meanings, and thus to have different control effects in the system of corporate management. For instance, profit and growth will continue to be important in the New World, but they will assume another function.

12. Reaching beyond economic dimensions, the new strategies will also provide solutions for the non-economic problems related to increasing societal disorientation and instability, as well as for mobilizing human energy, performance, and creativity. By cultivating new values, the new strategies will bring a new motivation for people. One focus of the new strategy will be a new meaning.

13. Together with other elements of my management systems, the new strategy concept also leads to a new social and economic order. I call it the *New Functionism*. This new order replaces both capitalism and socialism, as their traditional polarity prevents effective solutions for the new challenges. However, the *New Functionism* will comprise the best of both previous social orders: e.g., the performance principle from capitalism and the principle of solidarity from socialism.

A Word On the Terms Used

In addition to the glossary in the appendix section, it is important to explain a few terms at the beginning of each volume.

Bionics Coinage combining "biology" and "technics." It refers to the interdisciplinary field of research which studies nature's evolutionary solutions to apply their principles for the benefit of humans. So far, bionic findings have mainly been used in the field of technology. However, nature's solution can also be applied to management, e.g. to improve the functioning of organizations.

Control and Orientation Variables are terms used in the Malik-Gälweiler Navigation System. Control variables are the parameters an organization needs to get under control; orientation variables are the pieces of information which indicate whether the organization is under control.

Creative Destruction Term created by the Austrian economist Joseph Schumpeter. It refers to entrepreneurial innovativeness and the resulting large-scale substitution processes where the existing is replaced by the new.

Cyber-Tools Methods and approaches to diagnose and shape the cybernetic functionality of organizations.

Direttissima Name I use for the—methodically—fastest way to the right strategy.

Functioning is the most general term I could find to describe the reliable and optimal working of an organization in line with its basic purpose.

Great Transformation21 Profound secular transformation of business and society into the 21ˢᵗ-century society of complexity. What exactly this transformation entails is described in my 1990 book entitled "Krisengefahren in der Weltwirtschaft" "Risks of Crises in the Global Economy", and ever since then on a regular basis in my monthly management letters. The first time I used the term was in my 1997 book on corporate governance entitled "Wirksame Unternehmensaufsicht" "Effective Corporate Governance", where I dedicated a chapter to the dimensions of the ongoing metamorphosis of business and society, which was already recognizable back then, and on that basis presented my suggestions for right and good governance.

The term "Great Transformation" was first used by the Hungaro-Austrian economic sociologist Karl Polanyi in 1944. He used it in a similar sense but referring to a completely different era and to different manifestations, above all the spread of market economics and the nation state. Also, Peter F. Drucker used the term "transformation" in the headline of the introduction to his 1993 book "Post Capitalist Society," where he sketches out, among other things, the great lines of development of capitalism to the knowledge society and from the nation state to the transnational megastate.

By choosing this term, I am integrating some of its previous meanings to describe the generalized concept of a fundamental transformation process in the 21ˢᵗ century—a process characterized, among other things, by proliferating complexity, the emergency of globally interconnected systems and the dynamics of self-accelerating change. As a result, we are facing historically new challenges. Mastering them will require radically innovative bionic forms of organization, cybernetic systems for management, governance and leadership, and social technologies of no less than revolutionary effectiveness.

Innovation Phase in which something new, by being introduced to the market, starts to become effective in society.

Institution Most general term used for all kinds of societal organizations, both in business and the public sphere, as well as for the systems and rules guiding social behavior. In this sense, a business enterprise is both an institution and an organization.

The Integrierte ManagementSystem (IMS) One of the three basic models in my management systems, along with the General Management Model (GMM) and the Managerial Effectiveness Model (MEM).

Invention Stage within the overall transformation process in the course of which innovations are developed—from first inception to market launch.

Malik Gälweiler Navigation system / MG Navigator Complete and universally valid system for developing an effective strategy and reliably steering an organization.

Management System Audit MSA Method to reliably analyze my Integrated Management System (IMS) in an organization.

Master Controls The most fundamental regulations effective in an entire system, all the way to its peripheral elements, irrespective of their source— be it laws of nature, structural conditions, or man-made regulating decisions in the sense of principles or guidelines. The most important Master Controls are decisions and principles that bring about the cybernetic *self*-capabilites of a system, which are self-regulation, self-organization, self-direction, and self-control.

Old World and New World Pair of terms relating to the fundamental and secular change I refer to as "the Great Transformation21," in which the existing order is replaced by a new order.

Operational and Strategic Terms to describe the levels of reliable navigation of an enterprise or organization

Operations Room Informational sensory environment in which real-time decisions are made and implemented.

PIMS Look-Alike Term used in PIMS research to describe the similarity of businesses.

PIMS Par Term used in PIMS research, referring to the indicators of potential performance as opposed to actual perfomance.

Profit Impact of Market Strategy PIMS   So far the largest empirical-quantitative strategic research program ever carried out worldwide, in which the "Laws of the Marketplace" were discovered for both existing and new businesses, or start-ups (see Volume 3, Parts IV and V).

(R)Evolution   Coinage made up of "revolution" and "evolution." I use the term to describe a) the ongoing, profound changes taking place in the course of the Great Transformation21 and b) the innovations in management, leadership, governance, as well as their rules, systems and tools, that are required to cope with these changes.

S-Curves   Describe the typical, S-shaped course of healthy growth processes.

Sensitivity Model® (SensiMod®)   System-cybernetic procedure used to model the cybernetic regulation loops in complex systems and their cause-effect relationships. Its early development was under the guidance of Frederic Vester.

Solution-Invariant Customer Problem   One of the key terms and the "Archimedian point" of corporate strategy. It refers to the motive for a purchase, irrespective of existing solutions. For instance, a wrist watch is one of several possible solutions to the solution-invariant problem of indicating the time.

Start-up Business   Stage of a strategy that begins when something new, after having been invented and developed, is put on the market. The start-up phase markes the beginning of the actual innovation, which must always be defined based on market success and which requires a very specific strategy.

Strategy   Acting the right way, even when we do not know what the future will bring, and the rules required for right action. Strategy determines the path of development for an institution. The right strategy lays out the principles and guidelines that will guide an organization's activities in the long run. These principles and guidelines will be changed as newly arising circumstances require.

Substitution   Something existing being replaced by something new (see "Creative Destruction"). Examples include the replacement of analog photography by digital imaging, of terrestrial by mobile telephony, or of manual labor by machines.

Sustainability   Concept to determine time horizons for thoughts, decisions and actions.

Syntegration   High-performance social methodology which helps to master complex challenges and problems by simultaneously leveraging the knowledge of a large number of people. The procedure comprises a self-coordinating cybernetic communication proves and the synchronous application of cyber-tools.

Terms   Refers to the usual differentiation by short-, mid- and long-term. Defining management dimensions in this way, however, is misleading and thus extremely risky. Instead, the correct distinction is by "operative" vs. "strategic": this is the only way to arrive at the right timing, never the other way round. After all, there are long-term decisions that are largely operative and there are short-term decisions that have an enormous strategic impact.

Time Constants and Dead Time   Key terms within the Malik-Gälweiler Navigation System. They refer to the time elapsing between the point when the need for action is first identified and the point when strategic measures become effective, specifically generating new profit potential.

Part I:
Strategy for the Great Transformation21

Part I will deal with the Why referring to precisely the strategic management I present in this book.
Parts II through V will describe the What and Whereby.
Part VI will deal with the How.

Chapter 1

What Strategy Looks Like
When the Future is Unknown

Strategy means doing the right thing when we do not know what the future will bring but have to act nevertheless. In this context, "doing nothing" is considered one of numerous conceivable actions..

Strategy means, even before you start working on something, acting in such a way that you will be successful in the long run.

Strategy is not about future decisions but about the future effects of today's decisions, which also include non-decisions.

*

The first sentence reflects my own position. The second is by Aloys Gälweiler, the third by Peter F. Drucker. Each of these three sentences describes, in its very own way, the universal core of strategy that is and has always been valid for any age and time, irrespective of whether or not decision makers were aware of it, which made them build the wrong or the right strategies.

Strategy is dealing with an irremediable lack of knowledge. If we knew everything we needed to know to take far-reaching decisions we would not need a strategy but ordinary planning by deriving conclusions from existing data and information. The fact of the matter is, however, that we can never know everything we need to know because as executives we have to work and manage in the hypercomplexity of globally interconnected large-scale systems and in the dynamics of ever-accelerating change. We also face a constant lack of information and knowledge, as these systems are inscrutable by nature and will often change faster than we can make decisions.

As we will see in the next section, these three "definitions" of strategy are of particular, historically perhaps unprecedented importance for the Great

Transformation21, as the ongoing profound changes are creating a New World with many unknown variables.

All three positions do, however, not presume that we do not or cannot know anything about the future. Often, we could know far more than we would imagine, but to achieve that we have to let go of obsolete approaches and ways of thinking and focus on new methods, such as those I present in this book.

Managers often do not even know what and how much knowledge exists in the company because it is distributed across the organization and they do not know how to mobilize it. This is why critical knowledge is often dormant, again mainly due to unsuitable methods for which I suggest new alternatives here.

More often still, managers believe they know things they cannot really know, such as whether the crisis is really over. This creates a delusive sense of security and causes them to hold on to the old systems.

The most dangerous part of not knowing, however, is that we often do not know what exactly we need to know in order to design the right strategy. That was one of the main causes of the economic crisis, because strategies were based on information that was completely useless for strategic decisions and even misleading—to wit, on operational rather than strategic data. The solutions I present in this book also address this particular situation.

Gälweiler's, Drucker's, and my own positions are solutions for the above-mentioned cases of non-knowledge and for eliminating serious associated errors. These errors, some of which are systematically disseminated as false doctrines, are poisoning both the theory and practice of strategy; they are also the reason why we see corporate failures happen over and over again.

If these errors had been known the debacle of the financial industry would probably not have happened, as it was largely caused by such errors—which in the financial sector were committed with particular skill and perfection. It is therefore simply wrong when people say, in grave voices and with a knowing air, that it was impossible to foresee the crisis. Its seeds had long been sown in the strategies of numerous companies, including most financial institutions and regulators. Like them, many other influential and thought-leading organizations, such as rating agencies, consultancies, media firms and business schools, were set on a path of self-destruction.

What they celebrated as roaring successes for years—sometimes until just a few days before their demise—had actually been the "writing on the wall." Even the timing had been relatively easy to determine, albeit only with tools not affected by these errors. The demise of the U.S. automotive industry is one case in point: the fact it was caused by the wrong strategies was not revealed with hindsight—it had started to become apparent as early as in the mid-1970s.

On the other hand, there are numerous examples of companies where these errors were not committed and which have been managed excellently for decades and more: Nestlé since the early 1980s, VW since the early 1990s, and Microsoft since it began partnering with IBM. BMW and Warren Buffett's Berkshire Hathaway Group are further examples. Many family businesses—entrepreneurially led companies (ELC) as I call them—largely avoided the glaring mistakes that led to the world economic crisis, because they were not under pressure from the financial markets. Still, even ELCs will need new systems for navigation, information and control in order to cope with the challenges of the Great Transformation.

My own position eliminates, besides other misconceptions, the error of claiming to have knowledge where it is clearly lacking. Strategy therefore has to deal with constitutive non-knowledge, which—as mentioned before—results from the complexity and dynamic interconnectedness of todays's systems within which our actions take place. Bringing constitutive non-knowledge into the equation opens entirely new dimensions of quality in strategy design, and permits elegant solutions where conventional strategic thinking fails.

Gälweiler's position puts an end to the kind of errors that result from incorrect data, as well as to the entirely unnecessary and artificial limitations resulting from the setting of time horizons (short, medium, and long-term) which only obscures people's view of the open time horizon we call the future. By using a new navigation method, this position permits an almost magically effective solution for dealing with complex challenges, a solution that lets us think from the end to the beginning, not vice versa.

Drucker's position puts an end to the false belief that the future is predestined by fate and that we just need to predict it to know what will happen. His position—and this particular aspect is one I have often discussed with him—includes the extraordinarily hopeful thought that we can actively shape the future, rather than having to endure it passively. The resulting ethical mission for the top leadership elite is to go ahead and do just that—for they, and only they, have the necessary means and the power; in addition, they also have highly effective methods available to them today which are described in this book.

Here, I integrate these solutions with further elements to form a new approach to strategic corporate management, pointing out what you need to know in order to search for the right knowledge even under the most complex conditions, and to design and implement strategies that meet the following requirements: right, precise, fast, adaptable, and implementable with real-time control.

Before we get to that point, however, let us take a closer look at the Great Transformation and its drivers.

Chapter 2

The Great Transformation21

Both the word of business and society as a whole are going through one of the most fundamental transformations that ever occurred in history. This transformation can best be pictured as a transition from an Old World to a New World. What looks like an economic crisis on the surface are actually the birth pangs of this New World, in which everything will be different from the way it was before.

When in my 1997 book on corporate governance I chose the name "Great Transformation" for the fundamental change that was already beginning to show, it was plain to see that most organizations of society would face radical changes and those that would master it would fundamentally realign their management systems and the way they basically functioned. All management system components, such as strategy, structure, processes, culture, managers' competencies, policies and missions, as well as navigation, decision-making and problem-solving processes and communication systems would have to be adapted and, for the most part, changed to an extent both radical and revolutionary. This development has been in full swing ever since, and it is accelerating under the influence of an increasingly rapid succession of innovations in almost every relevant field.

This transformation process is far from being over. In just a few years' time, many of today's Global Fortune 500 companies will no longer exist, at least not in their present form. For instance, the U.S. Fortune 500 included eleven homebuilding companies in 2007—none of them is on the list today. Almost all of the corporate "Masters of the Financial Universe", including the most noble ones, have vanished over night. Others will follow and new ones will arise—but they will be very different. Microsoft will have to change dramatically just to keep its global position; the pharmaceutical industry is currently going through its greatest restructuring phase ever.

These are just a few examples, and hardly an industry will be spared. Transformation challenges will be even greater for the public sector. Healthcare and education, public transportation, energy, the trade unions, public administration and governments—they all will not be able to survive with their current structures, processes and decision-making routines. Last but not least, our democratic institutions will face the most profound transformation of their existence.

This transition from the 20th to the 21st century is comparable to the replacement of the agricultural by the industrial society, or of the feudal system by the rule of law and democracy. But judging from the changes we have seen so far, the Transformation21 will be even larger-scale and more profound than any previous transformation of society. Some of the most important differences compared to previous transformations are the unprecedented global scale, the unprecedented degree of global systemic interconnectedness, and the unprecedented pace of change. The superlatives used so far, such as *mega-change*, do not suffice to capture the new dimensions of change.

Historically, transformations of this kind have occurred every 200 to 300 years. One of them happened in the 13th century, marked by the beginning of the Gothic period, the birth of the modern city, the foundation of the first universities as centers of intellectual life, and the formation of the guilds as the dominant social structure.

Another, similarly profound transformation occurred between 1455 and 1517, starting with the invention of printing and then shaped by the Reformation. Milestones of the transformation process included the Renaissance, the discovery of America, the development of the sciences, the revival of medicine science, and the spread of Arab numerals.

The most recent transformation of this order of magnitude began in the mid-18th century. Key events included the Constitution of the United States, the development of the steam engine by James Watt, signaling the beginning of the age of industrialization, as well as the French Revolution and the Napoleonic Wars. Besides altering the political structure of Europe, this transformation also gave rise to modern universities, political parties and their ideologies, and a completely new structure of society in Europe.

The common denominator of these transformational periods is that each time, society and indeed the world changed radically within a period of about 50 years—so radically even that later generations would literally be unable to imagine what their parents' or grandparents' world had been like.

As a result of the current transformation of society, we will see fundamental changes in almost everything *that* we do, and also in *how* we do it and *why* we do it. In some way, even *who* we are will change. We will produce, consume, transport, distribute, and finance in new ways. We will also change the way we communicate, teach and learn, and almost any other human activity. The scientific insights and technological innovations for a new era are already there, and some of them have been used long enough for us to see their transformative power: the internet and the Smartphone are already changing people's lives, the way they work, consume, and communicate, and creating new values and motivations. Still there are many more new developments coming up, and they will increasingly—and more and more radpiyl—take hold.

To cope with such changes and also to drive and shape them, we need equally profound changes in management systems, organizational structures and strategies, as well as in our thinking. In sophisticated knowledge companies, the effects of the New World are already starting to show. One of them is the way we deal with knowledge as a new resource, a tool and a product, as well as the specifics of knowledge workers and knowledge work, and the new ways in which knowledge organizations function.

The Old World Ends as a New World Is Born

For all the above reasons, what is currently happening "out there" is much more than an ordinary financial and economic crisis, by far exceeding what the world can simply "handle" to then return to its previous state.

To this date, changes have already progressed to a point where turning back would be neither possible nor desirable. Just as a caterpillar in a quite dramatic metamorphosis turns into a butterfly, for which everything is different from what it used to be before, only very few things will be the same in the New World as they were in the Old World. For instance, the caterpillar is subject to the laws of geodynamics whereas the butterfly has to persist in the world of aerodynamics, which is quite a difference. To do that, it needs a different system of functions compared to the caterpillar: different sensory capabilities, different neuronal circuits, and a different biological navigation system. And while the laws of geodynamics have not ceased to apply to the butterfly, their relevance has dramatically changed.

Correspondingly, the Old World was governed mainly by the laws of money and economics, whereas the New World will be governed by the laws of information, knowledge, insight, complexity, and the dynamics of strongly interlinked systems.

It does not take any forecasts to realize this. It is visible from various new elements which have been making their way into the global societies ever since Soviet communism collapsed, if not before, and which have been changing the functional rules of society at an increasing pace. The collapse of communism was triggered, driven and supported by new realities that were coming into effect at the time. Of course it is also true that the economic system as such had failed, but the cybernetic forces of control and communication had a much stronger impact. Knowledge beats money, and information beats power—as I also wrote in my book *Corporate Policy and Governance*.

This takes us straight into the heart of the New World. One of its most outstanding features will be its proliferating, exponentially increasing complexity, which will accompany us throughout this book.

Megachange in Megasystems

I will begin by grouping the key elements of the Great Transformation around five complex drivers: The first is demography, the second is *knowledge and technology*, the third is *ecology*, the fourth is the all-contaminating greatest *debt* of all times, as a key factor of *economics*; the fifth factor results from the interaction of these four major areas: it is *complexity*.

These five factors reinforce and drive each other, creating more and more complexity and confronting an increasing number of organizations with ever greater surprises. Incidents and disturbances are becoming the new norm. Among many other areas this will happen in politics, which in an increasing number of countries is turning into a problem rather than a solution, due to its proliferating complexity and insistence on outdated methods. With the new methods now available this would instantly change.

These drivers involve enormous risks, above all the economic risk of bringing on one of the greatest deflations ever, with an almost total collapse of asset values due to the global debt mountain. That is why I am emphasizing this one aspect of economic life, for it is the crucial economic fact. At the same time, these drivers entail the knowledge and the power to mitigate and master this crisis and create a new society with a new and functional social order.

An essential part of the new solutions is contributed by wholistic and modular management systems, such as those I have modeled after most sophisticated steering and control systems we find in nature, also incorporating nature's laws of functioning. One reason that solutions have to be sought here is that conventional management thinking increasingly fails in the rapidly changing conditions of the New World. The new management systems are fundamentally different from conventional ones, almost to the extent that man's brain and nervous system differ from the simple neuronal circuits of lower organisms.

The Current Crisis as the New World's Birth Pangs

Whether the birth of the New World is going to be smooth or difficult is largely up to us: it all depends on how we deal with these new challenges and what concepts, knowledge, tools, and methods we select as solutions. We will need a new understanding of the network of societal organizations, and a new management approach that treats these organizations as complex, dynamically interconnected, incalculable and unpredictable systems. Compared to conventional management thinking, with its strong focus on economic categories, short-term profits, and generally financial parameters, it is going to be as different as night and day.

Complex systems have their own natural laws. I have pointed this out repeatedly; for instance, in my book *Strategie des Managements komplexer Systeme*[3] ["Strategy of the Management of Complex Systems"] I explained that the logic of a complexity-compatible strategy has to be of an evolutionary nature, just as the strategy itself. Once you have the neces-

---

3 Malik, Fredmund: *Strategie des Managements komplexer Systeme*, 10th revised edition, Berne/Stuttgart, 1984, 2008.

sary knowledge about the laws of complex systems, you can begin to understand, steer, shape and direct them at a meta-level and from a higher perspective. That, however, requires a new kind of knowledge. It provides the basis for my wholistic systems for an entirely new kind of management, which my book *Corporate Policy and Governance* describes for the top level of corporations, and which I will repeatedly refer to in this book on strategy.

It Takes More than Economics to Understand the Global Economic Crisis

The immediate financial and economic dimensions of the Great Transformation cannot be overrated. Its impact will be felt for many years—all the more so as we have not left the most difficult phases of the crisis behind us, as most people seem to think and the media purport. On the contrary: the greatest turbulences are still ahead.

Contrary to widespread opinion, however, these turbulences will not lead to inflation. Instead, we might be experiencing one of the worst *deflations* in history—that is, if we continue to rely on conventional economic tools. Even the governmental austerity programs alone, some of which are quite drastic, are having a deflationary effect in that they are strangling economic activity.

Moreover, these austerity measures will further depress the functionality of public sector organizations, which is already affected by the shortage of funds. Austerity measures never help to make old systems better; they can only make them worse. Unfortunately, conventional thinking knows no alternative. By contrast, the new methods enable organizations to work twice as well at half the cost. So if we accept that the crisis is much more than an economic crisis, even though it may appear to be economic on the surface, and if instead we consider it to be a crisis of functioning, there will be very different and much more powerful solutions coming into focus.

Another factor indicating that the crisis is not primarily an economic one is that almost all economists had failed to foresee the system breakdown of September 2008—although the first signs of it could be seen on the U.S. stock markets a least a year before. With appropriate tools, the imminent dangers could be made visible much earlier, some of them as far back as in the 1990s. I had pointed this out in my book *Effective Top Management* (first published in German in 1997) as well as in my monthly management letters, my other books, and numerous keynote speeches.[4]

As late as in summer 2008, only three months before the Lehman debacle, 98 percent of U.S. economists as well as the German-speaking economic research institutes, almost in unison, forecast a 2.5 to 3.5 percent growth for 2008, and apart from very few, rather infrequent exceptions there was no mention of the storm that had long been gathering and was about to break.[5]

Yet the general blindness for the debacle that was to shake the world only three months later could hardly be blamed on the economists, as is often claimed. It is much more likely to be a sign of something very different going on, something that cannot be detected by the conventional means of economics.

Anglo-Saxon Corporate Governance—A Machine of Destruction

To assess the imminent disaster, one had to look in a completely different direction: to the systematic mismanagement of an increasing number of businesses that had begun in the early 1990s, along with the growing popularity of the shareholder value doctrine. Having originated in the financial sector, it had spread across the real economy at an alarming rate. Aside from cheap loans, it was mainly the money-minded, 100-percent financially oriented corporate strategies that have caused the current crisis, as they led to an unprecedented misallocation of resources and generated the highest debt in history.

There were two main factors that (mis)led managers to believe they were on the right track: first, the supposedly good example of the U.S. economy, whichappeared to be the best in the world because only few people knew that the official numbers were wrong and, due to a 1994 change in statistical methods, glossed over the actual facts. That change, howev-

---

4 Revised and amended version entitled *The Right Corporate Governance* (2012); also see volume 1 of this book series Management. The Essence of the Craft (2010).
5 The rare examples of people who issued timely warnings include Robert Prechter, Paul C. Martin, Gunnar Heinsohn, and Otto Steiger.

er, could only be noticed by genuine experts; it never caught the attention of the media. The second reason is the global dissemination of the shareholder value doctrine through thousands of business schools worldwide, which uncritically adopted value creation and shareholder value strategies and presented them as ultimate truths. Therefore, of the millions of executives with MBA degrees only those who grasp every opportunity to rethink and learn from these past mistakes will master the upcoming challenges well. Solutions exist and are accessible to anyone.

Another contributing factor was the longest bull market in history, as well as constant and seemingly sustainable economic growth, much of which, however, was not growth of the real economy but of the *financial sector*, and which was actually funded through unproductive loans backed by less and less collateral. Additional factors included the influences of rating agencies, consulting firms, investment banks, private equity and hedge funds, the cheers from the media, and—as veritable turbo chargers—the bonus systems.

System Dynamics – Corporate Governance

The variables A through H show the system dynamics of the corporate governance system. The variables reinforce each other in short, positive feedback loops, forming a total of 79 feedback loops which are also interlaced with each other. The system is regulated by only 2 negative feedback control loops coming from the Unions variable.

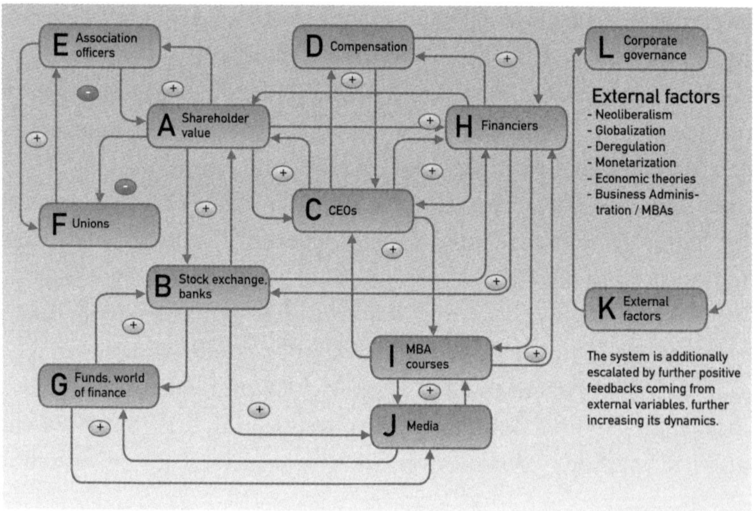

Figure 2: The corporate governance model

The variables A through H show the system dynamics of the corporate governance system. The variables reinforce each other in short, positive feedback loops, forming a total of 79 feedback loops which are also interlaced with each other. The system is regulated by only 2 negative feedback control loops coming from the Unions variable.

All these things were legitimized by national corporate governance codes focusing on *best practice* as a key criterion, neglecting the fact that best practice is something very different from *right* practice—and in this case was even the extreme opposite. Best practice is what everyone does, because everyone else does it, and that is a breeding ground for mass psychological misperceptions and lemming effects.

Back in the 1990s, I captured the growing instabilities in the overall system of corporate governance—which was not visible in the corporate balance sheets—in a cybernetic network model, first manually and later computer-based (see figure 2). It enabled me to reliably conclude that the corporate governance system was *out of control*: of 81 interlinked control loops, only two were stabilizing the system while 79 were destabilizing it. Largely unnoticed by the public, one of the most monstrous self-destruction machines in economic history had been created, and this was commonly believed to be the best economic system ever.

Once the instabilities forming within a system reach a certain level, the system is liable to collapse from one second to the next. It either explodes or implodes. This kind of system behavior is well known to those familiar with ecological systems, as well as to doctors and many managers

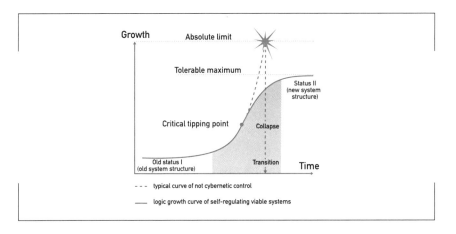

Figure 3: The growth trap

with a science background. Unlike most business school graduates they have learnt about the stability behavior of systems in the course of their studies. The same system laws apply to economic systems as well. Yet belief in unlimited linear growth continues regardless of modern systems research.

Complexity and Management Crisis: The Absence of Neuronal Systems

These system laws by far exceed mere economic dimensions. Conventional management systems can no longer cope with this complexity they have created. The "organisms" of society—i. e., its public and private-sector organizations—lack the sensory organs, steering and control systems to cope with the challenges of fundamental change. Communication and decision-making systems work much too slowly, and with too great a time lag, to permit correct decisions and quick adjustments. Also, many organizations lack the necessary traction systems to implement the decisions taken.

Or, to use a medical metaphor, with conventional management concepts we can fix the "anatomy" of an organization—that is, its structures—and the "physiology" of its processes quite well, but the "neurophysiological" part of conventional thinking (the analogy to management systems) has not kept pace. That, however, is precisely what organizations need to function under the difficult conditions of the Great Transformation with its crisis symptoms.

From the perspective of the higher system level, organizational control, we are facing something that encompasses much more than purely economic dimensions: it is a *crisis of the traditional functioning of society* and an increasing inability to steer and control its institutions.

Traditional forms of organization, as well as planning, decision-making and implementation processes, are often dramatically overwhelmed by the complexity and dynamic nature of today's globally interconnected systems. This is obvious from the way so many political decisions—and even more non-decisions—come to pass in hypercomplex organizational networks. The operating systems of functioning have not kept pace with the increase in complexity. No wonder even the best managers reach their limits when they do not have the necessary system support.

So, metaphorically speaking, the problem is not limited to the "blood circulation"—an analogy for the money cycle—which collapsed with the decline of Lehman Brothers, but goes on to the pending collapse of the societal "nervous systems", and thus of its capability to function.

In different ways, this concerns both private and public-sector organizations: after all, the banking industry would have imploded without immediate governmental intervention and would have pulled the real economy down with it. Public rescue plans, however, cannot do much more than stabilize things for the time being and help gain some breathing space. As important as they may have been in the acute emergency situation, these programs are not a permanent solution because they have not eliminated any of the main causes of the crisis. Instead they have created new ones, including the immense level of public debt which is another problem that had long been smoldering under the surface, as every expert knows, before fiercely erupting, threatening to pull even relatively healthy nations down into the mire of debt.

Launching public rescue programs is almost like giving hard liquor to an alcoholic at the height of his crisis to calm him down, and they have accomplished just that. The disease as such, however, has not been cured. Nor have the billions in additional funds changed all that much in the financial word; instead, they have been used to finance the revival and entrenchment of old structures and, above all, old behavior patterns. Business practices have remained largely unchanged; bonus schemes have yet to be redesigned.

Third Act of the Crisis: Deflation

The propagation of this self-destructive, American-style corporate governance throughout the world has led to the emergence of wrong strategies, of poor management in general, and of the explosive crisis we have on our hands today. If we fail to introduce the right management systems quickly, and in a sufficient number of societal institutions at all relevant levels, and thus to remedy the undesirable developments we have experienced—which is quite possible both technically and organizationally—the odds are that the further course of events will be left to the crisis's destructive economic forces, without any managerial counteraction. Politics alone cannot halt the process—not without the support provided by proper management in thousands of organizations. Otherwise we may well experience a repetition of the crisis of the 1930s, albeit on a much larger scale.

The current global economic crisis is not just one of the many economic disturbances that occur over and over again; nor does it belong in the category of *inflationary* crises. It is a *crisis of deflation. Deflationary crises* are much less frequent than inflationary ones, which is why hardly anybody is familiar with this kind of situation. In the history of the United States there have only been two deflations: one lasted from 1935 to 1942, the other from 1929 to 1932.

Deflation is the collapse of asset prices, from corporate stocks to real estate, precious metals and commodities, all the way to works of art. It is caused by *over-indebtedness* of almost all sectors of society. Starting with national governments, federal states and municipalities and going on to include private sector organizations and businesses, almost everyone has run up substantial debt, relying on the notion that there would be unlimited economic growth and the so-called "values" would keep rising, which has driven up prices to unprecedented highs. We have already passed through this phase: the inflation of share prices, real estate and commodity prices. These prices went up not because corporations were performing so well, or because of the inherent value of certain assets, but because more and more people bought these goods taking out higher and higher loans, blindly believing that prices would keep rising and that their increasing debt did not involve a major risk.

In the next phases of the crisis this debt will have to be repaid. It will bring about the liquidation of all liabilities that are no longer sufficiently collateralized, due to the destruction of asset values, and therefore have to be reduced. Or in other words, the mountain of debt previously piled up has to be levelled.

At current rates of indebtedness, this will lead to a massive collapse of share prices. Between 1929 and 1932, U.S. share prices fell 89 percent according to the Dow Jones Index. The share price charts of that period resemble current share price charts to an extent we cannot ignore. My over 40 years of daily experience in the hottest financial markets—which is probably more than most bankers today have—have taught me to be on the lookout for seemingly small signs, often to read them very differently than the zeitgeist calls for, and to notice the buildup of dangerously unstable system zones early on.

The economic tools even of the most well-intended and energetic anti-crisis programs will be hopelessly overstrained in this situation. Even at lowest interest rates, everyone will avoid leveraged investments; consumers will do the only thing that seems plausible; save up their money rather than spend it. All the more so as for most people consumption has reached a level of saturation where they can afford to forgo purchases without feeling they are missing out on anything essential. People will take precautions in anticipation of an uncertain future, for themselves and their families.

Economists will have to learn that most people are hardly maximizers of profit or utility, indeed that they are not even economic subjects at all. They are human beings, most of them with precisely those characteristics that econometric models cannot capture. Not only are conventional business models and management concepts wrong; in addition, economic management models have largely been programmed incorrectly.

The New Way of Functioning: Mastering Complexity

To prevent the crisis from continuing down that path, we need new solutions. One of the central challenges of the Great Transformation21 is the new way organizations need to function in order to master real complexity and be able to adjust to new and unprecedented conditions. The solution lies in wholistic cybernetic management systems of the kind that we at Malik Management have been developing for over thirty years. These systems do for organizations what nervous systems do for organisms: they make sure they function reliably.

Complexity-compatible strategies have an underlying evolutionary logic, and they emulate the strategy of evolution. Such strategies are necessary whenever the future is uncertain but there is a need for action. The course that the Great Transformation will take can only be roughly sketched out at present. But there are indications and signals—often rather weak ones—as well as patterns that are easy to overlook. These patterns do provide some orientation, provided we pay attention. So, strategies suitable for complexity are developed using sophisticated navigation systems which accomplish for business and society what satellite navigation accomplishes for shipping, aviation and space travel, or GPS for most motorists nowadays. Navigating correctly, knowing where you are at any point in time, steering in the right direction, finding the best routes although they keep changing, being warned about dangers early on and reacting promptly if required: these are capabilities that can only be built and maintained with complexity-compatible strategies.

"Greater skills can only result from higher complexity", is how the German biologist Carsten Bresch put it in 1977[6], and the pioneers of the cybernetics of complex systems had made this realization much earlier[7]. No modern car could function without cybernetic, feedback-driven steering and control, and nor could aviation or shipping, modern medicine or computer systems. Only cybernetic management will enable the organizations of society to function as required under the realities of tomorrow. Wherever something functions, it does so for cybernetic reasons and based on cybernetic laws. Wherever something does not function, there is a lack of cybernetic steering, control, and guidance. The knowledge about the new kind of functioning exists and has been fully captured in my wholistic management systems.

Leading organizations are applying these systems already. They are important for strategic leadership through the labyrinth of the Great Transformation, because they are the tool that provides the right orientation and helps to choose the right direction. The following chapters explain what kind of strategy and strategic management can complete the task.

6 Bresch, Carsten: *Zwischenstufe Leben—Evolution ohne Ziel?*, Munich, 1977.
7 Dörner, Dietrich: *The Logic of Failure. Recognizing and Avoiding Error in Complex Situations.* New York, 1989, 1997.

Chapter 3

When You Do Not Know What You Need to Know: The Minefield of Strategic Errors

Strategic Delusion by Operational Data

Next, let us take a look at the errors previously mentioned. Why do seemingly healthy businesses get into enormous trouble all of a sudden, and to everyone's surprise, and even slide into bankruptcy?

This is what happened in 2008 to Lehman and AIG (one of the world's largest insurance providers) in the U.S. and to Hypo Real Estate in Germany; in 2000 through 2002 it had happened to several of Switzerland's best companies at the time, such as the Zurich group (another leading global insurance company), Swiss Life (then one of the most renowned life insurance companies), and the CS Group, a corporation that was globally known for its outstandingly dynamic development. These companies needed billions in financial aid to survive; some could not be saved at all.

In the 1960s, the same thing had happened to the European office equipment industry, in the 1970s to the Swiss watch manufacturers, in the 1980s to the telephone services industry, and in the 1990s to the photographic industry. Starting from 1990, large parts of the Japanese industrial sector—which had seemed invincible—were affected, as was the U.S. automotive industry. All these supposed gems of business became turnaround candidates overnight—and in each case the majority of people did not understand the reasons. In these debacles, the proponents of business economics and business administration met their Waterloo, although they never realized it, apart from a few exceptions. Even after the company collapsed they did not realize that *operational* data are useless for *strategic* management.

The Right Kind of Information Is Lacking

In most cases, business disasters like these occur for the same reason: companies build their strategies on data that are completely useless and even misleading for strategic decisions, since they are purely *operational* data. So these companies evaluate their success based on operational data because they lack information on their strategic development. They do not even know where to look for it. As a result, they are regularly taken by surprise by unfortunate strategic developments and find it impossible to respond adequately and timely.

It is one consequence of shareholder value thinking that many corporate top managers rely exclusively on data from finance and accounting. Unfortunately, however, these data do not include even the slightest bit of information of the kind needed for strategic purposes—simply because that kind of information cannot be kept on the books.

Rating agencies, too, largely base their praise or criticism of companies on operational aspects. Annual financial reports, audit reports, and even the business media rarely contain anything truly meaningful in terms of strategy. Something similar can be said of controlling reports, and many supervisory boards use even more operational data today than they used to. Admittedly, you will hear the word "strategic" quite often in these organizations. But you can be fairly sure that the more often the word is used in senior management and supervisory bodies, the less the actual strategic insight.

Conventional Strategic Wisdom Is Wrong

Faced with the new challenges of the Great Transformation21, conventional strategic concepts and methods increasingly prove useless. Even worse, they drive, exacerbate and prolong the crisis. For instance, most of the growth strategies pursued are extremely dangerous and can cause the system to collapse. While growth will continue to be important, its direction and significance will change under deflationary conditions. To give you some examples: Over 60 percent of M & A strategies have failed, with DaimlerChrysler as one case in point; also all those failed banks' strategies can hardly have been right, just as many private equity schemes and maneuvers turned out to have been strategically ill-conceived.

To sum it up, previous key business concepts and control variables will continue to be used with the new strategic way of thinking, but they will assume a different position and function within the new navigation system. For instance, the information content of profit will be radically changed in several respects. What has been positive in the old way of thinking will become negative, and vice versa.

In the following sections I will point out the errors and mistakes of traditional thinking, to make very clear why and how business schools' conventional strategy concepts can no longer be used. Indeed, they have been leading us astray for quite a while.

Too Much Emphasis on Financial Figures

Since the early 1990s, many managers' attention has been steered predominantly to the financial aspects of doing business. This was a direct result of shareholder value thinking and of the sophisticated systems of financial indicators that emerged along with it. The more sophisticated these systems became, the further away they moved from strategic information content.

The difference between *operational* and *strategic* management was practically eliminated in the process. And while the words "strategy" and "strategic" were used abundantly, they increasingly referred to mere operational facts and, after a while, to financial transactions alone. Consequently, the general understanding of genuine corporate strategy and strategic management went down the drain.

Throughout history, whenever companies were predominantly or exclusively managed by financial aspects and businesses were assessed based on financial terms only, this usually marked the beginning of what was later to become a recession, sometimes even a dramatic crisis.

So, when I observed this trend towards finance-based corporate management I realized that a system of systematic mismanagement was taking shape, although on the outside it bore the appearance of modern corporate management. Over an extended period of time, this unfortunate development could have been corrected. But since most business economics courses at university, U.S. business schools, auditing firms and rating agencies worldwide, and almost the entire consulting industry proclaimed this disorientation to be good corporate management, the error only became apparent several years later.

No doubt financial discipline is important, as financial results provide the *foundation* for corporate success. But *they are not the reason for* it. So, setting the highest standards for financial management does not mean paying special attention to financial figures but quite the opposite: it means questioning their origins.

Misleading Time Horizons

Every strategic decision takes its effect over time. That is why strategy must not be determined by time periods. A "5-year strategy" is usually wrong, as is a "medium-term 3-year plan". To provide effective guidance, time horizons for strategy or planning always have to be based on the nature and inner logic of the business, which means that time horizons are a consequence rather than a precondition of strategic decisions.

The usual categorization by short, medium and long-term is dangerous because it overrules the far more important distinction between strategic and operational plans. Before time periods can reasonably be determined there must be clarity with regard to the *content* of a plan, since it determines what parts are operational and what are *strategic*; only when this is known does it make any sense at all to discuss time horizons.

To this date it is impossible to define in general terms how long "long-term" really is. A definition can only be given for the *individual* case but it will never be generally valid. Neither business administration academics nor economists have been able to find a solution because clearly there is none. As a way out of these, discussions about profit maximization usually revolve around "long-term" or "sustainable" profits. Neither of the two is definable.

The fact that "short-term" usually refers to the current fiscal year—because that is something clearly defined by law—is usually not harmful to management practice. But the words "medium-term" and "long-term" can only be defined—at least in a way useful for management—by means of the cybernetic navigation system I will introduce later, as "operational" and "strategic" are defined by the different nature of the tasks rather than their temporal range. The time periods spanned by operational and strategic decisions are a consequence of their different nature.

Profit, Fitness, Viability

There is no question that businesses must make profits. That does not mean, however, that profit generation and maximization have to be a company's ultimate goals. As a matter of fact, I have found that precisely those companies that achieve the highest profits usually do not pursue specific profit objectives; rather, profit is an outcome of well-defined strategic goals.

It seems unknown to many people that companies making profit are not necessarily healthy. Most of the businesses that collapsed had generated good profits shortly before, which is why nobody questioned their strategies.

Profit can only be a top-level goal for operational management. By contrast, strategic management focuses on the *conditions* that have to be met for the organization to be profitable. In other words, strategy is about creating the sources of later profits while operational management is about utilizing these sources. Consequently, a strategy that provides guidance for correct management action will focus on the viability and functionability of the business—for an indefinite period of time—, or its ability to remain in existence.

Profit itself is just one of several factors of entrepreneurial navigation. *Reducing* corporate management to profit alone will inevitably lead to a restriction of managerial decision and control systems, confining them to the *operational* dimension of management and driving management into shortsightedness and short-term thinking. The fixation on operational management causes a *neglect* of strategic management—the company ultimately throws away its future.

Operational and Strategic

There are operational tasks and there are strategic ones. By virtue of their very nature they determine the time horizons of planning—not the other way round. Most so-called long-term plans are purely operational, providing no strategic guidance whatsoever. They feign a kind of planning and management quality they do not have. Quite to the contrary, they inevitably lead to undesirable developments.

Common usage of the words "strategy" and "strategic" is so vague—even among supposed experts—that the terms have almost lost their original meanings. They threaten to become useless and misleading, although they are among the concepts that are key to the right management approach. As long as it remains unclear what the difference is between, say, strategic and operational marketing, or even what the opposite of strategic marketing is, both terms are useless. The same is true of strategic controlling, strategic human resources management, strategic asset management, and many more.

As a result of the inflationary and unthinking use of the word "strategy", one of the key *insight*s into the logic of reliable corporate management is being diluted, as I will show in the next section. This is aggravated by the fact that in public debate—following both the zeitgeist and the financial markets—shareholder value continues to be the preferred variable for evaluation and target-setting purposes. Shareholder value is a purely operational parameter and strategies must not be based on it, particularly if you want to ensure that your shareholders are paid well.

The following seven propositions will provide clarity in these questions. They describe the lessons learnt from the errors and false doctrines that have driven many companies into bankruptcy and caused the present global economic crisis.

Operational and Strategic Management

1. Operational data are systematically misleading in corporate management.

You cannot make strategic decisions based on operational data. You cannot even recognize whether there is a need for strategic decisions.

Operational data are *systematically* misleading—and I am not talking about the mistakes that can typically happen in business, even with excellent strategies. There is a great difference between ordinary mistakes and systematic errors; that is, being *systematically* and thus inevitably *misled*. In this latter sense, operational data are systematically misleading. But what are operational data anyway?

2. The control and information systems used by business economics, in particular finance and accounting, provide operational data only.

Operational data include turnover, costs, profits, returns, contribution margins, liquidity, cash flows, cash flow rates, and anything derived from these. It does not matter whether these numbers are recorded for the short or long-term, whether they are discounted or not. Even a 10-year cash-flow analysis is purely operational information. Even if it was extrapolated over the long-term this would not change anything about its operational nature.

Note that I am not questioning the accounting system as such. I am referring to its *misuse* for purposes it was never intended to serve, as will be shown in the next chapter. It provides operational data for *operational* management, reliably and well—no more and no less, because that is what it was invented for.

Strategic management, by its very nature, is something very *different* from operational management. It has to serve other purposes, solve other problems, and generate other decisions. For strategic management, *different* reference variables are needed; different laws and rules need to be known, and they must meet *different* criteria.

That does not mean that strategic management can replace operational management; nor is the reverse possible. Both kinds of management are needed simultaneously. They are largely independent of each other but have to complement each other. None of the two "halves" of management can be dispensed with.

The respective tasks can be clearly defined. Operational management has to *realize the company's success*. Strategic management has to create the conditions for that—it has to provide the *potential* for corporate success. When there is no potential, even the best operational management will not be able to achieve any success in the longer term, as great as that success may be at present.

3. The brighter the picture painted by operational data, the greater the risk of strategic mistakes.

Favorable operational data, such as high profits, attractive returns, turnover growth and so on, work like tranquilizers. When these figures—as found in companies' annual reports, in balance sheets and profit and loss statements—look healthy, people will feel there is no reason to worry. Supervisory board members will hardly dare ask irritating questions; and if they do, their questions can easily be brushed aside referring to the splendid numbers. It takes an extraordinarily strong supervisory body to muster the strength to question good operational figures.

As numerous examples show, the worst mistakes are never made at times when companies are doing *badly*. They are made when operating results are *good*. Entrepreneurial vigilance is lulled by good results. It has happened to DaimlerChrysler, General Motors, the former IBM, the steel industry, and to many banks and financial institutions. Numerous examples can also be found among the less lesser-known, small and medium-sized businesses.

At times of *poor* operating performance, all senses are alert, the antennae are raised and it is considered OK to question everything. Change readiness is great, through the ability to change is sometimes lacking, and all of management's intelligence and experience are focused on solving the problems at hand.

In Part III of this book I will introduce our navigation system and show how effectively it can help avoid these very mistakes. In part IV I will address the PIMS® (Profit Impact of Market Strategy) methodology and explain what enormously important achievements PIMS research has given us, and how it helps build the kind of leadership that takes precautions for bad times while times are good.

4.   Strategic mistakes are irreversible.

My third proposition above could be shrugged off by pointing out that making mistakes is part of doing business. That attitude, however, would be too shortsighted. Worse still, it would seal the company's fate and imply surrender right before the breakthrough.

Strategic mistakes have a very dangerous quality: once detected, they *are past being corrected* any more. Or, to be more precise: They can no longer be corrected by *ordinary* means. Correcting them will always require particular and exceptional measures—such as cut-throat cost reductions, large-scale redundancies and turnarounds, closing down entire plants, business units or sites, giving up independence, or entering forced alliances.

It is therefore important to distinguish sharply between ordinary mistakes and *strategic* ones. Ordinary mistakes are an inevitable part of doing business and of entrepreneurial activity. They involve setbacks, sacrifices and disappointments, but they do not jeopardize the *livelihood of the company*. Strategic mistakes *always do that*. Why is that so?

5. Strategic mistakes cannot be corrected because time is working against you.

The consequences of strategic mistakes will *eventually* always show in the company's *financial figures*, but their causes can rarely be found there. Rather, that is where they take effect and where the consequences inevitably become *visible*.

Approximately 75 percent of all bankruptcies are only discovered based on financial analysis indicators; an astonishing 55 percent are only detected based on liquidity ratios. About 25 percent of all bankruptcies are discovered six to twelve months before the actual breakdown, about 40 percent as late as in the final six months. That fact alone indicates a complete lack of effective early-warning navigation systems, and thus the systematic uselessness of traditional management tools.

Still, in most cases the core of the problem is not so much the money itself but the fact that, after the impending disaster has been noticed, there is not enough *time* left to correct the mistakes that were made. Anyone who has ever been through a turnaround knows what I am talking about. If only there were enough time … for further negotiations, for taking the necessary countermeasures, for settling one's liabilities, and so on.

This is where the full implications of the distinction between operational and strategic become obvious: *Once a strategic mistake becomes visible in the operational figures, it is too late for truly effective counter-measures.*

So, one central purpose of corporate strategy is to gain time. The earlier you discover a problem, the more time you have to avert it. The time gained, however, never appears on balance sheets, least of all in the bottom line so beloved of managers; and I have never heard of any rating agencies or financial analysts that were even aware of the significance of this parameter—which just goes to show how massively they contribute to the short-sightedness and blindness in corporate management.

When a problem is manifest in the bottom line, the patient is at the intensive-care stage. It is the same as with cancer: once the patient starts feeling pain, it is usually too late to cure the disease—or, if it can be done, this often requires serious interventions in the patient's organism through surgery and/or chemotherapy.

6. Operational data are strategically insignificant because they cannot support or refute a strategy.

It is generally wrong to say, *"But we are making profits—so our strategy cannot be off the track."* Even when a company is terminally ill and cannot be rescued, it may still be generating enormous profits and meeting all the financial analysts' criteria. By the same token, it is wrong to say, *"We are making losses, so we need to change our strategy."* Often, the best strategies will push a business into the red over several years, especially when they are aimed at fundamental innovations.

Few of the great innovations we know of would have ever been implemented if those in charge had focused on accounting figures only. Fundamental innovations would even have to be vetoed by the CFO if he only used accounting logic. Carl Benz and Peter von Siemens, Henri Nestlé and Thomas Watson Sr.—they all would have had to give up quickly, had they applied the logic of a financial controller.

Operational figures can only justify operational measures. And strategic measures can only be substantiated by strategic arguments and information.

7. What may appear reasonable based on operational data can be utterly wrong strategically—and vice versa.

An exclusive focus on operational data and numbers will almost always lead to measures that are harmful from a strategic point of view. Current profits are not necessarily an outcome of pursuing the right strategy. Very often, profits—especially very high ones—are owed to the fact that strategic potential is excessively exploited, and thus ruined. For example, operational figures can easily be improved by reducing the expenditure for research and development, human resources development, or marketing. From an operational point of view this may be justified, even inevitable in certain situations. But the strategic potential of the business is often put at risk that way.

On the other hand, as pointed out before, even a strategy that is clearly good and right will not necessarily generate high profits, cash flows, or returns, but often the opposite—at least initially. So the related actions may seem wrong from an operational point of view, even when they are strategically right and perhaps even necessary for the company's survival.

That is the *original dilemma* of corporate management. A company in a tight squeeze may have to separate from businesses which have lots of potential but would require years of investment—that is, it may have to sacrifice its future. On the other hand, a company determined to build future potential and to persevere will have to be prepared to accept deteriorating operational figures, possibly for several years—in short, it sacrifices its present.

This company's management can hardly expect a lot of praise from financial analysts and shareholders, for the only thing it can promise them is future results, which, when discounted, often appear rather pathetic. By contrast, if managers cut down on future potential, striving to maintain and optimize current business results instead, they will be able to enjoy the grace of the moment at the expense of the future. Which may not bother them too much if they are looking at retirement or holding a limited work contract, or when brief tenures in top management positions happen to be the norm, as was the case during the stock market boom. Or if their bonuses are tied to operational figures, as is almost always the case—although very different, even strategic solutions are available. All of these things are signs of systematic poor programming, a direct consequence of traditional strategic thinking and in particular of the shareholder approach.

Any manager focusing on only *one* dimension of corporate management will always have a relatively easy task. It is seldom difficult to maximize current profits if you do not have to think about the future. And most managers won't have a problem focusing on the future if they do not have to worry about current results.

The art of corporate management begins where both have to be done *at the same time*. Making provisions for the future *and* achieving good current results; achieving good results today and safeguarding the future.

Making this art a profession that can be taught and learned is the purpose of sound management theory, and the navigation system presented in this book makes it possible.

Doing business is not easy, but *staying* in business is the entrepreneur's true mission. It is the more difficult, strategic task.

In times of major change, it is particularly important to have a corporate strategy. The future of a company does not simply happen—it is created and shaped by strategic management.

So, as important as financial figures may be—it is just as important to be always aware of their operational nature. If a company is managed by financial aspects *only* it is managed *operationally*. And even if this is done brilliantly, the danger of neglecting strategic management aspects automatically exists.

Replacing the words by other terms does not change anything. A dog will remain a dog even if you call it a cat. Strategy will not result from *renaming* operational management and operational facts. It only results from using strategic management and control variables. It is a matter of logic and of the *principles* of corporate management, not of language.

The next chapter will explain what strategic principles actually are.

Strategic Thinking Traps

The more collective misdirection there is—e.g., through uncritical MBA courses and incompetent media—and the more difficult the economic situation, the more important it is to know the logic of correct strategic management and to avoid the errors typically inherent in conventional strategies. That alone will lift strategy work to another quality level. In addition, the new methods of SuperSyntegration I will describe in part VI generate completely new possibilities for solving key questions such as growth, size, and diversification, for which, beyond a certain level of complexity, traditional methods have been unable to find solutions.

Why Growth is Not an Aim but a Result

Contrary to popular belief, growth, as important as it may be, must never be a company's ultimate goal—least of all if it refers to an increase in sales. Therefore growth targets must not be used as inputs to a strategy: they are the result—the output—of a good strategy.

If the conventional approach is reversed in this way, you will usually end up with much higher growth targets than you would have had the courage to set. Moreover, growth targets resulting as an output from strategy have a much better foundation, for the only way to determine whether a company *must* grow, *can* grow, or *must not* grow any further (yes, that is possible, too) is through strategic information. It can be derived among other things from the PIMS program which I will introduce in part IV.

Under certain circumstances, a company may urgently need a strong growth phase for strategic reasons, such as to build a defendable market position quickly enough to outpace competitors. This can be particularly important for start-ups. But there are also situations in which a company could move itself into an unsustainable position through further growth, and thus bring about its own demise.

It is not that important to keep growing—it is much more important to keep getting *better*. Even companies which can no longer grow due to market limits can still keep improving their quality and, above all, their productivity. Another extremely important question is *how* growth is achieved—if it is a definite goal. Is it achieved by increasing volume in a *growing* market or by increasing market share in a *saturated* market? Through acquisitions? Through innovation? Or through diversification? The latter is very difficult, as numerous examples have shown, most notably DaimlerChrysler. Or is the company going for growth through diversification and innovation *at the same time*—which is even more difficult? Growth through diversification and acquisition makes a company larger, so it will seem increasingly successful to many people. But in fact it will become weaker and weaker until it reaches the end of its tether.

Another, seemingly easy growth approach with very far-reaching consequences is to expand the company's product range. Taking a look at fast-growing companies, one will frequently find that the increase in sales figures has been achieved through product range proliferation—that is, an exploding number of products or variants. Almost always, the result is proliferating complexity, along with a rapid decrease in transparency and an erosion of contribution margins, profitability, and liquidity.

Size Will Have Two Faces

"How big can a company be?" is a question I am often asked. Years ago, the answer used to be simple. Now, I find the issue quite intriguing because in the New World, size will be a two-faced strategy variable. On the one hand, companies will be *able to be much bigger* than before, as the new management systems will provide them with the necessary tools. Readers will understand this part as soon once they have seen Part VI. I can easily imagine corporations with a million employees and more, yet without lots of red tape and with excellent productivity levels. Companies which feel their size is being limited at present, and that they have further market opportunities will be absolutely delighted with the new tools.

On the other hand, nobody has to be big in the New World, as there are new possibilities for small players to serve large markets, even dominate them.

What matters is not so much size but *strength*, not volume but *speed*, *quality*, *adaptability*, and above all, *manageability*. Mastering complexity will be crucial because in the past every growth in size brought an ever greater increase in complexity. But the tools presented here allow you to master it well.

There are companies which are considered large by common standards but which are weak in each of their lines of business. This is often true of highly diversified groups and holding structures. Then there are companies which, by conventional measures, are small or medium-sized at best, but almost unbeatable in their fields. In Part IV we will see that successful stand-alone strategies are largely independent of size.

Diversification Requires Skillful Complexity Management

100 years of economic history teach us that diversification almost never works. Instances of success are few and far between, so obviously the approach is not really advisable—least of all for small and medium-sized

companies because they usually lack two major prerequisites: financial re-sources and management.

Larger firms often have the money—though not always enough to bear the follow-up costs of diversification—but they, too, often lack a sufficient number of able managers. Even more frequently, they lack the management systems to cope with the complexity of diversification.

As far as conventional methods are concerned, my recommendations remain unchanged. Not so with the new, complexity-compatible management systems and methods: they will trigger changes in this field, too, as they enable companies to overcome the previous obstacles of diversification management.

Eliminating Deficiencies is Hardly a Strategic Goal

Eliminating its weaknesses makes a company mediocre, not excellent. Of course, every strategy has to deal with the weaknesses of the specific organization, and there may be cases where their elimination is the key to success. True entrepreneurial achievement, however, is always a result of exploiting strengths. Often enough, there is only *one* strength—and one that the company already has, not one it needs to build over the next five years, for in business you rarely have that much time available.

That is why, in developing a corporate strategy, first and foremost you need to focus on identifying strengths. Also, consultants should never be paid for telling you what the weaknesses of your company are. Finding those is usually easy; often they are hard to overlook. It is much more difficult to identify an organization's strengths. The same is true of employees, by the way: usually, any number of people can tell you what is impossible, and why. In a way, they also make a contribution; but more important are those who realize what capabilities the organization has and what you can do with them.

Anyone identifying a company's true strengths, however, is worthy of virtually any consulting fee. As a young and inexperienced consultant, I was often proud of the many deficits we had found and which we would present to management after thorough analysis. Based on these we were also able to develop the most wonderful package of measures. The mountain of work that resulted for the company seemed to justify our invoice; after all, I had done a lot for the company. Later, it became my most important mission to help companies identify their strengths, very clearly and precisely, and to make sure they were used. Weaknesses not eliminated may interfere with the success of a company, but the elimination of weaknesses itself will seldom be a source or driver of success.

Right Strategies are Resistant to Inaccurate Data

With regard to data *completeness* and *accuracy*, people sometimes make demands that simply cannot be met. How exactly can quantities such as market potential, market volume, market share, substitution effects and so on really be determined? Some industries, such as the insurance industry, have very precise market data because they are neatly structured by associations; in other industries, such as the retail trade, there is a wealth of experience based on decades on broad-based market research.

But in most cases—especially when new developments in technologies, products, and markets have to be assessed—it would be an illusion to think that the relevant factors can be *accurately* determined. This is particularly true of small and mid-sized companies, which cannot afford the human resources required to do so.

So, any reasonable strategic planning process has to be designed in such a way that strategies will not depend on *data accuracy*. This is one of the key methodological principles particularly for coping with great complexity. Any strategy depending on precise data is bound to involve a great deal of risk, for it will hardly be *resistant* to the fluctuations and inaccuracies that are bound to occur.

The Best Strategies Do Not Depend on Forecasts

There are very different kinds of forecasts; the most useful, however, are hardly known. Some of them will be dealt with in this book. The most widespread forecasts are linear extrapolations, which are barely useful but definitely misleading. Therefore, my navigation systems are designed to keep companies largely independent of forecasts.

A good strategy involves deriving consequences from past occurrences, working with assumptions and boundary conditions and exploring typical patterns, such as the S-Curve I will talk about later, as well as the results of PIMS research, which will be discussed in detail.

Also, it is important to remain open to singular events, which can hardly be predicted but often involve the best opportunities or the greatest risks. Most of the things that happen every day were not forecast by anybody, not even considered possible by the experts, before they became a reality. A simple analysis of the current forecast literature will quickly prove my point. The hit rate is embarrassingly small, even if the forecasts were made by renowned think tanks.

For all their attempts to identify the future with forecasts, people often fail to fully understand the present and the past. *Peter Drucker* presented some striking examples of how the truly crucial events are not those that have yet to happen but those that have already happened: the changes that many people fail to see or draw consequences from, even though they are already behind us.

One prime example is the demographic changes that can be predicted for several decades in advance, but which in many companies are not adequately taken account of. Even if in most cases we cannot predict what the impact of these changes will be, it is usually possible to say that serious consequences have to be expected. Often, the *kind* of changes can be specified as well.

The more we know about the present and the historical developments that led to it, the less we have to depend on forecasts; what is more, the more we will recognize how hollow, useless, and misleading many of them are. One case in point is the widespread naiveté in the financial markets. Just being familiar with the history of the 20th century would be enough to raise serious doubts and call for modesty, but it would also help to gain much better knowledge. Without any knowledge of the history of financial crises, it is almost impossible to understand what is going on in the financial system and where the risks lie.

Finally, another thought of *Drucker's* applies here as well: the best way to predict the future is to create it. That is the entrepreneurial element in the free economy, irrespective of whether or not entrepreneurs are also owners.

Buzzwords and Empty Phrases Get in the Way of Good Strategies

Wrong thinking and very specific errors result from using meaning less catchwords and empty phrases, first in designing strategies and then in formulating them. Both in literature and in companies' planning documents, one can usually find rather meaningless words and statements.

For instance, descriptions of strategic thrusts frequently contain expressions like "building market share", "increasing sales", "forward strategy", "maintaining position", "pushing for growth", and so on. Such vague terms may suffice in exceptional situations, if at all. They are hardly suitable to give a company and its business units what they need from a strategic point of view: orientation.

For instance, "building market share" can be a possible strategy in almost any situation. The art—and the necessary step—is to *specify how, with what, where, at whose expense, and through what actions* the company's market share is to be increased, and then to assess whether that would be a reasonable aim at all, in the light of all the known and given factors, as well as whether the company can actually afford that strategy or whether it would be likely to get into serious trouble.

Serious damage is done by the idea of management needing visions because they are at the core of every strategy. That is an open invitation to produce the very opposite of a useful strategy: meaningless phrases. Missions are a different matter. A mission is definitely necessary, and I will get to that shortly. It often follows from a very broad and far-reaching idea which could be called a vision or a dream. That dream, however, first has to be transformed into a viable mission: this is the only way to distinguish useful from useless visions.

Particularly tempting are *"empty phrases"* or tautologies. They enable a certain type of manager to stay in their positions much too long: it is the logically gifted bluffer. An "empty phrase" or a "tautology" is a phrase which is linguistically and grammatically correct, but only *seemingly* meaningful. In truth it is *devoid of meaning*. Empty phrases are used particularly often in forecasts. An obvious and instantly clear example is an old German proverb which can loosely be translated as "If the cockerel crows from his favorite spot, the weather may change, or again it may not". This forecast will certainly *always* come true—which is why it is completely meaningless. It conveys no information whatsoever.

Now, economic and management forecasts are usually not phrased that way because it would make their emptiness all too obvious. Instead, they usually meander along, ornately frilled and stretching across several book pages, so that it requires a special effort to see their true nature.

Typical examples of empty phrases in strategy are: "… need to take targeted action …; prepare adequate measures …; create optimal conditions …; take appropriate decisions …; set competitive prices …" and so on.

The easiest and best way to test a grammatically correct sentence for true content is to check whether its logic negation could also be a conceivable alternative. It then becomes clear very quickly that "*taking untargeted measures*" or "*inappropriate decisions*" could never qualify as alternatives. Their lack of meaning is obvious, and this goes to show that the original phrase only appeared to convey information.

We come across such statements at every turn, and not only in business: they are even more frequent—and more brazen—in politics. No wonder many plans are never implemented, and others are carried out in very arbitrary ways.

Responsible strategic planning requires thorough and careful thinking, and often what is almost an obsession with the company's key issues—the issues that its *livelihood* depends on. Many failed strategies were based on errors of the kind discussed here. Mergers and acquisitions, growth strategies and the like would not have failed so grossly had these errors been avoided from the start.

Part II:
Strategy as Master Control in the Wholistic Management Systems

"Cybernetics offers a method for the scientific treatment of the system in which complexity is outstanding and too important to be ignored."

Ross W. Ashby, Doyen of the cybernetics of complex systems

Having addressed the Why in Part I, Parts II through V will now deal with the What of Strategy. Main topics will be the Malik Management Systems with the navigation tools entailed by them, as well as the necessary strategic knowledge, the Strategy Map, and the Strategic Intelligence Models.

Part VI will deal with the *How.*

Chapter 1

Making Companies Function Well

The logic, architecture, and content of my Wholistic Management Systems1 are designed to enable managers to meet the challenges that the Great Transformation21 will bring: high complexity, interconnectedness and dynamic change, uncertainty about the future, the inscrutability of complex systems, and the unpredictability of their behavior.

For these conditions of complexity, our management systems work as universal *management support tools*, enabling executives at all levels not only to fully bring their skills to bear and do so in a coordinated manner, but also to increase their management effectiveness by several orders of magnitude. They do that because they are modular and scalable and unfold their effect across the whole organization in a quasi-holographic manner. As a result, organizations of any size become complexity-compatible down to their very capillaries, almost like modern computer networks. What this implies is no less than a "Corporate REvolution", as I have pointed out in my book *Corporate Policy and Governance*, another volume of this series.

Enhancing Management Impact Through Management Support Systems

Within certain limits, our systems are comparable to the *driver assistance systems* in modern cars. ABS, speed and distance control systems, traction controls, and intelligent engine management enable the driver to better perform the tasks at which human beings will always be superior to any technology. At the same time, they relieve the driver of all the things that technology can accomplish better. Not only does this help to better cope with the growing complexity of modern-day traffic, it also makes driving more economical and ecological—and it adds to the driving pleasure even of those of us who would not call themselves the most gifted of motorists. But this analogy has its limits in that management systems have to cope with far more complexity than any of those technical systems.

Yet it can be achieved by means of our management systems. We have equipped them with the systemic-cybernetic qualities that evolution, over eons of experimentation, has given to living organisms, including the human one, enabling them to function even when conditions are extremely complex and circumstances constantly change.

The keys are multilevel feedback controls and capabilities such as self-regulation and self-organization. This will become very clear in Part VI of this book when I describe the new, radically different methods we have developed, in particular the Syntegration method for strategic management.

Right and Good Management—Universally Valid

With our methods it is possible to move even very large and complex organizations with ease and at maximum speed. Previous limits to manageability, which resulted from the size, diversity and complexity of organizations, can now be overcome. What is more, these characteristics can be turned into competitive strengths. Compared to the relatively modest means available in the past century, even the name *Corporate ^{R}Evolution* is an understatement.

These new achievements are possible because, far beyond business administration and economics, we have focused on the sciences of complexity which deal with the secrets of functioning systems: systemics, cybernetics, and bionics. Systemics is the science of entities, cybernetics the science of functioning, and bionics the science of how to apply evolution's solutions to the problems that mankind and its organizations face.

None of these disciplines would alone suffice to create a management system with the capabilities described. Only at the intersection of all three fields could we gather all the insights we needed to create these management systems which are certain to work even under hyper-complex conditions. Only with these systems can executives compensate for their lack of knowledge about complex systems, and skillfully manage them even under

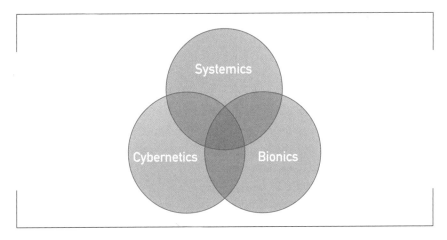

Figure 4: Relevant management knowledge in the intersection of three complexity disciplines

most difficult circumstances. They also enable the strategic errors and logic traps to be avoided and eliminated for good.

One of the outputs of my management systems is the definition of universally and globally valid professional standards of *Right and Good Management*®—as opposed to wrong and bad management. The terms "right" and "good" are therefore used quite often in this book, as in my previous publications, because they refer to the basic qualities of management and management systems. This also puts an end to the arbitrariness of the subjective approaches that prevailed in the organization and management of the 20th century. Even recurring fashions can no longer do any damage. Finally, this book is not about "strategy in general" but about my own strategic approach, which is fundamentally different from almost any other approach.

I was guided towards my concept of right management by decades of scientific research on management, together with such outstanding mentors and colleagues as Hans Ulrich, Walter Krieg, Aloys Gälweiler, Frederic Vester, Stafford Beer, Peter F. Drucker, and many others. Another key aspect is the fact that before my university studies I spent almost six years in an executive function in a mid-sized company, thus gathering real-life experience, and so as a student I was able to tell quite clearly what did and did not make sense in academic business economics. I was also able to see where connections existed between business economics and management and where they were lacking.

A key factor influencing my position on right and good management is my long-standing experience in the training and consulting of entrepreneurs, managers, and leaders at virtually all kinds of organizations, age groups and hierarchical levels: in the course of these more than 30 years I was able to see for myself what works and what doesn't. Even in China, where one would expect the greatest differences, our management systems have proved effective. Our concept of right and good management has passed one of its biggest acid tests there.

Another field of practical experience was the founding and building of our own organization, above all to be able to test our management innovations by way of self-experiment before recommending them to others as effective solutions.

Finally, a key factor driving the current state of development of my management system is the practical experience I have been gaining in the "centers of power", as it were, having served as a member and chairman of several corporate governance, supervisory, and foundation boards for over 20 years. After all, any outside-in analysis relying on the meager resources used in academia, such as questionnaires or interviews, will only capture about 10 percent—if that much—of the realities of management.

The direct personal experience of being involved in the making of a high-risk decision—and even being responsible for it—leads to an entirely different way of thinking about management than any academic activity ever will. Of course the latter has its merits, too, but regrettably it is forced to work on limited resources and often with rather blunt instruments.

By combining science and practice in this way, I was able to experience first-hand what makes companies function: those companies which already work with sophisticated, complexity-compatible and dynamic management and control systems—while others still have clear development needs, struggling as they are with conventional management tools which dramatically curtail the capabilities of their executives. Even the best and most gifted managers cannot deliver their full performance without high-performance systems.

On the other hand, I was a witness to the sensational impact achieved by introducing just a few of the modern tools available, such as the Central Performance Controls I will discuss later. One of its impressive effects is an almost immediate 180-degree shift in the use of the shareholder value concept: it moves from the top to the bottom of the list of economic targets and decisions.

Management, Financial Markets, and Alpinism

Finally, there are two experiences I should mention in this context because they have enormously helped me to understand complex, dynamic systems and to develop my management systems and strategy concepts. The first is my over 40 years of experience with international financial markets, most notably the hottest ones: the U.S. futures markets. The second is my passion for sports, specifically extreme mountaineering in all its different variants, both on rock and on ice.

Even before I took up my university studies, I had gained my first practical experiences in stock trading. This was the beginning of my life-long vital interest in all matters financial, in particular in the history of the great financial crises and crashes, which I studied meticulously and with great fascination over the years.

Along with my knowledge of cybernetics, this enabled me to see much earlier than most how a *perfect storm* was brewing in the financial system. I am more familiar with these markets than most bankers, and have been for a much longer time. While bankers, in their active time, have only been able to experience the bull side of the market, I was perfectly familiar with the whole picture, including excesses in both bull and bear markets: on the futures exchange they happen three to four times a year. So anyone active in that market has plenty of opportunity to get used to them.

That is also why I am familiar with the dynamics of the leverage effect—both its positive and its negative sides and the associated risks—from everyday practice. It enabled me to recognize the looming disaster, based on many indicators from very different fields, and to put together the pieces of the puzzle.

Climbing is another activity that taught me how to deal with high-risk situations. I am not saying you need to be an active climber to know something about managers or be a good manager, or even a leader. But when you have to cope with difficult conditions in the mountains, including your own physical condition, it sharpens your senses for the difference between good and bad teams, the significance of true professionalism—for instance, when it comes to taking safety measures—, and for the thoroughness with which people approach a task. It also enables you to handle unforeseen events better and to cope with real dangers such as falling rocks, thunderstorms, or avalanches, as well as with the dangers that lie deep in yourself and which determine how you deal with your own limitations, be they perceived or real.

From all these different ingredients, over time I have put together the "menu" of my management systems, as well as my position on what is right and good in management, and what is wrong and bad.

A Practical Hint for Readers in the Know

At this point, I would recommend to all those readers already familiar with my management systems, in particular those who have read the previous volume, *Corporate Policy and Governance*, to proceed directly to Part III. For all others: this part contains a summary of my management systems and models, so you can see where strategy fits in—including the upstream input systems for strategy, corporate purpose and mission, as well as the Central Performance Controls which permit the transition to the Strategic Navigation System1.

Systems in general, and hence management systems as well, are difficult to put into words due to their outward and inward interconnectedness, which is one of the reasons why so many people find them hard to understand. Illustrations are helpful here, which is why I use them quite extensively in my books.

But even illustrations in a book are only two-dimensional and static, while the reality of systems is multi-dimensional and dynamic. The much easier and faster access to my management systems is through state-of-the-art Web technology with its almost limitless possibilities of making dynamic and complex interrelationships visible, I therefore recommend using both the book and the Web as they complement each other. On the Internet, you can interactively explore my management systems on www.malik-management.com. (See appendix for more information.) To facilitate readers' orientation, I will keep using the most important graphs as icons.

What are Master Controls?

To tackle the issue of complexity, I will begin by explaining how strategy works as a master control. *"Master controls" is the term I use for the top-level basic principles that are binding for the organization as a whole, all the way to its capillaries.* They determine the organization's function in all dimensions. They are the universal means of design, control, and management, which in my system are primarily aimed at enabling the organization to self-organize and self-regulate.

The central underlying rule is: *Design a system in such a way that it will be able to organize and regulate itself.* This corresponds to one of the laws of cybernetics, the science of functioning. Only through a maximum of self-organization and self-regulation can companies enable themselves to function reliably, grow, adapt, and respond flexibly in a constant succession of new and unfamiliar situations.

With their rather modest means, both business economics and U.S.-style business administration are increasingly unable to capture the key challenge to management, let alone meet it; on the contrary, they are moving further and further away from it. *This challenge consists in mastering complexity.*

The way my General Management System works is almost comparable to the operating system of a computer: *it ensures that the right tasks are performed by the right people in the right way, so that the company as a whole can function well.* It requires the subsystems, functions, and interrelationships shown in the graphs.

Please note for all my systems that interconnections between elements are just as important as the elements themselves, sometimes even more so. The step from the elements to the connections between them is one of the keys to understanding the systems and their properties. Many find this step hard to take, as these connections are usually as invisible as the forces of nature and can only be concluded from the elements' behavior.

It is these interconnections which turn the individual elements into a system—and specifically, it is the regulatory connections which give the system coherence, dynamics, and the ability to act. That is what in cybernetics we refer to as *control.* For connections to have a regulating effect, we also need *communication.* Cybernetics is therefore often defined as *Control and Communication in the Animal and the Machine.*[8]

---

8 Subtitle of Norbert Wiener's book *Cybernetics.*

The Basic Management Model and Its Basic Concepts

The basic model located on the left-hand side of the graph shows the "object" to be managed by corporate management.[9] This "object" is the *organization in its environment*, as well as the mutual interaction between both, which in reality is a highly complex and dynamic system with its own laws.

To be successful, a company has to prove itself over and over again and every day in its specific environment, which is made up of markets, customers, competitors, suppliers, investors, the media, the government, and many more institutions that management has to take into consideration in its decisions.

So this is where the company faces the megachanges of the Great Transformation21, as well as the megasystems which permanently restructure themselves and their dynamic complexity.

Corporate management, located in the top field of the graph, is linked directly to the company and indirectly to its environment, so it constantly has the overall system "on its screen". I will later show how this works in practice, using the Navigator and Strategy Map.

On the right-hand side of figure 5, the basic model has been moved to the center and for each of the subsystems a specific *concept* has been added: the *business concept*, the *environment concept*, and the *management concept*. In addition to these static illustrations, our website also shows the dynamics of the model's architecture, building up step by step in a perfect system and process logic.

These three concepts contain the knowledge required to fulfill the tasks of the overall management. The set of several tools for organizing the relevant information into knowledge—the Knowledge Organizers—have already been described in volume 2 on corporate policy. They include the environment and the business concept, as well as the sensitivity model for the control levers, which is one of the most efficient and powerful tools to capture interconnectedness and complexity. Further components of the concepts are the Navigation System and the Strategy Map, which I will describe in Part III. At that point, the reader will understand why so many executives are intrigued by the fact that there are such straightforward

---

9 For a better understanding of the models, animated graphic depictions can be found on www.malik-management.com.

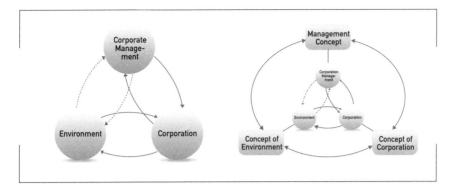

Figure 5: Left-hand side: basic management model; right-hand side: basic model with concepts

tools available for organizing the complexity of strategic issues and for steering a business.

Management of Institutions: The General Management Model

Now let us zoom in on corporate management and the management concept, and explore their contents step by step.

At the level of overall institutions, my General Management Model is used for management assistance. It comprises the necessary subsystems for the *overall management* of institutions of any kind and size. I use the term "institution" to refer to all kinds of organizations.

To facilitate the reader's understanding, the elements of my General Management Systems are briefly described in figure 6. All parts are interconnected, and together they form a single whole. At the same time, they are embedded in the subsystems of Corporate Governance and Corporate Policy which, in turn, are embedded in the Environment and act as an in-terface with it. So, it should now be obvious where the subject of this book, strategy, is located within the overall system and what its neighboring systems and its embedded systems are.

All elements of my General Management Model are described in Volume 1 of this series on "Mastering Complexity". Volume 2 deals with the

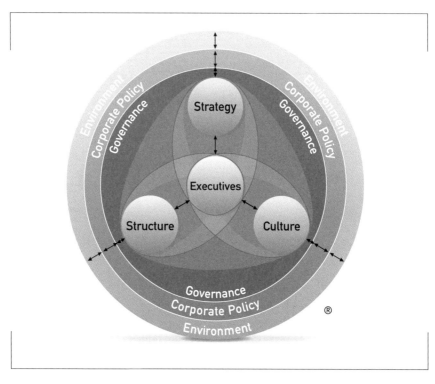

Figure 6: Malik General Management Model (GMM) ®

two outer rings; the present Volume 3 is dedicated to strategy, while Volumes 4, 5, and 6 will deal with the remaining elements.

For the purposes of this book, I will focus on the shaded area in figure 8. Please note that I do not single out "strategy" alone but, in line with the logical structure of the model, include the respective interconnections.

So, while in this third volume I particularly focus on strategy, it will not be described separately from other elements and relationships. It *remains interconnected*, as is the case in real-life corporate management.

This mode of thinking and of seeing and understanding management opens the way for managers to the right generalist approach in which their expertise—which is just as important and necessary—is maintained.

This approach to modeling the function that shapes and guides, the function we refer to as management in a very broad sense and which also includes governance and leadership, permits error-free orientation and navigation through any degree of complexity.

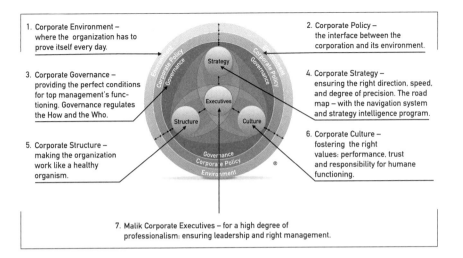

1. Corporate Environment – where the organization has to prove itself every day.

2. Corporate Policy – the interface between the corporation and its environment.

3. Corporate Governance – providing the perfect conditions for top management's functioning. Governance regulates the How and the Who.

4. Corporate Strategy – ensuring the right direction, speed, and degree of precision. The road map – with the navigation system and strategy intelligence program.

5. Corporate Structure – making the organization work like a healthy organism.

6. Corporate Culture – fostering the right values: performance, trust and responsibility for humane functioning.

7. Malik Corporate Executives – for a high degree of professionalism: ensuring leadership and right management.

Figure 7: The elements of the General Management Model

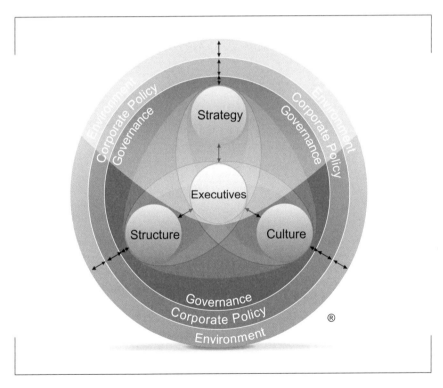

Figure 8: Focus on strategy, including its relationships with other system components

Management of People: The Standard Model of Effectiveness, or "Management Wheel"

At the level of managing individuals or teams, the standard tool is my Model of Managerial Effectiveness, for which the name *Management Wheel* soon became established. It comprises the necessary and sufficient components of professional effectiveness: principles, tasks, and tools for effective action, as well as the necessary communication and accountability. In my book *Managing Performing Living* the Management Wheel is described in detail.

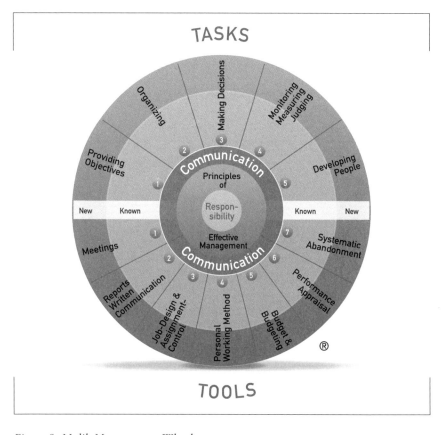

Figure 9: Malik Management Wheel

The two models are inseparable. They complement and enhance each other, as shown by the illustration in figure 10—although certain compromises in geometric accuracy had to be made in order to for both halves to be visible.

Figure 10: Relationship between GMM and Management Wheel

The Integrated Management System—IMS

Figure 10 shows how both individual models are integrated into one, the "Integrated Malik Management System". It is the model for managing people in institutions, comprising the entire organization.

The IMS comprises all the system components necessary and sufficient for the functioning of an organization, and comprises two dimensions: The first is *time*, i.e. the present and future, on the vertical axis; the second is *content*, referring to both the organization as a whole and the individuals in it, on the horizontal axis.

In the volume on *Management*, I have described the "*Integrated Management System*" and its logic at length. Strategy, the subject of this book, is located in the top left-hand corner of the IMS, in element 2. With its corporate strategy, the top management of an organization answers the ques-

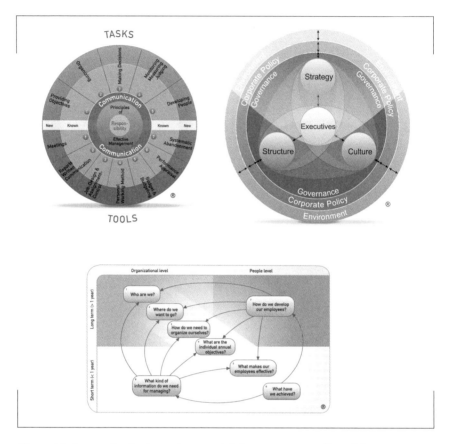

Figure 11: Integrating both previous models into a new overall model

tion: *Where are we headed?* Inputs to strategy are the company purpose and its mission, which answer the question: *Who are we?*

Figure 13 shows the IMS using the technical terms instead of the management questions. More details can be found in the volumes *Management* and *Corporate Policy and Governance*, as well as in a book by Dr. Marius Klauser on management processes which is based on the IMS and expands on its process dimension.[10]

Even these few basic models for wholistic management provide comprehensive solutions for most management problems, enhancing organiza-

---

10 Klauser, Marius: *Lenke, was dein Unternehmen lenkt: Management-Prozess-Architektur (MPA) als Quantensprung in der Unternehmens- und Mitarbeiterführung*, Frankfurt/New York 2010.

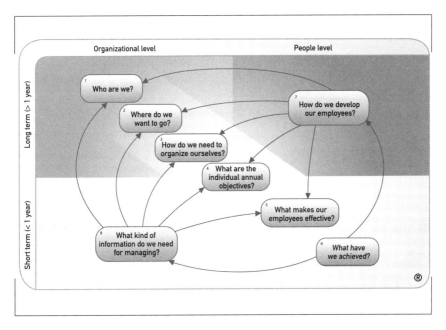

Figure 12: The Integrated Management System®—overview and questions

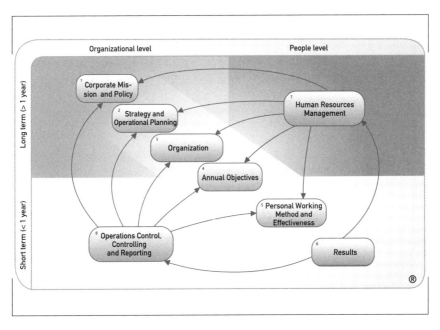

Figure 13: The Integrated Management System®—overview and technical terms

tions' manageability by several orders of magnitude. Above all, they revolutionize the ability to master change effectively, as well as the power to transform actions into results. As these systems are applied further down the organizational periphery, on an adequate scale and at adequate levels, their effects multiply. No more endless meetings, no more tiresome discussion about innumerable details. These models create the conditions for system-immanent coordination and coherence through self-regulation and self-organization, down to the capillaries of an organization.

Integrated Strategy as a Top Cross-Divisional Function

Corporate strategy has to integrate all organizational entities to fulfill its direction-setting purpose. It therefore runs across all business areas (divisions) and all functional units, as shown in figure 14. There are close interactions between both levels because strategy has to take into account the developments in businesses and functions. But its integrated perspective takes top priority.

It is a basic insight from systems theory that the total of all sub-strategies almost never adds up to one consistent overall strategy. It has to be the overall strategy, then, not the individual strategies, which provides the foundation. That is why the navigation system (see part II of this book) is so important for strategy: by organizing data and knowledge in a very

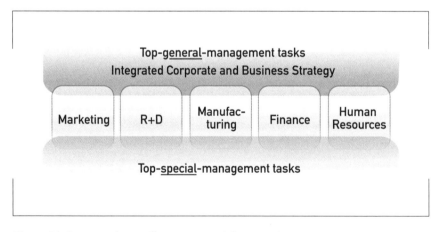

Figure 14: Integrated overall strategies and functional areas

specific way it ensures that the overall perspective will never be lost out of sight.

Just like there is one overall symphony, with each individual instrument—the violin, the cello, the trumpet, the horn—making its own specific contribution, there is only *one* corporate strategy to which business units and functional units make their contributions. Consequently, there cannot be a separate financial or HR strategy; rather, it has to be derived from the overall strategy. It follows from the latter in a very natural, almost self-evident way. So, this book deals with the overall strategy. In the chapter on the Strategy Map we will see how everything results from it organically.

At the level of the overall company, I use the term "corporate strategy"; at the level of individual business units I use "business strategy", wherever the distinction is important for understanding. Otherwise, I simply use the term *strategy*. Beyond the business strategies as such, the corporate strategy comprises consolidating elements, such as financial, legal, or geographical overall decisions, e.g., in branding. The boundaries between corporate policy and corporate strategy are flexible but can be determined quite accurately in the individual case.

At both levels, the same basic principles apply for strategy, in terms of the key challenges of dealing with complexity, interconnected dynamics, and uncertainty. Consequently, the navigation systems and strategic information of the PIMS program, which will be introduced later, apply at both levels.

Figure 15: Business and functional units embedded in the integrated strategy

Only in this system logic and with the content outlined in the following chapters will corporate strategy, in its function as master control, meet four criteria that are critical for success: They determine the right direction for the company with greatest precision and maximum speed, while maintaining the inner cohesion of the company *as a whole*.

This is true of any conceivable situation the company might get into, but it is particularly important and critical for survival and success in times of major change, such as the Great Transformation21.

Chapter 2

Providing Direction Through Corporate Policy and Business Mission

In the logic of my management systems, strategy is embedded in the more comprehensive subsystems of *corporate policy and corporate governance*, I consider the latter to be a part of corporate policy and not the other way round, as is often done as a consequence of the corporate governance dogma. Corporate strategy receives as its inputs from corporate policy the purpose and mission of the business.

The Right Purpose

If the purpose of the company has been wrongly defined, its strategy cannot be right. So, according to the General Management Model, it is necessary to define the corporate purpose before determining the strategy. In a free economy, anyone basically has the freedom to define the purpose of his company ad libitum. That, however, is a rather deceptive freedom, and perhaps the main source of bad management decisions, which then work as wrongly programmed master controls, steering the company in a wrong and possibly irreversible direction. I have explained my reasoning in my books *The Right Corporate Governance* and in *Corporate Policy and Governance*, which is why I will keep the following explanations brief and to the point.

Using the Corporate Purpose to Self-Program for Success

Examples of wrong corporate purposes are *shareholder value* and *value creation*. Equally wrong is the supposedly reformed *stakeholder approach*.

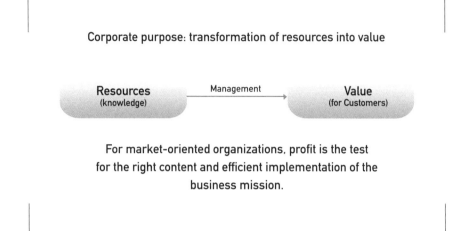

Figure 16: Corporate purpose as transformation if resources into customer value

Both hamper and prevent the very things they are supposed to promote: high profits, happy owners, and a prospering business. Especially when you are determined to make big profit, the last thing you should do is make profit your direct objective.

These wrong purpose decisions of the early 1990s are what actually caused the centennial economic crisis. The things that are currently blamed on governments and economic policies are almost inevitable consequences of "programming errors" committed in the corporate world. This has largely gone unnoticed to date, which is why most national rescue programs miss the point and cannot really solve the problem.

There is only one suitable definition of corporate purpose: *The purpose of the company is to transform resources into customer value. Or, as Peter Drucker put it: The purpose of the organization is to create satisfied customers.*

Value comprises any kind of problem solutions for which customers are prepared to settle a bill. So the right corporate purpose is customer value.

Consequently, the two guiding lights for the navigation of the company are:

customer value, not shareholder value
and
competitiveness, not value creation.

Profit is not an aim in itself, but the result of fulfilling the corporate purpose. That does not mean, of course, that a business can or should go without profits. The economic functions of profit as a capital return and a risk premium remain.

From the point of view of navigating and steering the company, however, profit has a different function: it is *control information*. I suggest viewing profit as a test for the rightness of the company mission, and as a gauge of the *quality of its fulfillment*.

Profit provides two pieces of key information for managerial navigation: one, whether the organization is doing the right thing—referring to the *effectiveness* of its activities—and, two, whether the organization is doing the right thing well—referring to the *efficiency* of its activities.

These are the solutions, and the only ones that work. So while you are basically free to decide whether the purpose of your company is profit maximization or satisfied customers (as in a free society everyone is free even to make the wrong decisions), the consequences of these two different purpose definitions are completely different. Opting for profit means programming the company for failure and for doing harm to society; opting for the customers means programming it for success.

It doesn't make any difference, by the way, whether you avoid talking about "maximization" and go for "optimization" instead, or whether you speak of "sustainable" or "long-term" profits. This becomes very obvious from the navigation logic of the corporate strategy, as we will see in the next part of this book. All these efforts to qualify the term "profit" are ineffective and sometimes desperate attempts to save a bad decision. The problem must be tackled at its roots, correcting the underlying definition purpose. It is the only way to find true solutions.

Shareholder value is adverse to investment and to innovation. The stock market environment inevitably resulting from this programming error leads to a very one-sided approach to corporate management, one that is exclusively guided by financial considerations—which actually not even focus on capital but simply on money, and ultimately on debt money. The former economic concept of capital did not refer to money only, but to machines, factories, products—in other words, real things rather than monetary fiction.

Examples of how it is done are provided by the numerous small and mid-sized businesses that are sometimes treated with condescension: most of them are not managed by shareholder value but they focus on customer satisfaction, which is why they often make much more money than the proponents of the shareholder concept could imagine.

Focus on a Healthy Business

A healthy business will, of course, make profit—but not because this is its ultimate goal. Well-managed companies have very different goals, as I will show in the next part. The widespread fear of profits being diminished by customer orientation is completely unfounded—the opposite is true. Typically, profits are higher when based on customer orientation—and, as a pleasant side effect, "sustainably" so—due to the very fact that they are not directly targeted but *result* from achieving very different objectives.

Defining a company's purpose with a focus on customers meets two key criteria for success: *First*, it provides a solution to the question of organization's social responsibility by defining its purpose not as a money-making machine but as a productive cell of society, without falling into old ideological molds of socialism or of the state-run economic order.

Second, this corporate purpose maximizes the chance that the organization's management boards will make more right than wrong *decisions*, thus contributing to the entrenchment of right and good management.

So, with the rigorous focus on customers, I let the *enterprise itself* take center stage, rather than any of the two interest groups, shareholders or stakeholders. Since the early 1950s, stakeholders have been skulking around the fringes of economic history as a potential corporate purpose; the shareholder approach has been dominating and misguiding corporate leaders since the early 1990s. Both have proved to be inappropriate corporate goals or purposes.

My 180-degree turn toward customer orientation does not mean that the interests of both these groups should not be taken into account. On the contrary, their legitimate interests will be optimally met with the corporate and customer approach. Only if a company has satisfied customers can it meet any kind of aspirations, perhaps even to the fullest. If, however, shareholders' and stakeholders' interests take higher or even top priority, customer value will inevitably rank second. Distributing the business's output among shareholders and stakeholders will take priority over generating that output.

Nobody is forced to accept my solution, as we are now at the heart of *normative* management, dealing with true *value decisions*.

These values I am talking about should, however, not preempt a decision; rather, they should result from the potential consequences of a decision. Only a decision in favor of customer value will result in the right management of the company. It is the customer who pays the bills. That, in turn, results in all interests being served as well as possible.

No other purpose can achieve that. It is logically impossible to find the right strategy unless it is explicitly directed at solving customer problems and creating customer value. There is not one strategically relevant question that can be answered without focusing on customer value.

What is Our Purpose?

Once this general definition of purpose is accepted, it needs to be adjusted to the individual situation of the specific organization when working out the company policy and its core element, the business mission. Questions to be asked are:

- What is *our* purpose?
- What resources do we transform into what value?
- Who are *our* customers? Who should and could they be, and who should they not be?

Resources include all kinds of goods and services required to create value for customers. The key resource of the 21st century will be knowledge, which is already true of numerous sectors, such as pharmaceuticals or IT. In the knowledge society, knowledge is the raw material for production, the means of production, and the production tool, all at once; more and more often it is also the product itself.

An additional factor is the (meta-) knowledge of a higher level which is required and effectively transform knowledge into value. At the control and system level, this knowledge is identical to management; in the context of the New World it is the management in and of complex systems.

The Right Mission

After the purpose of the company, the second basic decision that is needed as input for the strategy is the corporate or business *mission*—the mission that the company aspires to fulfill in tangible business terms.

I can keep this section short because the related part of my management systems makes it very clear what to consider and what to decide. Here we have one of the cases where the simplicity of good master control decisions becomes very clear even for extremely complex systems. As such, the business mission is so simple, clear and effective for the control of a company as a roundabout is for traffic. This is a metaphor I like to use when it comes to self-organization. By contrast, the *answers* to the key questions of the business mission and the *decisions* to be taken for the business mission are anything but simple.

The Three Elements of the Right Business Mission

A business mission that really works has to comprise three elements: needs, capabilities, and beliefs.

Something to be clearly distinguished from the business mission is the *mission statements*. It would be a mistake to begin with the *wording* of the mission statement right away, as is so often done, and even worse to start by searching for a catchy *slogan* or claim. These things belong at the very end of the process of shaping the business mission, not its beginning. They are tasks to be handled by the corporate communication, the marketing, and the advertising functions.

At the beginning of the process it is important to think through one's business operations, asking the three key questions listed below. The next step consists in clarifying the associated sub-questions, which I will introduce in the following paragraphs. Only after this step has been completed does it make sense to search for catchy words and phrases.

The key questions are:

1. What is the need we are satisfying? Or: What do customers pay us for?
2. What are our strengths? Or: What can we do better than others and where are we superior?

3. What are our beliefs based on? Or: From where will we get the power that we are going to need when motivation starts fading?

What the World Lacks: The Need

The first question forces us to focus outside the company, to the market and the customers corresponding to the business purpose; e.g., to the key need—or to the center and source of proliferating complexity.

I am talking about *need*, not (yet) about want, and least of all about demand. Need is more comprehensive, and it is something objective. Sometimes need and want are congruent, sometimes a perceived want has to arise from an objective need. Anything that is a want is also a need. These logical relations provide the basis for assessing the market and approximating its size for strategy purposes.

Not all wants are satisfied, not all create a demand. As you can tell, we are in the midst of the difficult questions of strategy, marketing, and—a key element in the age of *complexity*—communication. One of the starting points is the available income and its use by customers, so the following three questions need to be answered:

- What do customers pay us for?
- What do they *really* pay us for?
- What do *non*-customers pay for?

These questions are aimed at the heart of the business. As simple as they may appear, it is usually quite a demanding task to find substantial, action-oriented answers. Managers unwilling to settle for superficial slogans will be familiar with the experience.

In less than a third of all companies the answers have been thought through carefully, although the master control effect of a mission decision calls for particular thoroughness. Even when people believe they have answered the first two questions well, the third is a challenge to most corporate leaders.

For most executives permanently think about their customers—but who ever remembers to think of non-customers? For instance, if you have a 30 percent market share you will rightly be proud of your business performance. But the question is: what makes 70 percent of potential customers buy somewhere else?

Where We Are Better Than Others: The Skills

The second element of the business mission is defined by asking:

- What are our strengths?
- What can we do better than others?
- What is our superiority based on?

These questions draw the attention from the company's environment to the organization itself and its strengths, to the inside, but always *in comparison to others and to the need*, i.e., using points of reference which are located in the environment. So this is not simply an inside perspective, it is an *inside-outside-inside* perspective.

Identifying an organization's strengths usually is not very difficult. But finding out where its specific skills lie, and what it can do better to just the extent that will cause the customer to prefer that company over its competitors, that is a high art and a top management responsibility.

What Moves Us Deep Inside: The Beliefs

The third pillar of a business mission is what really moves people deep inside, what drives their power of achievement and their performance reserves. Related questions are these:

- What do we really believe in?
- What are we convinced of?
- What drives our commitment?
- What gives us the strength to deliver performance?
- More specifically, what can give us that strength when our motivation starts fading?

This is not about motivation, incentives and such—as important as they may be—but about something much more profound: it is about the power that enables us to master even what seem to be hopeless situations. When you can still *motivate* people in the ordinary sense, there are seldom truly serious problems. But when it comes to the point where motivation is exhausted, yet the aim is still far from having been reached, this is where this particular element of the business mission comes in, mobilizing the last reserves even beyond the "dead end". I have not come across even one successful company which has never gone through this particular test. Endurance athletes, or perhaps even better: doctors and nurses, are familiar with this situation. It occurs in the lives of many people at some point or other. Whether you face up to it or not is a matter of conscience.

Organizations which fail to give their employees good reasons to mobilize their last reserves, beyond motivational factors and any thoughts of money, can hardly be successful on a permanent basis as they will fail in times of crisis. The most important reasons lie in what the company is actually good at and what the customer really needs.

Emerging From the Interaction of Elements: The New Whole

The synergetic interaction of the three elements described generates a new whole—a new system with new properties and capabilities. The new arises as three further systemic capabilities or properties result from the interaction: value, pride, and meaning. In systems sciences, such properties which seem to emerge "from nothing" are called *emerging properties*. They are typical results of indirect control, which only occurs in complex, self-organizing systems.

Sources of Value

Customer value results from the interaction of need and strengths. When there is a need but the company does not have the required strengths there can be no value. On the other hand, there can be no value if the company has strengths for which there is no need. It takes both to generate value—value to the customer. Value is a phenomenon emerging from the interaction of need and skill, that is, an indirect result of directly created conditions.

Source of Pride, Self-Respect, and Self-Confidence

From the interaction of what the company is capable of and what its people believe in—precisely because the company has those strengths—result the crucial *collective* and *personal* values of corporate culture: pride in the company and its achievements, as well as *self-respect* and *self-confidence*. Anything the company is not capable of will hardly be a source of pride, so under these conditions there will hardly be conviction and commitment. Quite clearly, we are now moving toward the heart of the corporate culture.

Source of Meaning

Meaning results from the interaction of belief and need. The term does not have a metaphysical-philosophical meaning here; I am using it in the same practical sense as Viktor Frankl, the great Austrian psychiatrist, did in his book on the meaning of life.[11]

It is the meaning—both individual and collective—that is inherent in the service to a cause or mission. Meaning is much more than motivation in the usual sense, and so meaning is a key parameter of corporate culture. Motivation is rarely sufficient to mobilize someone's last energy reserves; usually that is only possible if the person can see a meaning in his task or in his service to an organization's cause. Meaning is the basis of motivation. In this context, Frankl uses Fried rich Nietzsche's famous quote: "*Whoever has a Why to live for can bear almost any How …*" Conversely, if things are pointless, motivational measures are useless.

Business Mission in a Systemic Overview

The following figure 17 shows an overview of the pillars of the business mission and their interrelationships, both as a whole and an interacting system. Depending on how the terms are interpreted, the path leading from the specific to the general runs from *business mission to corporate mission* and, beyond that, to what you might call *organizational mission or institutional mission.*

With sensible adjustments, all organizations—schools, hospitals, administrative authorities, cultural organizations, universities, and so on—need a mission, and they need to ask the same questions to determine what it is. Only on this basis is it possible to have the right strategies, plans, decisions, and actions.

---

11 Frankl, Viktor: *Man's Search for Meaning*, Washington, 1984.

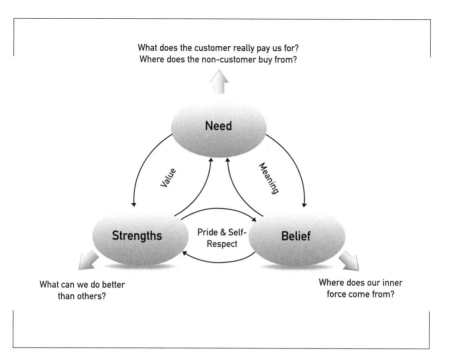

Figure 17: The elements of the business mission

Focus as an Effect of Master Control

Implementing the business mission gets easier the more it compels the organization to *concentrate* its force. This is another master control effect which strongly influences the strategy form the very start. Disciplining oneself to focus on few things, just a small number of key areas, is among the most important rules for the effectiveness both of people and of organizations.[12]

The need for *master control* through a business mission is all the greater,

- the more complex, fast-moving and intransparent the environment is;
- the larger the organization is;
- the more experts and mind-workers it has;
- the more risks it faces.

---

12 See Malik, Fredmund: *Managing, Performing, Living. Effective Management for a New Era.* Frankfurt/New York, 2006.

It is also even more important then, to communicate the business mission effectively and to interpret it correctly. In today's organizations, decisions are taken at many levels and by many people, and chances are that each of these individuals has another business mission in mind and applies another mental model. Alignment and cohesion are hardly possible without the *master control* effect of the business mission.

The Right Performance

At this point in my General Management Model, we move from corporate policy to strategy.

An organization's business mission has to prove its worth in six groups of variables. I refer to this set of variables as *Central Performance Controls* (CPC). They belong to the few *constants* in change and are therefore suitable for safe navigation and orientation. They are the system's *essential variables*, which together determine the organization's success and longevity.

These six key variables are:

- Market position
- Innovation performance
- Productivities
- Attractiveness to the right people
- Liquidity and cash flow
- Profitability.

These six variables have a double function: they are master controls for the present as well as the future business, or for innovation.

The following chapters will deal with the function of these six variables in strategic navigation; after that, in the chapters on PIMS I will explain what we know about them and how they provide help in steering an organization.

Whatever a business or any other kind of organization does, it shows in these six key variables. The market position of a business organization will be strengthened by increasing customer value, while a non-profit organization will focus on the recipients of their services. But even the latter will have to deal with the issue of market position at some point: sooner or later, not even public sector organizations will have monopolies, so they, too, will have to compete in the marketplace.

Central Performance Control (CPC)

If you have these six parameters under control you are on the safe side—which, however, does not mean you are bound to be successful. But if you do not have control of these six variables, failure is almost a certainty. Most corporate risks are located here.

The complex of *Central Performance Control*, made up of these six relevant control variables, is located at the *highest tier of master controls, together with purpose and mission*. It creates cohesion and ensures *central control* in the entire system. Metaphorically speaking, it is the neuronal power center, the "six-pack of control" with a highly sensitive "solar plexus". Should more variables be needed for central control at some point, we can easily add them to the system as new modules, in line with the logic of all my models which is evolutionary and open to new developments.

The purpose and the mission show the way. In the definition given here, it is quite clear that these master controls take effect down to the capillaries of an organization: they enable us to distinguish performance from non-performance. In doing this, they establish another one of the major feedback loops required to master complexity.

The CPC Complex and Its Threefold Function

The interaction of the six variables listed above has a *threefold effect*: They are *performance areas and assessment parameters, both at once*. In other words, the organization has to perform in these six areas; all entrepreneurial activities have to be aligned accordingly. At the same time, the results achieved form the basis for the continuous assessment of corporate performance. They provide the yardstick against which performance is measured. So they are both *risk sensors* and *risk controls*.

But the essential variables concept goes far beyond the so-called *Balanced Scorecard*. The latter was a step forward, compared to the one-sidedness of the shareholder value approach, but it still falls short of meeting all requirements. The variables typically measured in the Balanced Scorecard are largely arbitrary and usually much too finance-focused.

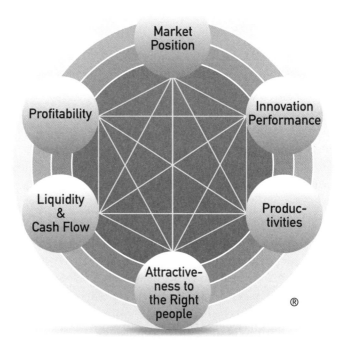

Figure 18: The complex of the six interconnected Central Performance Control

The control-relevant parameters for overall systems control, such as the essential variables, have to be *right* (and empirically demonstrably so); they have to have sufficient *control impact*, provide the means to control complexity, and safeguard the *viability* of an organization in its environment. This is exactly what can be achieved with the six key variables of *Central Performance Control.*

Figure 18 shows the six key variables and their connections. They form a network *system* because they are interconnected and interdependent. Any kind of isolated consideration or analysis, let alone isolated interventions, would typically be unsystemic and reductionist. They would preclude the true understanding and control of the system.

Each of the six essential variables is, in itself, a complex field of influencing factors and sub-variables, but organizing them in six groups they become easier to handle and transparent. It is one example of how you can get complex facts under control, structuring knowledge in the right way and creating an elegant and simple solution—without ruining the complexity of the underlying facts, for these are required to make the system work.

The contents of the individual performance fields are not predefined, as they partly depend on the specifics of the organization's business or activity, and thus have to be adaptable to the particular situation. Besides, the inner structure of the six variables may change, depending on the evolution of markets and economies, and most of all on the success of the organization itself. In other words, the system needs to be capable of evolving.[13] The fundamental factors, however, originate from PIMS research.

One of the key tasks of *corporate strategy* is to do exactly that: to determine those contents and limits of the six CPC variables that are crucial in each individual case, and to keep adjusting them to changing conditions. This takes us to a new understanding of strategy: as a continuous process of anticipatory and adaptive evolution.

---

13 In order to have sufficient complexity for the control of the overall system consisting of the organization and its environment, the aim of our research was to project the developments in an organization onto the smallest possible number of variables. Nevertheless, the system is expandable.

Part III:

Mastering Complexity Through Reliable Navigation in Any Circumstance

The What and the Wherewith of strategy are covered by the Navigator and the Strategy Map. They will be dealt with in this part of the book.

Chapter 1

Revolutionizing Strategic Navigation

Now let us move right on to the ^REvolution of navigating the hypercomplex, dynamic systems of economy and society. The central question addressed here is: What do we have to look out for, in order to find the right destinations and routes and to master the complexity and dynamics of such systems?

I am speaking of a revolution because most of what has so far been regarded as strategy is no longer useful, and has actually been wrong all along. As this part of the book makes particularly clear, shareholder value and value creation strategies are the wrong points of reference for strategic management decisions, in particular as the Great Transformation and the transition from the Old to the New World present new challenges. An increasing number of corporate leaders are realizing that conventional strategy concepts are misleading. But what they usually lack is a new solution, one that really works.

This solution is the subject of this chapter: the currently most effective, always reliable and globally unique *navigation system* as a tool of assistance for corporate top management. When I make bold statements of this kind in seminars and speeches there is often strong opposition, which is not very surprising, in particular from those managers who never had the opportunity to learn anything other than conventional MBA and economics knowledge. But it usually takes less than an hour to convince them that what I say is true. After that they are usually impressed, even enthusiastic about the clear and compelling nature of the navigation logic I shall present on the following pages, as it opens the way to a new universe of orientation, one they had not even been able to imagine.

The most positive responses tend to come from scientists, mathematicians, computer scientists, doctors, and often from lawyers: they realize that in some areas, management can have the same quality they know and appreciate from their own studies. I include lawyers, too, because they are accustomed to working with logic, precision and clarity of expression, without being able to quantify everything. It is often the same with management.

After the navigation system, I will then introduce another assistance system, the *Strategy Map*, and in the subsequent chapters I will explain how strategies are operationalized and quantified.

The Malik-Gälweiler Navigation System

When embarking on this expedition into unknown territories, companies with superior navigation systems have an advantage. It is important to understand precisely which operational and strategic *control and orientation variables* you can always rely on, whatever the circumstance.

Under conditions of profound and radical change, strategy has to be suitable for dealing with complexity, and it has to work even when there is constitutive ignorance regarding the "white spots" on the strategic landscape. Adaptability and robustness are essential, and above all, strategy must be objectively *right*. The *Malik-Gälweiler Navigation System, MG Navigator®* for short, meets these requirements like no other system currently does, being built according to cybernetic principles and integrated in the context of our Wholistic Management Systems. With these properties, the navigation system can be linked to the neighboring systems of Strategy: Structure, Culture, Executives, Corporate Governance, and Corporate Policy.

Together, they form the perfectly functioning overall control system for determining and controlling the organization's direction. It comprises all orientation and steering mechanisms required for success, sustainability, and viability. In figure 19 below, this is depicted graphically by embedding the navigation icon in the Strategy subsystem.

The MG Navigation System focuses on the *healthy business* and the *viability* of the organization. Other strategy variables which have traditionally been considered important, such as profit and growth, are integrated in the concept but assume a new meaning in the context of the much more comprehensive MG Navigation System. Thus it becomes possible to answer virtually all related strategic questions that are yet unsolved;

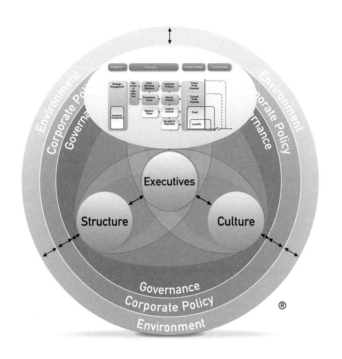

Figure 19: Navigation System embedded in strategy

for instance, how long "long-term" really is or what "sustainable profit" is—these and other questions that business economics and business administration have yet to resolve.

The foundation for this navigation system was created by *Aloys Gälweiler* who, during his time as Chief Representative of Brown Boveri in Mannheim, Germany (which later became ABB) was one of the most seasoned planning and strategy experts ever. When I first read a publication written by Gälweiler I instantly realized that I was looking at one of the greatest breakthroughs for strategic management.[14]

---

14 My long-standing collaboration with Gälweiler, who also taught in many of our seminars, ended with his untimely death in 1984. I was able to publish posthumously twelve of his working papers and articles (written between 1977 and 1984), thanks to the outstanding initiative commitment of our then head of research, Prof. Dr. Markus Schwan-

In the following years I complemented and expanded Gälweiler's basic concept by adding the necessary cybernetic tools, including the insights and tools from PIMS, S-Curve analyses, and network models—which I will deal with later—as well as the instruments and methods required to use them. Today, Gälweiler's framework forms an integral part of our Wholistic Management System, and so could unfold its full potential.

Based on the rich industry experience he gained in a major corporation, Aloys Gälweiler knew that sustainable success requires more than profits and growth. He had also seen that especially large profits and fast growth can be seeds of later failure, and even of the decline of a company. He had seen it happen in real life, and it had shaped his concept of strategy.

Back then, Gälweiler was far ahead of his time, just like other pioneers of system-focused and cybernetic management, such as Stafford Beer, Hans Ulrich, Walter Krieg, and Frederic Vester.[15] When conventional approaches were still applicable, only the technological leaders among the businesses had a need for cybernetic management and strategy solutions, especially if they used sophisticated control and regulation logic in their own products or if this logic was a product innovation in its own right. Now, under the complex conditions of dynamic and globally inter-connected systems, the true significance of this pioneer work is becoming evident. Gälweiler's strategy logic is universal, and thus valid and industry-relevant through time, which is why it is a perfect match for our management systems. Although Gälweiler held an honorary professorship at the University of Mannheim, in addition to his position in industry, the enormous progress his groundbreaking concept represented was never noticed by the established business economists of his time. But that is something we often see with breakthrough innovations.

---

inger. See Gälweiler, Aloys: *Strategische Unternehmensführung*. Campus Verlag, Frankfurt/New York 1987; 3rd edition 2005.

15 As for keeping the works of Stafford Beer and Frederic Vester available to corporate managers, see appendix.

The Right Strategy for a Future Unknown

Let me stress again at this point that one of the core problems in strategic navigation is corporate management's systematically being misled by operational data, as provided by finance and accounting.

This focus on operational data is one of the main reasons why a management team solely aiming for profits will notice undesirable developments too late, and therefore run the risk of missing out on the future because appropriate countermeasures are not taken in time. As a consequence, this approach will inevitably create a need to manage crises caused by one's own mismanagement. Examples include the former DaimlerChrysler Group and the failure of Swissair, as well as the collapses of renowned banks that have occurred since 2007.

Contrary to what common theory and practice suggest, the main purpose of strategic management cannot be to detect deviations from target figures, based on corresponding analyses, and to take *corrective* measures. The key purpose of strategic management is *to bring about* desired developments for the business, and *to prevent* undesirable and disastrous ones.

A comparison of target and actual figures, of the kind that is usually done in profit/loss statements, cannot accomplish that because the signals needed to trigger corrective action will always appear too late. It is therefore necessary to identify points of orientation which, due to the factual information they provide—and not, mind you, by extrapolation—permit exploring a longer time period. This will result in time gained to identify the need for action and to initiate measures to secure the company's livelihood and further success.

The MG Navigator is comparable to the natural evolution of sensory organs, which become ever more efficient in higher organisms and thus permit ever improved orientation. In this sense, even the original achievements of *Aloys Gälweiler* represented an *evolutionary* leap in corporate management.

Putting an End to Arbitrariness in Strategy Design

Contrary to both traditional business economics and conventional management theory, Gälweiler's system had a *compelling* inner logic to it, even

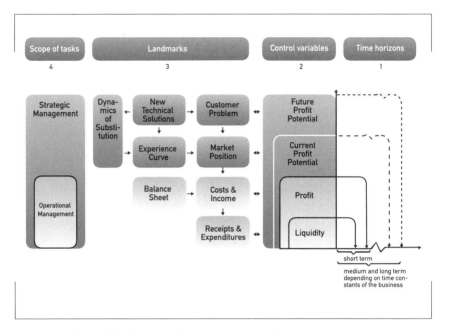

Figure 20: The Malik-Gälweiler Navigation System for integral strategic navigation logic

in its earlier version. It is due to this logic, among other things, that *Gälweiler's* work represents a significant step forward in corporate management.

Gälweiler's system marks the end of arbitrariness and mere subjectivity, because it raises the management of corporations to the level of reliable functioning based on the cybernetic laws of nature. This is massively reinforced by the possibilities of quantification, as provided by the PIMS program which will be the topic of the next part but one.

With ingenious simplicity, the MG Navigation System comprises all the essential facts that are *necessary* for the overall management of a company, both *operational* and *strategic*, and therefore covering the short, medium, and long-term.

As mentioned before, this will clarify the different questions still unsolved, such as how long "long-term" can actually be, under what circumstances and how growth can be healthy and from what point it gets unhealthy, and under what circumstances innovation is urgently required and cannot be left to random, wild creativity.

Together with the *Strategy Map* used for navigating unknown "territories", which will be discussed in the next chapter, we now have the universal system for the orientation and management of all activities of an organization. Since it is omnifunctional, its application is independent of how the global economic will play out.

Looking Further Into the Future—Without Forecasts

The MG Navigator puts an end to corporate management's dependency on conventional forecasts, projections, and extrapolations—and in particular on the linear projections which unfortunately have become so popular. Thanks to its logic and feedback control, the system permits more substantiated and reliable assumptions about the future. As we will see in a moment, it takes advantage of the cybernetic law of integration of higher system levels, thus permitting the functions of early warning and anticipative control which are so essential to survival and success.

Looking even further into the future, yet doing so without forecasts—this seems to be a contradiction. In fact, it is the practical application of an insight by *Peter F. Drucker*, according to whom strategies are not about "future decisions" but about the "futurity of present decisions".

Time Constants and System Dead Time

One groundbreaking achievement of this navigation system is that it solves the question of timing in strategic planning. Instead of arbitrarily defining time periods as short, medium, and long-term, the overall management of an institution is structured in two areas: operational and strategic management. Operational management is about *using* and *exploiting* existing profit potential, while strategic management is about *maintaining* current and *building* future profit potential.

This is both a convincing and elegant solution to the issue of time periods, for they are not isolated variables that can be squeezed into arbitrarily defined categories or derived from mainstream thinking.

What mid-term and what long-term is depends on the objective facts of the business: namely the *business-specific time constants. Time constants* are the periods for which the company has to make irreversible decisions because the nature of the business calls for it. In other words, it is the time required to generate the conditions that are key to business success.

For instance, creating a completely new automobile rarely takes less than five years, even for the fastest automotive companies. Five years from the point the development project is launched until the new model can be seen in the streets. Now, this new car may or may not be successful in the market. If it is not, another model has to be developed, which will take another five or so years. So the time constant is ten years in this case: twice the development time until a car can be put to market which will hopefully be accepted by consumers.

This is the *system dead time* during which hardly anything can be changed. During this time, the company is restricted to a certain course, and this time period has to be covered by strategy.

In the pharmaceuticals industry, aviation, and the energy sector, time constants are much longer: Companies in these industries are strategically tied down for 15 to 50 years and unable to make major changes, so the decisions that management takes today had better be right for the entire duration. These decisions have to be taken for an uncertain future.

By contrast, in the fashion industry, for instance, lots of things can be changed rather quickly because collections appear in rapid succession. Yet changes cannot be made at arbitrary intervals, as even this industry depends on manufacturing, marketing, and sales infrastructures.

Remember how I defined strategy at the beginning of this book: How to act when we do not know what the future will bring? How to start off acting in such a way as to be successful in the long run? How to think about future effects of current decisions?

Limitations of the Market Economy: Why Economists Do Not See Far Enough

At this point, let me add a critical remark regarding the workings of the market economy which most economists value so highly. To do this I distinguish between a critical and a naïve market theory. The latter served as justification of such things as the shareholder approach, the bonus systems, and generally all the developments in the global financial system, above all its excesses. That is why the proponents of main stream economics failed to notice the coming even of this crisis of centennial proportions.

According to the naïve theory of the market, economic subjects let themselves be guided by the signals coming from the market, in particular by relative prices and costs, and then steer their resources and business activities to where they can make the highest profits.

These signals, however, are largely useless for companies specializing in technologies that span several decades or even centuries—and we will come to that later—and therefore have to make irreversible investment decisions for these periods. Current prices and costs do not tell these companies whether or not to invest in a certain future technology. For instance, the costs of road traffic are largely irrelevant for the construction of airplanes and airports.

This market economy theory is therefore meaningless for many businesses. It is important to be aware of the limitations of the markets, especially for those who, like me, basically favor a free market economy. Not knowing these limitations means expecting too much of the market economy.

In this context, strategy is an expedition into unknown territory. Traditional thinking, conventional strategic approaches and methods are virtually useless here. It takes different tools to master situations like these, including those I describe in this book. For further details, see parts IV, V, and VI.

What Must Be Monitored: Variables for Control and Orientation

The MG Navigator comprises two kinds of navigation aids for the management of the business and of the entire organization: *control variables* and *orientation variables* (see figure 19). There are four control variables and eight parameters of orientation.

Control variables are the parameters that management absolutely has to keep under control if it wants a strong, controllable and viable company, a company that survives and prospers.

Orientation variables indicate whether these control variables are or are not under control. In other words, they provide knowledge and information on whether the control variables are on target. Let me give you an example: For motorists, one relevant control variable is speed. To assess and control it effectively we can use the speedometer as a reference.

The four *control variables* of the navigation system are *liquidity, profit, current profit potential* (CPP) and *future profit potential* (FPP).

The eight *orientation variables* are *receipts* and *expenditures, income* and *cost, market position* and *cost position* (which actually refers to the lowest cost limit) as well as *new technical solutions* and the *customer problem.*

Reliable Function With Cybernetic Control Systems

With the variables specified above, the navigation system spans a total of four system levels which are defined by cybernetic control relationships, interrelated and interdependent (see figure 19). Going from bottom to top, the first two levels comprise the tasks of operational management and the two levels above comprise the strategic management tasks.

Together, they permit organizations to be reliably controlled both operationally and strategically. In sum, the MG Navigation system permits *wholistic* and *simultaneous* management across all dimensions—for both the present and the *future*, from an internal and an *external* perspective.

All of these four system levels *have* to be considered. If even one of them is overlooked, this will inevitably trigger undesirable developments which will not even be noticed at first. Once they become visible it will usually be too late for corrective action.

The following description of cybernetic control logic refers to figure 21. The navigation system should be read from bottom to top, starting with liquidity, following the historical emergence of commercial management. Up until the early renaissance, merchants used to manage their businesses by means of cash and promissory notes, or in other words, with liquidity-based instruments. Back then this was enough to keep the business under control. But as businesses grew increasingly complex and more and more long-term commitments were necessary, as people had to invest in things

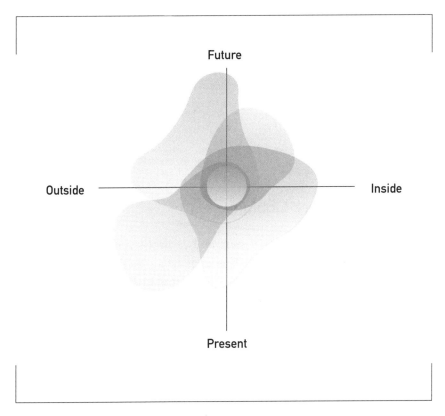

Future

Outside ─────────────── Inside

Present

Figure 21: The universal coordinate system for top management

like ship construction and equipment, an additional, new and higher navigation level was called for.

An ingenious solution was presented with the invention of *double-entry book-keeping*. Its first conclusive description was published in a 1494 book by Luca Pacioli, a Franciscan monk and mathematician. It was then referred to as the "Venetian method." Early users included the Medici and the merchants of Genoa, to whom it provided invaluable benefits for the management of their businesses. Double-entry bookkeeping permitted them to capture a new kind of information on business *success* in terms of profit and loss. It enabled them to not only control their businesses but even to apply anticipatory control. Similarly, as complexity kept growing, further navigation levels were explored which all followed the same principles.

Chapter 2

Reliable Control Through Cybernetic Navigation

First System Level: Liquidity

As mentioned before, the first system and control level is dedicated to liquidity. I will describe this level in greater detail than the three remaining ones because the logical connections essential for effective navigation keep recurring, so they will apply to each of the subsequent system levels as well.

This is one of the enormous time-saving advantages of the MG Navigator: Once you have understood the underlying logic, you can apply it at all levels—a typical example of how complex control problems often have surprisingly simple solutions.

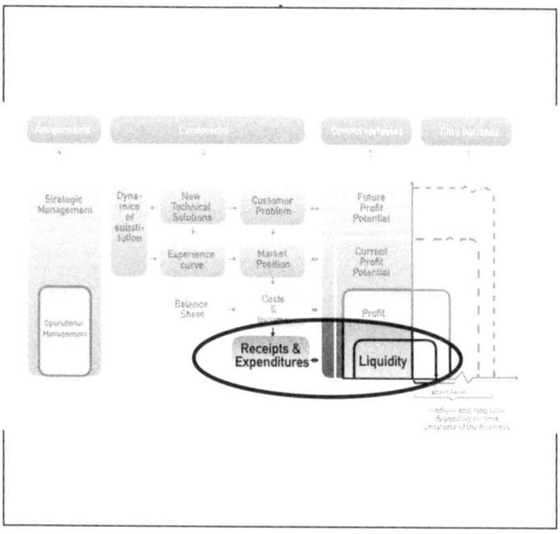

Figure 22: Controlling liquidity

It enables you to disseminate this strategic navigation tool through the capillaries of your organization, thus ensuring that all managers who have to be involved in shaping and implementing strategy will think and act according to the same principles. In other words, the foundations for self-organization are laid across the entire organization, following the maxim I mentioned before: *Organize a system so that it can self-organize.*

Market Economy Means Survival by Paying Bills

The first and most fundamental control variable of a company is not profit, as mainstream thinking would have us believe, but *liquidity*—the ability to make necessary payments at any given time. This, and nothing else, is the key to survival or failure in a market economy.

Even a high-performing company will inevitably perish if it does not manage to remain solvent at all times. It will go bankrupt or be subject to a takeover. In a market economy, not profit but liquidity is crucial for survival, in both economic and legal terms. Consequently, liquidity has to be kept under control—or managed—at all times.

So the management of a company is not so much about the factors that everyone always talks about—profit, growth, profitability, and so on—but about safeguarding the company's solvency.

And contrary to widespread opinion, the market economy as a system is not defined from the profit angle but from the liquidity angle. Actually it does not even matter in a market economy whether or not you make profit—as long as you are able to pay your bills you are part of the capitalist game. Where exactly you take the money from to pay those bills does not matter so much—which is not to say that profit is not an issue. It will come into play once we address the next higher system level.

Controlling Liquidity

For liquidity control, companies today usually have a dedicated, often highly specialized function called *Finance* or *Treasury*. After all, in a globally interconnected world full of turbulences and unpredictable financial streams and interest rates, liquidity control is a highly complex task.

But no matter how complex this task may be, ultimately it all comes down to the two orientation variables relevant for liquidity, *revenues* and *expenditure*, as shown in figure 21. The difference between the two is crucial for the survival of the company.

Liquidity Is Always Short-Term

By its very nature, liquidity is a typical short-term variable which cannot be turned into a "long-term" one. Of course, a CEO today will typically have reliable knowledge of whether the business is able to meet its financial obligations, in particular when the head of Finance has given him the current state of liquidity first thing in the morning. But how far does this knowledge reach into the *future?*

As such, liquidity management can always capture the *short term only*, for solvency is always a momentary state. Depending on the characteristics of a business, one may be able to make an estimate as to whether it will be solvent over the next few weeks or months (or in some industries, over the next few days only) but that is not enough by far to make decisions that will bind a company for many years to come. How, then, can we extend the time horizon into the future? Not by reverting to the usual method—extrapolative projections—but by changing the navigation level.

Looking to the Future By Switching System Levels

It would make no sense at all to say, "*We have never been short of cash over the past ten years, so we will surely remain solvent over the next ten years.*" This is immediately obvious. Yet it is the same (lack of) logic that is inherent in one of the standard forecast approaches, and even human thinking processes work in much the same manner. *The future will largely be like the past ...*—this is how most people think, and managers are not excluded.

Even the most sophisticated analyses of current and past liquidity and its drivers—receipts and expenditures—will not provide any information on future liquidity, since it depends not on current liquidity but other factors.

To look further into the future and capture a longer period of time, which is indispensable for strategy development, a typical cybernetic approach is useful: the change of system levels. It is the only way to explore new orientation and control variables that provide additional information.

This integration of a higher system level brings *profit* and the corresponding orientation variables onto the navigator's screen. "Higher system level" means that you can survey a longer time horizon when you look at a different kind of information, just as an elevated vantage point will give you a broader view of the land beneath.

That is why I mentioned the historical example of double-entry book-keeping. It enabled people to look at things from the *profit* point of view, which was completely new to them, and it enabled them to survey a longer time period because profit logically *precedes liquidity*. So in my historical example, double-entry bookkeeping was the tool that enabled even the medieval merchants to look into the future.

Protection against Preprogrammed Control Errors

We are now getting to a very important property of the MG Navigator. It applies to all four levels of the system and, to my knowledge, is only known to a minority of managers outside the accounting function: it is the protection from preprogrammed mismanagement. What does this mean?

The control variable *liquidity* can be systematically misleading for the following reason:

Liquidity can be high even when profits are low—and vice versa.

Without profit and loss calculation this potentially contradictory mutual relation between control and orientation variables is impossible to see, but with the P+L it becomes very obvious. Even the most sophisticated liquidity extrapolation will not reveal the contrary trends of the two variables liquidity and profit. It takes a completely different type of information system to recognize them—which is double-entry bookkeeping.

The prerequisite for and source of liquidity, profit, may already be sending negative control signals (losses) when liquidity as such is still sending positive ones (full cash boxes). Paying attention only to liquidity would be a surefire way right into bankruptcy, as one would not be able to see the need for

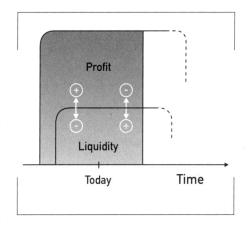

Figure 23: Logically opposed relationships between control variables

action and, reassured by the stacks of cash available, would remain inactive. Conversely, liquidity can be low or even negative while the business is yielding high profits.

In short, the liquidity situation can be contrary to the profit situation, which generates wrong control signals. This cannot go on forever because sooner or later profits or losses will also affect liquidity, but the state of affairs may well continue long enough to encourage systematic control errors, and by the time they are detected it may be too late to change course.

In sum, an exclusive focus on liquidity would automatically incur wrong decisions because managers would fail to take timely precautions to ensure sufficient liquidity in the future, for instance by entering into negotiations with banks early on. If a loss then materializes in the accounts, it may well be too late for counter-measures.

A lack of control know-how is one of the key causes of undesirable developments in business, and one of the main risks in corporate management. This will become even more obvious at the higher levels of the navigation system. Systems are not controlled through cash or power but through information, and they control themselves through information. Self-regulation and self-organization are therefore only possible if the necessary information systems are in place.

Early Warning and Anticipatory Control

The conclusion from the above is that you can never derive insights from bottom to top—that is, draw conclusions from the state of liquidity for the profit situation—while the opposite, drawing conclusions from profits with regard to liquidity, is always possible, and reliably so.

The higher-level control variable profit has two extremely important cybernetic control qualities: It is both an *early-warning variable* and a *pre- (or anticipatory) control variable* for liquidity. Proceeding from the profit perspective, one can look further into the future because earnings precede liquidity both chronologically and in terms of cause and effect. This is the only way to extend the time horizon and make valid forecasts for liquidity development—by system analysis, not by extrapolation.

Second System Level: Profit

If one were to choose one single variable for the financial success of a business, *return on investment (ROI)*, would be the best suited. It is defined as EBIT (earnings before interest and tax) in relation to the fixed and working capital required for operations.

This is the current ROI figure provided by the accounting system. We will soon see that there is another ROI figure, *return on potential*, which can help achieve sensational solutions to some of the problems that have so far seemed unsolvable.

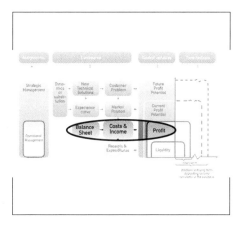

Figure 24: Controlling success

Extending the Time Horizon

So, exploring a longer time horizon and improving anticipatory liquidity control are *only* possible by means of the profit variable. Let me emphasize this again: earnings *precede* liquidity in terms of logic, cause and effect, and time. Only by means of liquidity can we eliminate the risk of being systematically deceived by liquidity.

Note that profit control cannot replace liquidity control—profits provide the basis for *anticipatory* liquidity control. As such, profit control extends the time horizon for liquidity control by focusing on different factors following different laws, not by extrapolating liquidity itself.

Exploring the Second System Level: New Information for Orientation

Liquidity control on the one hand and *anticipatory* liquidity control on the other—each of the two has its own framework of reference and its own measurements. While liquidity control focuses on receipts and expenditures, *anticipatory* liquidity control factors in a whole new set of components which are placed at a higher level in terms of logic, time, and cause relations and effect relations: *income and costs*. They are direct orientation variables for monitoring profit.

The very fact that the profit drivers are different from the drivers of liquidity explains why they are effective parameters for anticipatory liquidity control. Logically, profit control including everything it requires—the calculation and analysis of profits and losses—is allocated to another business function: It is one of the core tasks of *accounting*.

For exactly the same *logical* reasons, the orientation variables relevant to profit cannot be used for anticipatory profit control, because the same *potential* contradictions between control levels that we have seen for liquidity now recur—this time for profit and profit potential. Again, control has to focus on different orientation variables which, *earlier* than the direct profit drivers, will help recognize how the profit situation will develop in the future.

The reason is that the navigation variable "profit" involves the same potentially misleading signals—which can trigger control errors—as the variable "liquidity" does. Profits can be positive when their source—the profit potential—is already turning negative. Conversely, they can be negative although the profit potential is excellent. There is no way to infer future profits from previous ones. To identify future profits, it is once again necessary to go to the next higher level of information.

The danger is that handsome profits can lull management into a false sense of safety, so no one realizes that the profit potential is waning. On the other hand, a business may have slumped into the red although its profit potential is on an upward track. This is a typical case of simple mismanagement, where managers do not know how to take advantage of existing potential. It is actually easy to solve.

Third System Level: Current Profit Potential (CPP)

From Operational to Strategic Management

For the first two system levels, traditional business administration has served its purpose well; in fact this is where it originated. Now we are about to go beyond this point, again trying to obtain control of even greater complexity and larger periods of time, and the information we get from accounting figures is no longer enough for these new horizons of navigation.

So far we have been dealing with operational management. The next step leads us into the spheres of strategic management.

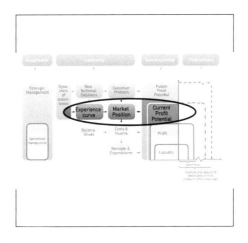

Figure 25: Controlling current profit potentials

The next-higher control level, above the earnings level, is *profit potentials*—or more *precisely, current or existing* profit potentials, abbreviated CPPs.

While many strategy authors interpret "potentials" as general advantages or strengths, Gälweiler precisely defined the term as *"the entire set of product and market-specific conditions of success, which have to be fulfilled by the time that success is to be realized"*. In specific terms, this means: What all has to be accomplished before we can even start thinking of profits?

Switching to the Strategic Business Unit (SBU)

We now have to change our object of reference, switching from the *overall company* to the *Strategic Business Unit (SBU)*, because this is where the profit potential lies.

While operational information about things like liquidity, cash flow, or earnings can be provided for the company as a whole, strategic statements only make sense for individual SBUs. After all, the company generates a profit but, as an overall organization, it does not have a market share.

Profit potentials in the sense described by *Gälweiler* are not identical to the widely popular *core competencies*. There are core competencies that will never turn into profit potentials; on the other hand, it is an ideal case when both coincide and profit potentials can be built on core competencies.

Exploring the Third System Level

Anticipatory profit control requires another change of system level and a focus on yet other control and orientation variables: current *profit potentials* and their extent and durability. If neglect and wrong decisions are only recognized after the fact—that is, when the business generates a loss—it is usually too late to build potentials: that would require much more time than you have available between the point where a dangerous situation is detected and the point where it affects the company's liquidity. This shows very clearly how important it is to distinguish between operational and strategic data, as explained in part I, chapter 4.

If you introduce your profit- or liquidity-enhancing measures *after* having detected the effects of lacking or eroding potentials in your accounting figures, these measures will usually have short-term effects only, and sometimes they will diminish profit potentials rather than save them.

There are more than enough examples to prove this point. For instance, most cost reduction programs will not only cut those costs that represent a waste of funds, but also those that actually represent *potentials*, such as advertising and promotions, all in an attempt to increase profits. That may be necessary on a temporary basis, to secure both profits and liquidity, but it involves the risk of diminishing potentials: if competitors increase their advertising efforts during the same period they will probably gain market share and increase *their* potential.

Any unexploited potential will temporarily cause more costs than it generates revenues. This does not necessarily mean that these costs should be reduced; yet it is often done because it is the only way to enhance the profit situation. The stock markets will reward it—but the potential is ruined, although management never notices because accounting figures do not show it. This is a typical example of what I said earlier, that measures can be right from an operational standpoint and at the same time be strategically wrong, and vice versa.

Quantifying Potentials: Actual ROI versus Par ROI

I have mentioned before that ROI is the figure used to quantify the control variable "profit". Since it is a figure taken from operational management, it can only be the *actual ROI*—as this is the only one that appears in the accounting figures.

The question now is: would it be possible to quantify a *potential* in any meaningful way—that is, not only answering the question of "How much profit are we making?" but also "How much profit is this business capable of generating?"

Indeed, this has become possible with the world's largest empirical strategy research program "PIMS—Profit Impact of Market Strategy", which today forms a part of the *Malik Strategy Intelligence Programs—MSIP®*.1 Part IV and V will deal with how PIMS research can be used for strategic management.

Thanks to PIMS, it is now possible to determine the profit potential just as precisely as the current ROI. The relevant variable is the Par ROI. While the ROI tells us how much money a business is actually making, the Par ROI tells us how much it ought to be making when the relevant strategic parameters are taken into account. In other words, Par ROI expresses the potential return. It permits very innovative comparisons to current profit-ability, and it enables us to answer questions that are among the most intriguing that exist at the interface of strategic and operational management—such as: *Why are we making less or even more than Par in a certain business? Is business unit management unable to exploit the potential, or—in the latter case—are we facing a case of "overgrazing", with the substance of our potentials gradually being eaten up? Who deserves the higher bonus—the manager with the highest ROI or the one with the highest Par ROI?* We will come back to that later.

Experience Effect and Defendable Market Position

Two orientation variables which help to assess the existing profit potential—and thus permit anticipatory profit control—are market position, expressed as *relative market share*, and its *implications for productivity* and *costs*. To be more precise, this refers to *market share relationship* versus *main direct* competitors.

One key objective of a strategy must be to achieve a *defendable market share* at minimum: only then will a business have managed to create sufficient and somewhat sustainable profit potentials for itself. Allied to this must be a strong customer preference for this business's offering versus the competitors' offerings.

As such, market share is not important. It is only a figure which approximately expresses the *cumulative experience* gathered in and with a business, and the proof of past customer preferences. Of course, one can never have first-hand knowledge of competitors' cumulative experience; but market share is a pretty good indicator.

With the right management approach, cumulative experience will manifest itself in productivity increases and cost reductions. The business with the higher market share is likely to have generated more output in the past, so the odds are that this advantage in experience and routine can be transformed into a plus in productivity.

Consequently, the business with the highest relative market share will also have the potential to achieve the *lowest cost*, and thus price leadership. This cost effect of market share is also referred to as experience effect, and the so-called experience or learning curve precisely describes it.

The experience effect theorem goes something like this: *Every doubling of the cumulative output comes with a 20 to 30 percent cost reduction potential per reference unit in constant prices.*

The resulting *experience curve clearly* determines the bottom cost limit a business can achieve, so cost reduction potentials and targets are clearly defined at any time. The mere fact that many (I dare say most) companies have higher costs than would be necessary is not a valuable argument against the existence of the experience effect. What it does prove is that cost reduction potentials are yet to be fully exploited. It is one of the great challenges to many companies of all types and sizes and to their business units.

This is not about conventional cost cutting and profit improvement, but about fundamental strategic direction-setting. That is why our strategy experts and management training teams are often faced with doubts and resistance against these insights, as they are still far from being standard in business administration courses at colleges, universities, and business schools. After dealing with the subject more thoroughly, however, skeptics are usually convinced.

So, since there is clear evidence of the existence of the experience effect, there should be no need to ask *whether* or not there is such a thing as an experience curve. Rather, from a *strategic* point of view the question should be: *How do we have to organize ourselves in order to capitalize on the experience effect?*

Solving this task often requires profound restructuring—starting with the engineering and design of products and services, via continuous development and production, all the way to commercialization). That, in turn, can be accomplished with the modern frameworks of wholistic process management[16], as the full exploitation of the experience effect reaches far beyond conventional cost cutting.

By far the best approach to cost cutting and profit improvement worldwide is the *Syntegration method*: to anyone who has not experienced it in practice, its efficiency and speed may seem downright utopian. For more on Syntegration see part VI.

Quantifying Profit Potentials: PIMS Research

So, ultimately it is the orientation variables *market position* and *bottom cost limit* which are key to success in the final game—market saturation—, if not earlier. Behind these two final variables there is a whole universe of strategic knowledge and strategic intelligence: the sensational findings from the PIMS program I mentioned earlier. The significance of PIMS cannot be overestimated—only with PIMS research results is it possible at all to meet the control conditions that will be absolutely essential in the New World: *getting the demonstrably right strategy in ultra speed and with*

---

16 Klauser, Marius: *Lenke, was dein Unternehmen lenkt: Management-Prozess-Architektur (MPA) als Quantensprung in der Unternehmens- und Mitarbeiterführung*, Frankfurt/New York 2010. Also, Stöger, Roman: *Prozessmanagement: Qualität, Produktivität, Konkurrenzfähigkeit*, Stuttgart 2009.

measurable maximum, and being able to modify it just as quickly whenever circumstances require.

Back in the 1970s when the project's very first research results were published, PIMS was a sensation. Companies striving to be innovative in their management systems instantly realized the ground breaking possibilities PIMS provided in strategy design. A sizeable number of Fortune 500 companies owe their current market dominance to the early application of PIMS, foremost among them the General Electric Corporation where PIMS originated. It has made the market position of some companies so unassailable that they can only be endangered by gross management errors, for instance in strategic navigation.

In the turmoil of the Great Transformation, the insights from PIMS will be particularly valuable, for without them strategic navigation errors will be almost inevitable. With its sophisticated databases and strategic intelligence models, PIMS research has reached a globally unique level of perfection and it enables us to elegantly master the challenges of the Great Transformation.

Fourth System Level: Future Profit Potentials (FPPs)

When Even the Best Market Share Gets You Nowhere

As we have seen, the basis for profit potentials is sufficient market share—that is, sufficient to be defendable through pricing. Still, some readers may feel uneasy due to my strong emphasis on market position and market share. And rightly so, for the navigation horizon has yet to be extended further. Market share, as important as it is, cannot be the end of strategy.

Market share is where the strength of the business lies; the strength that translates into size. In large markets, large market shares mean high sales volumes.

In small markets, even high market shares mean relatively small sales volumes—but still the business will be strong, as due to its higher market share it will also have a stronger pricing position, provided it takes advantage of its cost opportunities. Obviously, *small* market shares are threatened by rival businesses with *larger* market shares because they have potentially lower costs, enabling them to set lower prices and still make more money. At the end of the day, a price war with the market leader cannot be won. What, then, is the greatest threat to the *largest* market shares and even to monopolies? Why do even market leaders perish or dwindle to marginal positions—as has happened, amongst others, to the erstwhile gold mines in communications, engineering and photography which were heading their markets up until 15 years ago?

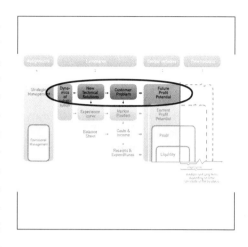

Figure 26: Controlling of future profit potentials

The greatest threat even to state monopolies is *technological substitution.* Market positions, experience effects and cost reductions all have their limits when there are certain fundamental *restructuring processes* going on in the market, in the course of which previous solutions to customer problems are replaced by completely new ones. Countless new solutions will be thrown on the market as the Great Transformation takes place and New World emerges. Many of them are already here, only they are yet to unfold their full power.

Greatest Innovation and Most Dangerous Competition

At this fourth system level, we encounter a very different and much more dangerous kind of competition than exists between direct competitors battling over market shares: it is *substitution competition.*

Direct competitors usually know each other quite well. Often, they know all about each other and try to spare each other unnecessary trouble, such as ruinous price wars. By contrast, only the very best companies are alert to substitution competitors. These competitors are usually ignored, the reason being that they are noticed too late or not taken seriously, because after all they *"make very different products ...", "are in another industry ..." or "use a completely different technology ...".*

This is why substitution competition is usually the most dangerous kind: it is the substitution of existing things by new things, based on new technologies that permit new solutions to *the same* customer problem. So, this is where the center of real key innovations lies. At all other navigation levels there is also innovation, but of the kind that follows the familiar logic of the familiar business. Here, however, we have a yet unknown logic of a new business, and so this is the core of the company's viability without time limits. By analogy, this holds true for any other kind of organization. Anyone speaking of "sustainable" profits is fooling himself unless he is referring to the fourth system level and substitution competition.

Although there is not only *technological* substitution innovation but also social and cultural and other kinds of substitution innovation, I usually begin with *technology* when talking about substitution dynamic in practical strategy work. Often, new values, changed consumption habits, esthetic perceptions and the like are considered to be just as important. However, upon closer inspection I usually realize that they are *consequences* rather than *causes* of new technological possibilities. For instance, no one missed the telephone before it was invented, and the automobile was considered superfluous for several decades because nobody sensed a lack of mobility. New value systems and also needs have often emerged as a consequence of new technical possibilities; hence it is seldom wrong to begin with technology.

Exploring the Fourth System Level

The quality, extent and durability of current profit potentials can only be controlled and precontrolled if another, yet higher system level is integrated, with yet another set of orientation variables. Again, we have the same logical opposite relations as with all other control variables. For instance, the last blacksmith in the village must have had 100 percent market share on the day before he went bankrupt, which was an enormously positive signal at the CPP level—but he was no longer in the right market. Even the highest market shares in dying markets are potentials that are dwindling away. Their positive signals are therefore grossly, even fatally misleading: once the previous solutions started to fail there is not enough time to build new potentials.

How, then, can we discover the right market in time? In what market do we need high market shares? These questions can only be answered by focusing on FPPs—future profit potentials.

Current potentials may be excellent while a look to the future will reveal that there is nothing in the development pipeline. Conversely, current potentials may be eroding while future potentials are about to be in full bloom.

Again, anticipatory orientation and control are only possible by focusing on factually *different* points of orientation, which are at yet another control level and therefore follow different laws.

The better a company's existing profit potential is, in terms of market share in a given market, the lower—due to the resulting positive effects on profit and liquidity—will be the pressure to question the basis for current profit potentials; as a result, the higher the risk of overlooking orientation variables for future profit potentials. That is why we often hear managers talk about *surprises*, although in truth the developments they refer to could have been recognized long before they took their effects in the markets—if only they had focused on the MG control system described here, its orientation variables and its inner logic.

Substitution Concealed by Innovation Masquerade

Substitution comes veiled as innovation. Although innovation should always be taken seriously, not everything new is important. There are new developments that the management of a company may just as well ignore; then there are those that can pose a fatal threat if they are not detected in time—but which can also open great opportunities for a new future.

How can we differentiate between these two kinds of new developments? There is only one differentiator: the *substitution* effect of an innovation—which, in turn, can only be determined when focusing on the *customer problem* addressed by it.

I am talking about fundamental innovation here, based on fundamental technologies. The chronology of *fundamental technologies* provides clues as to the *speed* and *frequency* of substitution processes, and thus for the *time* remaining to take advantage of ongoing structural change and launch an adequate response.

These points of orientation, which refer to yet another set of facts, open up the *longest* possible time horizon of all for management and control, a period sufficient for any strategic decision.[17]

More on this highly important and very intriguing issue in part V of this book.

The Archimedean Point of Every Strategy

At the core of controlling new profit potentials is the *customer's* or *user's problem*. In order for it to have the power of orientation that triggers the right decisions, it has to be understood in a certain way. The customer's problem has to be understood in its original, *solution-independent* form.

From a strategic perspective, every product and service that is successful in the market presents a *solution* to a customer problem—but to exactly which problem? This is one of the most important questions of strategy, as it defines the market and competition. To find the right answer we need to move away from current solutions. We need to take a step that is essential to economic survival, and which leads us to the solution-independent or solution-invariant definition of the customer problem. It requires abstract thinking—something that many executives seem to find enormously difficult, while others are true masters of it. The key to the right answer lies in precise phrasing. The key question to be asked must not be: What is our product? It must be: What does our product do? What does it achieve for the customer?

Coming Full Circle—Back to Corporate Purpose and Business Mission

We have now completed the entrepreneurial navigation loop. We are back to where we started: at the corporate purpose and business mission. Both of them center on customer needs, for the purpose of a company is to cre-

---

17 We have developed and refined special approaches to analyzing substitution processes and their dynamics, and to using their factual and chronological sequence for strategic decisions. Metaphorically speaking, these approaches are like telescopes permitting insights into faraway galaxies—that is, into future technologies, products, manufacturing processes, and markets, which often emerge much faster than anyone would think.

ate satisfied customers. The key question asked was: What do customers pay for? Customers pay for a solution to a problem, offered by someone whose solution is better than everybody else's, due to specific strengths that translate into a superior position. Customers pay for the utility and the value created by the solution to their problem.

Customer value and competitiveness were the two relative fixed points in the stream of continuously changing, self-restructuring systems, and in the complexity of dynamic cross-linkage, unpredictability, and uncontrollability. The circle closes, from the corporate purpose and the business mission, on to the four system levels of navigation, back to mission and purpose. This shows that managing a company can never be a linear process if the company is to function well. It has to be a continuous circle which, logically, has no starting point or end. Mastering circular processes is one of the secrets to effective and right strategy.

Circle of Survival and Viability

Historically, the evolution of corporate management began with liquidity management. But the only type of enterprise that managed to survive as the complexity of the business and economy increased was the kind that developed better orientation and control systems—just as in nature, better sensory faculties have emerged to deal with complex navigation tasks. We have seen that effective control is not possible from the bottom up, so we cannot start with liquidity. It does work perfectly the other way around.

Only if we know the customer problem in its purest form can we discover what and how many solutions there are. Only then can we know what innovations are important for us. Only on this basis can we know in what market we need defendable market shares, what effect they will have on our productivity and costs—due to the experience curve—and what is necessary and possible in terms of pricing. That, in turn, permits reliable conclusions as to future revenues and expenditures, as well as to the resulting profit and ultimately the liquidity to be expected. Liquidity is the criterion for surviving in a capitalist market economy—but not a guarantee for long-term viability. Liquidity has to be available for 1) the continued cultivation and exploitation of current profit potentials, and 2) building future profit potentials in due time. If we manage to do that, we meet the criteria for viability.

The fundamental errors regarding operational versus strategic management, as described in part I, can be fully and effectively eliminated with this wholistic navigation approach. It is also obvious now why the shareholder value approach was bound to fail, and why it caused the greatest strategic control errors of all times—outside wartime—in the world of business, as well as the grossest misallocation of economic resources. Shareholder value stretches no higher than to the profit level—to return on investment (ROI) or on capital employed (ROCE), which are essentially the same. That is almost as though the human "navigation system" ended where the spinal cord enters the base of the skull.

A management approach focusing exclusively on business economics or even financial aspects, or which is even exclusively guided by profit and growth, will inevitably lead into a fatal trap. It will drive a suicidal program because of the lack of wholistic navigation and control. The question as to whether a company is able to grow, or whether it perhaps must not grow any further in order not to get into a strategically unfavorable position, or whether it *has to grow* to gain a strategically sustainable position—all this cannot be subject to mere declarations of intent or best-practice trends, and it cannot be the starting point of strategic deliberations. Growth and profit are *results* of applying this navigation system. They will be higher the better the higher-level navigation works and the better managerial decisions therefore are. Only if growth and profit are based on strategic foundations can they be sustainable. In and by themselves they cannot be. So, having sustainability as an aim is very acceptable, but the risk of choosing the wrong course is high—unless top management has the MG Navigator ever at hand.

The systematic function of the MG Navigation System has essentially been completed in both theory and practice. Relations between the individual elements and parameters are largely known, PIMS findings on the quantification of individual variables have been integrated, methods and tools have been developed and tested. Together with the Strategy Map, which will be dealt with in the next section, the MG Navigator is the central tool of strategic management. To my knowledge, there is no remotely comparable concept worldwide with the same stringent logic and full coverage of all strategic factors.

Chapter 3

Setting the Right Strategy, Irrespective of Economic Climate: The Strategy Map

In addition to their northward-oriented compasses, the navigators of old also used to consult various land and sea maps. Their invention and refinement by Portuguese seafarers, among others, represented such enormous progress that the resulting navigation and orientation information provided the basis for Portuguese world domination which lasting over 100 years. The same principle applies to navigation in the world of business. Here, too, we need maps to get some orientation—*"Where am I, where can I go, where am I headed, how do I get there?"*—*What we need, in other words, is a Strategy Map.*

And just as compasses and maps have been digitalized and are available in one single device which provides real-time information, satellite-supported, in all kinds of weather, we are rapidly approaching this kind of progress in corporate management as well.

In this chapter, we will now deal with the *Strategy Map*, for Navigating and Steering Organizations through their strategic universe.

Brain-Like (Re-)Organization of Knowledge

The key contents here are basically the same as in the preceding chapter because the strategy universe is the same. But the contents are organized and sorted in a different way. This is immensely important, as the ability to reorganize knowledge by different aspects is crucial in a knowledge society, when it comes to mastering rapid change. It is also necessary for strategies under megachange conditions.

The human brain performs this very reorganization, while a computer does not. It is one of the extraordinary qualities of the brain that, depending on the particular focus of attention, it configures essentially the same information in a new way so it will precisely match the situation at hand. Especially higher forms of learning work that way: whenever a new insight is added, previous findings are not deleted or isolated but *reshuffled*. After integrating the new finding, previous contents are still available but they usually have new positions of significance. So, learning is not a static addition of new insights but, above all, the reorganization and reallocation of previous findings in the context of the new information.

That is an advantage for top executives, for their previous insights gain all the more value, the better they are reorganized and reconfigured.

The Strategy Map

This chapter deals with the basic structured approach to developing an adequate corporate strategy (as shown in figure 27 below). I call it *Strategy Map*. While it was developed with a view to business organizations, in terms of the language used, it is basically applicable to all organizations.

At present, different terminologies are (still) used in the public and the private sector; however, I expect them to converge each other rather quickly because the Great Transformation will have an even stronger impact on public organizations than on businesses. Both areas will then work together much more than they have so far, in comprehensive systems and structures, in order to find joint solutions to the greatest challenges. This will also lead to certain adaptations in the language used.

Aloys Gälweiler also developed the underlying concept of the Strategy Map, which I have integrated and further refined in the course of our collaboration. Gälweiler himself was only able to contribute to its further development for a relatively short while; also, his professional commitments left him little time for that. But he cared very much about its continued progress. He was intrigued by the possibilities offered by cybernetics, which was quite advanced at the time, and by the first bionic experiments; for we had already started emulating the nervous system for management purposes and had published reports and articles about our efforts.

The basic idea for that had emerged back in the late 1960s. Also, he had a keen interest in the integration of PIMS research results.

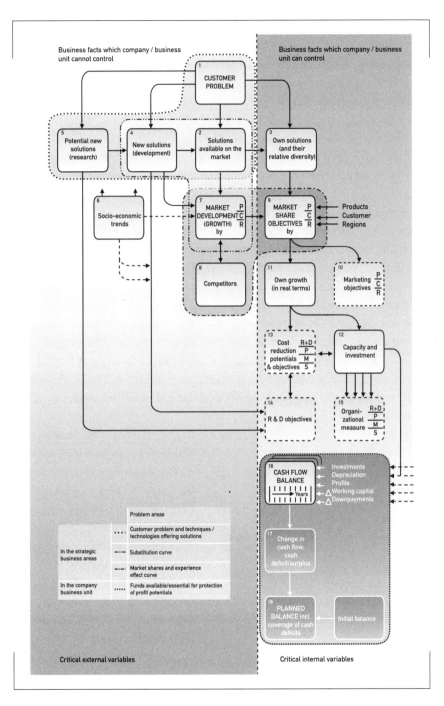

Figure 27: The Strategy Map

Strategy as Interface and Cross-Border Function

This chapter will guide the reader through the Strategy Map, step by step. The clear terminology used in this Strategic Map gives the user perfect orientation through the Great Transformation21 and the universe of change it involves. Almost all executives I have introduced to this world of strategic thinking and acting began to see their strategy, their company, and the economy overall with new eyes. Far beyond mere economic theory, they now understand economic processes and their interaction with technological progress; they see customer value, research and development, marketing and all the other corporate functions in a new light, for the first time understanding them as an integrated, dynamic system. This means an evolutionary leap in their world view.

First off, please note that the graph showing the Strategy Map has a vertical dashed line running through its middle. It distinguishes the external factors on the left-hand side from *internal ones* on the right. The line does not *separate*—it *distinguishes*, so the systemic *integration* of the environment and the company is possible and guaranteed. At this point, the reader may find it useful to go back to the Basic Management Model in part II, to see how we move from abstract model relations to very concrete tools and methods, in order to provide practical solutions to the strategic tasks top executives face.

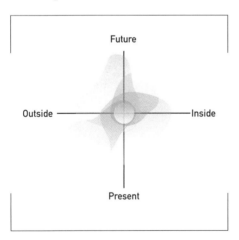

Figure 28: The universal coordinate system for the strategy map

Right from the beginning, the Strategy Map enables me to clarify some of the basic issues of every strategy, which other authors and strategy experts either fail to recognize or leave unanswered so they can continue to confuse the users.

The question is: What is part of the company and can thus be influenced by management— and what is part of the environment to which the company needs to adapt proactively because it is the source of opportunities and risks?

At this point it becomes clear that strategy is the interface between an organization and its environment, assuming a cross-border function by which the organization integrates into its environment and forms an overall system with it.

Strategy Map for Right Action

All elements of the Strategy Map are numbered for easier orientation. For practical purposes, this numbering system corresponds to Web-based check lists, guides, templates, and special Web tools to be used for neat, methodical and efficient strategy development, supporting the enormous speed with which strategies today increasingly have to be developed and adapted.

The fastest approach, the Direttissima method I have developed and which can be refined by Syntegration, will be dealt with in part VI. It goes without saying that in the era of the Internet everything is available in digital form and interlinked. I have already explained how the Strategy Map is integrated in my General Management Systems®, especially in the General Management Model (see part II).

While in the previous section I explained the navigation system going from bottom to top, this time the presentation starts at the top. So the Strategy Map starts where the navigation system ends: at the solution-invariant customer problem.

The Solution-Invariant Customer Problem

Strategy begins with the *customer problem*. This term can only unfold its full power of orientation if it is understood in a very specific way that may seem unorthodox at first: it is the *solution-invariant* form which describes the problem as such, irrespective of any solutions that may have existed or still exist. The term "user problem" is just as appropriate, depending on what products and services we are dealing with. Please note that in our depiction of the Strategy Map, the customer problem is located to the left of the vertical dashed line, meaning outside the company, which does

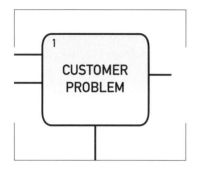

Figure 29: The customer problem

not necessarily mean that the company is unable to actively create or influence customer problems.

Peter Drucker, after having shown in one of his books how to analyze a business, adds: *"... we can answer the question: How are we doing? But how do we know whether we are doing the right things? ..."*[18]

Well, we will know once we know the customer problem. Knowing customer problems is key to solving most of the aberrations in today's corporate governance debate. Everything starts with the customer problem, not the shareholder problem, as I have explained before and for which I now present the corresponding methodical approach. The better a customer problem is captured and solved, the better a company can satisfy the legitimate demands of its shareholders and stakeholders. With the aid of the Strategy Map and its logic, it is easy to see where the shareholder value theory is flawed, and why this faulty theory was bound to get companies in trouble.

From a strategy point of view, every product and service is a *solution* to a problem that a customer or customer group is having. Now the *product* itself is known throughout the company, people are familiar with it, constantly deal with it, are proud of it—in short, it is at the center of attention. *But what is the problem that the product solves?* Here, the strategic maxim is: Customers never just buy a product. They buy what the product does for them—they buy a *solution* to a problem, they buy customer value. So customer value is the guiding star, as discussed in part II. Part IV will explain how to design for optimum customer value.

The product perspective and the solution perspective lead in very different directions. For instance, watches can be viewed as miracles of high-precision mechanics—or as devices indicating the time. Who needs horologic high-precision mechanics, and for what? To see what time it is—that is, as a *time indicator?*, as a *status symbol?*, as an expensive *luxury gift?*

A watch can be all of the above, and more. Anyone seeing only the current form in which a watch is presented, and failing to wonder about the

---

18 Drucker, Peter., *Managing for Results*, Oxford 1999, p. 85.

invariant problem solution, runs the risk of ignoring ongoing substitution dynamics. Almost any problem can be solved in very different ways, so a company's own solution can be swiped off the market so quickly there is no time left to respond. That is something which should always be taken into account in strategy. Hardly anything can be more risky than to believe that you have reached the end of solution development—with your own product, which is and will probably remain an undisputed market leader.

The same kinds of questions arise in every company, with every product. Cars can be viewed as machines to overcome distances, or as flirting devices, or in countless other ways. The consequences of these different views for corporate policy and strategy could not be greater, and they affect virtually everything from technology to branding, from design to pricing, from management to shop-floor execution.

Ray Crock, the man who turned McDonald's into a global empire, saw the solution-invariant customer problem in young mothers' nagging children. So his business mission was to calm them down. His solution was not to sell hamburgers—*"they can get hamburgers everywhere"* he would say—but to get the children to calm down. It was the beginning of an entrepreneurial success story, which led to more and more new, self-unfolding solutions to customers' problems.

Original and Derived Customer Problems

Since current profit potentials are replaced by new profit potentials, based on technological change, it is crucial that we expand our perspective to cover the largest possible range. This includes differentiating between two kinds of customer problems: original and derived ones.

Original customer problems hardly change. They correspond to people's basic needs and wants. Here we are getting to some kind of *"Archimedean Point"* in a system of problems, solutions, and technologies that otherwise keeps changing autodynamically. Examples of original customer problems include the need to eat and drink, to dress, to be mobile, to communicate, to converse and—in the New World—to get an education.

Derived customer problems are those that only exist because the original problem was solved in a certain way. For instance, we need buttons when certain kinds of clothes (original problem) are closed with buttons (solution). The technologies and materials needed to manufacture buttons and buttonholes present derived user problems. If the solution to the original problems changes, derived solution technologies ("button and buttonhole manufacturing") may disappear or, if possible, be used to solve other problems. Also, it is possible for one solution (button) to coexist with other solutions. For instance, while the zipper has not replaced the button it has taken a sizeable share of its potential market.

Another example is chemical films, which were needed before digital technology emerged. Meanwhile the films of earlier times have almost disappeared—some, it seemed, overnight. Solutions to derived problems share the fate of solutions to original problems: the entire chain of derived solutions becomes obsolete once the original customer problem is solved in a completely new way. That can make entire industries disappear—and others emerge from scratch.

The question as to whether a given company and its offerings are addressing an original or a derived customer problem can be clarified quickly, reliably, and comprehensively by analyzing the entire system of services and effects that have emerged around a customer problem. The best suited approach is the cybernetic sensitivity analysis, a highly effective tool we have refined for application. It will be dealt with in part VI.

Surfing the Tidal Wave

Only if we manage to gain a *solution-invariant* understanding of the customer problem do we have a change to surf the waves of technology, and thus to judge the substitution dynamics in a market correctly. Only then can we answer the question as to whether and to what extent new solutions can actually *replace* the previous ones.

Substitution processes, which today essentially replace Old World knowledge with New World knowledge, are one of the drivers of the Great Transformation because there is such a host of fundamental scientific and technological innovations in store for us. As I already said in part I, they will change just about everything people do, how and why they do it, and they will also change themselves in the process. There is no shortage of examples for this.

Let me continue the photo example here. One of the most striking substitution processes since the early 1990s has been the replacement of chemical photography by digital image recording. As late as in 1995, I had some people from the photo industry attending one of my strategy seminars, telling me that there would never be such a thing as digital photography for everyday use, only for marginal and niche applications. Their arguments—too expensive, poor quality—were understandable though only superficially convincing, but these people enormously underestimated the dynamics of substitution. None of them knew any historical examples. When I gave them a few, they thought that they were irrelevant to their case. It was typical Old World thinking.

One historical example is the replacement of the horse by the automobile. In 1900, the horse was still the number one means of transportation in the U.S., with a 100 percent market share. By 1930 it had been replaced by the car—all 100 percent. We will come back to that in part V.

As I have mentioned earlier, strategy work is much less about forecasts than many people think. Scenarios are also of secondary importance. Many of the usual scenario techniques are of little use because they are often built on linear forecasts. So, discussing forecasts and scenarios with the photo people made little sense, as they were relatively confined in their thinking. One of my most proven methods, however, is working with premises. In simple terms, this means:

Instead of discussing forecasts, let us ask ourselves: *How would the company fare if this new development came to pass?* In my experience, this approach facilitates dealing with the subject, even for executives who are less familiar with challenges of this kind.

Drivers of Megachange

In the course of the Great Transformation21, new *fundamental technologies,* their frequency, speed, and potential substitution effects are among the key drivers of megachange.

They determine the direction of change, its risks, its complexity, and the solutions to master them.

Being able to recognize the enormous proportions of such fundamental change is one of the greatest challenges presented by the ongoing change process. The term "vision" comes to mind. The meaning it should entail to be of any use at all is: the ability to find the solution-invariant definition of the customer problem and the imagination needed to picture substitution dynamics realistically. This is where I see one of the essential components of true leadership. Both contrast sharply with the host of trivial books on these topics.

Here, we have one of the most important, if not the most important source of centennial change, the kind of major change that affects entire industries, societies, and cultures, the kind that leads to crises, revolutions and wars and makes world powers emerge and collapse.

Hence the question must be: Of the assumed customer problem, what remains unchanged with all possible and sensible solutions? This way, invariant problem patterns might crystallize even without any special methods or tools being used. Definite requirements, however, are open-mindedness to inventions and innovations and some history knowledge about previous transformation epochs; also, it requires stepping back mentally from the company's current activities to understand what significance the respective change might have for customers. It is a matter of analyzing, as much as it is one of philosophizing and exploring.

Every strategy stands and falls with the knowledge of the solution-invariant customer or user problem. A strategy failing to take a stance on this point is usually worthless and will only prevail as long as there is no change in the way of solving the customer problem—which is something that should never be taken for granted, no matter how long the "quiet times" may have lasted so far. On the contrary, the premise must be: *The longer the period during which nothing has changed the greater the probability of fundamental change, which is then all the more likely to catch the company off guard.* Most cases of corporate failure have their reasons in a lack of knowledge of the solution-invariant customer problem, or in a complete failure to know it or deal with it.

In over 30 years of strategy consulting, less than 20 percent of the companies I encountered had made the professional analysis of user problems a natural component of strategy work. So desperately did many of them cling to profit as their key point of orientation that they were not aware of the changes going on "out there". I have seen dramatic and even tragic cases in the telecommunications industry, among others: companies completely taken by surprise by the advances in computer technology and which lost their entire telephony business as a result—despite the fact that the emergence of digital technology had been visible even to laypeople for a decade, if not longer. In fact, it had been on the cards since the 1940s, when the mathematician John von Neumann presented his groundbreaking research. As late the early 1990s, in a discussion on mobile telephony, the board member in charge of telecommunications at one of these companies told me in very amiable terms that I knew precious little about telecommunications and there would never be a significant number of cell phones because due to physical reasons it would never be possible to build stable radio links in major cities. And in 2008 the long-serving head of strategy at another corporation in the same industry told me that the dangers of digitalization could not have been noticed earlier.

The problem of insufficient deliberation on strategic key questions is further aggravated by the fact that some corporate top managements have retreated to some kind of investor role, assuming the tasks of a holding unit, while shifting strategic responsibility to the business units. In itself, the decentralization of strategy work is fine, but too often it comes with insufficient strategy training for business heads. As a result, there are enormous opportunities for improvement which can be tapped with the tool described further below, often in a very short time; if left unexploited, they give strategy-minded competitors the chance to take the lead. One thing is certain: gaps like these will always be filled.

At this point, let me clarify two potential misunderstandings:

First, I do not automatically assume clients to know their own problems, or even to be able to specify them if they were asked to. In most cases they can't, or at least not well enough for the question about the customer problem to be of any use. That is why a customer value analysis, which I will deal with in the following sections, is so extremely important. There are still too many companies who try to scrimp here or content themselves with superficial analyses, for which they will have to pay dearly at a later point.

Second, the customer problem does not necessarily have to exist first. On the contrary—quite often, new technologies cause new problems to arise or be perceived which can be solved with these technologies but did not exist before. A *business*, however, can only emerge if there is someone willing to pay. This has to be a customer who has a problem and us searching for corresponding solutions.

Another factor directly linked to the customer problem is the primary source of diversification, which is often subject to lively discussion in the strategy context because, for complexity reasons, it poses great challenges.

The most difficult approach to diversification is to simultaneously offer several fundamentally different solutions to customer problems, which are also based on different technologies. One example is General Electric, with their product portfolio including such diverse things as household devices and aircraft turbines, and many more. Another example is Nestlé, with product families ranging from coffee to yoghurt.

Solution Technologies

Solution Technologies Existing in the Market

Our next stop in the strategy universe is field No. 2: the question as to what solutions to the customer problem currently exist in the market. What products and services, and above all, what basic technologies currently exist to solve the customer problem? In other words, the target of our assessment is the solution-relevant *fundamental technologies existing in the market*. In photography, for instance, for roughly 100 years there was only one basic technology: chemical image generation. Actually, however, photography was only one of *several* basic technologies for image generation. The 1950s then saw the emergence of Polaroid technology, permitting instant photography. While this was not a fundamentally new basic technology, it was different enough to solve one variant of the customer problem even better—which in this case meant: instantly. Since then, digital technology has entered the scene, along with electronic picture generation, which replaces almost all other problem solutions.

The term "solution technologies" in field No. 2 (figure 30) is used in a very broad sense, as the "fundamental kinds of possible solutions". In this broader sense, technologies also include variants of sales channels or service types—such as "full-service restaurant" versus "self-service restaurant".

Own Solution Techniques

Up to this point we have been looking at the external world; field No. 3 is the first element *inside* the company. These are the *solution techniques* existing in one's own company. In parentheses we read *range of products*. This shows how this framework can help create clarity in distinguishing between *strategic* and *operational* questions, which would otherwise be constantly confused. While the number of different *items or product variants* represents the operational range of products, the number of different *solution technologies* that the company masters is a *strategic* variable.

In this field we find the second source of diversification: solving the same customer problem with different solution techniques. This kind of diversification is a bit easier than the first one, but still demanding enough.

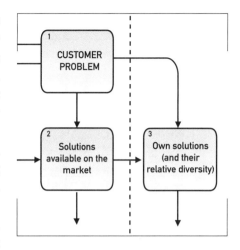

Figure 30: Own solution technologies

Future Solution Technologies

Fields Nos. 4 and 5 cover the entire problem area of *solution substitution*—of replacing current solutions with future ones. These are the basic fields of innovation management. They span the longest possible time horizon that the company is able to discern—all without requiring any forecasts, as pointed out earlier. In a good strategy, nothing is forecast or projected. Everything is determined by reasoning. Deliberations do not, as is common in forecasting, start from the present and go into the future but

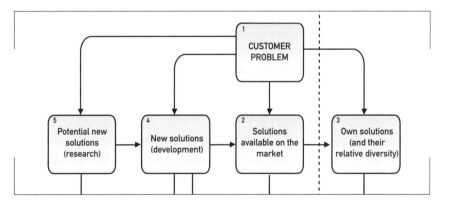

Figure 31: Future solution technologies

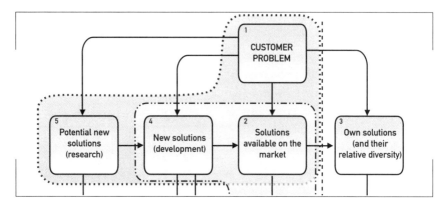

Figure 32: Subsystem of future profit potentials

the other way round: from a bold look to the future they proceed to the first signs of new solutions, and from then on to the significance these solutions have for the present.

Field No. 4 represents the new solution technologies, which are currently in their *development* stage—that is, research is largely completed and the development phase leading to market launch is in full swing—and will then join the solution technologies available in the market.

Field No. 5 shows the *completely* new, the *potential* solution technologies which are still in their research stage. Note that I am not referring to fundamental research here but to *applied* research, because this is a field that is already related to the customer problem, which fundamental research is not.

The result is a first subsystem of interconnected elements, which in figure 31 is encircled by a dotted frame: it is the subsystem of future profit potentials in the sense of our navigation system.

The most important tool to capture these potentials is the analysis of system and *substitution dynamics*, which the Italian physicist Cesare Marchetti has developed and refined over the past 30 years[19], and which will make for a rather exciting chapter later in this book.

As the direction of the arrows in figure 31 shows, all kinds of solution technologies are driven by *the* customer problem, again proving its significance. The customer problem is the Archimedean point par excellence. If

---

19 e.g. Marchetti, Cesare: *Society as a Learning System—Discovery, Invention, and Innovation Cycles Revisited*, Laxenburg 1981.

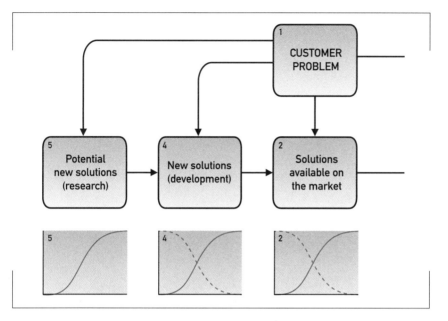

Figure 33: S-Curves are the drivers

the solution-invariant definition of the customer problem is wrong, all efforts to create the right strategy will be futile because mistakes will have become engrained. Another thing that becomes very obvious here is the enormous reach of this kind of navigation, compared to things like profits, turnover growth, or shareholder value.

Fields Nos. 1, 2, 4, and 5 are dominated by what I call the "magic" of the S-Curve and the "pulsations of a hidden engine" From one field to the next, S-Curves and their interaction drive developments. In part V, readers will understand why I choose this kind of language.

Socioeconomic Trends

Field No. 6 is the *logical* place for situation analysis, which is the comprehensive assessment of economic and social developments. Contrary to its logical place, situation analysis is usually the starting point both in *chronological* and *psychological* terms. Fields Nos. 4 and 5 are among the main drivers of social-economic trends, as I will explain in greater detail at a

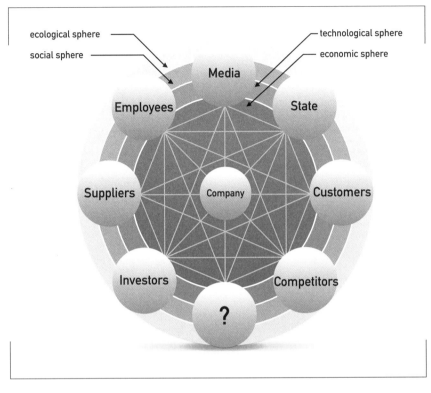

Figure 34: The Environment Model

later point. Two additional factors located here are the early detection of crises and the assessment of the course they take.

Just how frequently situation analyses have to be conducted depends on the dynamics of the particular situation. In any case, one should be prepared to do them real-time and continuously, in situations like turn-arounds and crises perhaps even daily. Here, our Master Model "Environment" acts as a *knowledge organizer and controller* for necessary discussions, which tend to get out of control in the absence of such a framework. The clear, wholistic and interconnected logic of our environment model helps to control easily and efficiently what would otherwise be tenuous discussions. The Master Model "Environment" acts as a network to capture and organize data, information, and knowledge fragments.

A good situation analysis can largely do without conventional forecasts in the sense of extrapolations. As far as methods are concerned, two things are key: *first*, recognizing dynamic patterns, and *second*, identifying premises and boundary conditions[20]. Dynamic patterns are best identified using certain forms of system analysis, such as sensitivity modeling and S-Curve analysis, as well as the Elliott Wave Theory and the pioneering discipline based on it: socionomics. This young scientific research discipline is about to revolutionize the common understanding of complex social systems and to turn conventional cause-effect perceptions of social processes upside down.[21]

Market Position

The subsystem discussed so far is dominated by customer problems defined in their solution-independent form. In modern chaos theory this would be referred to as a "strange attractor". Next is the system evolution to the current profit potentials centered around the market position. The first step leads us along the substitution time curve and to market development.

Market Development

Field No. 7 shows the development of the market in the sense of real market growth. For strategy purposes, markets must be expressed in units of quantity wherever possible; only later can they be expressed in currency units. This way, experience effects can be identified which can lead to cost-reduction potentials.

As you can see from the logic of the Strategy Map, the market development is influenced by the preceding fields 1, 2, 4, and 5 as well as by field No. 6, the systemic trends and tendencies in the company's environment. Market development, which is located outside the company, is not primarily driven by marketing, as many people believe (although marketing does play a certain role). It is driven much more by the technological solutions offered for the customer problem.

---

20 See my book *Managing Performing Living. Effective Management for a New Era*. Frankfurt/New York, 2006, in particular the chapter on decision making.
21 Prechter, Robert: *Socionomics. The Science of History and Social Prediction*.

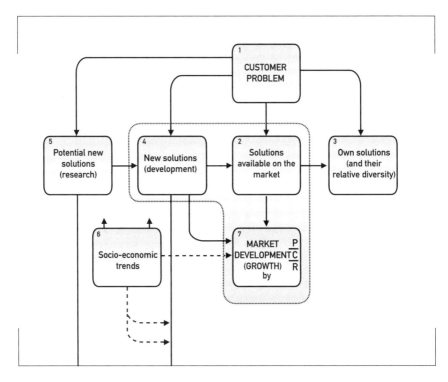

Figure 35: Market development

We are now getting to a second subsystem, framed by a dashed-and-dotted frame. It is the so-called *substitution time* curve. It provides the answer to the question as to how long a solution technology available in the market (Field No. 2) will continue to drive market development, and how long it will take until a new solution technology starts and ultimately succeeds in replacing it. This is another point where the system analysis approach by *Cesare Marchetti* finds a special application.

Market development generally has to be structured by products, user groups and regions, symbolized by the letters P, U, and R in Field No. 7.

Gainesville, 2003; Malik, Constantin: Ahead of Change. How Crowd Psychology and Cybernetics Transform the Way We Govern, Frankfurt/ New York 2010; Casti, John L.: Mood Matters. From Rising Skirt Lengths to the Collapse of World Powers, Berlin/New York 2010.

Further structural aspects may be added, such as sales channels. In the pharmaceutical industry, for instance, three channels—pharmacies, pre-scribing doctors, and hospitals—have to be considered, as well as the internet as a fourth channel for certain kinds of drugs. Further criteria may include target groups, application situations method of administration, and so on. All of these might be important for capturing the structure of the markets.

Another noteworthy point is that buyers are not always identical to payers, meaning that both groups have to be taken into account. Finally, in virtually all cases it is important to view consumers and the different trade levels as an entity.

Market Share Targets

The following step takes us to the next subsystem (framed by a dashed line) of the navigation system, the known *current profit potentials or CPPs*.

Up to this point we have focused on the world outside the company— except for field No. 3—and on factors that the company cannot influence,

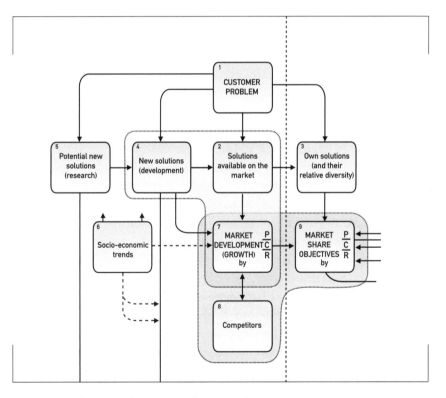

Figure 36: Subsystem of current profit potentials

or if so, only to a very limited extent. Now we are entering the company's internal world, specifically focusing on market share targets. Obviously they are very easy to influence because they are set by the company.

What market share does a business need to be successful in the long run? The appropriate *market share target* depends on two variables—market development (field No. 7) and in-house solution technologies (field No. 3)—and of course it is also influenced by the competition (field No. 8). Just like market development, market share targets have to be distinguished by products, buyer groups and regions, perhaps also by sales channels, applications, and possible further criteria influencing the buying decision.

So this is the field of market and *competitive dynamics*, of the logic and structure of competition and its autodynamic change. At the end of the day, these interactions determine the profitability the company can achieve, in the sense of a potential *return on capital employed*, which in the MG Navigator I refer to as Par ROI.

As I have pointed out before, the objective of a strategy must be to achieve at least a *defendable share of the market*—only then has a business managed to create sufficient and somewhat sustainable profit potentials for itself. When I coined this term many years ago these relationships were largely unknown, but successful executives and entrepreneurs quickly realized that this was the source of their own business success. They understood it intuitively, even though they had not been able to put it in words.

What does "defendable" mean? Against what or whom do market shares have to be "defended"? The answer is: against any conceivable competitive attack in the phase of market saturation, which usually means that the final game is on for players and some of them will drop out. Such attacks are usually run via price. As much as marketing, advertising, quality, service, and many other differentiating factors matter, and will continue to matter, companies still have to take into consideration, as markets are entering the final-game phase, that price may increasingly gain importance.

All players still in the market during the stage of saturation are obviously able to meet customer requirements; otherwise they would long ago have dropped out, so price gets more and more important. Consequently, each player had better be prepared to counter all price attacks, which is only possible if costs are low enough to leave room for profit. This, in turn, is only possible with sufficient market share and the experience that comes with it, which is used to lower the bottom cost limit to the optimum level.

How large is a defendable market share? It depends on the number of competitors left in the market's final-game phase. Experience suggests that this number is usually around seven, plus/minus two, which translates into a critical and defendable market share of around 15 percent per player. In some cases a slightly smaller share of, say, 12 or even 10 percent may be in order, but to be on the safe side one should go for more. This is one example of how my initial strategy definition is applied in practice: "*From the very beginning, act so as to be successful in the long run*", which in this case means acting so as to ensure you will have at least 15 percent market share in the final game, so nobody will be able to push you out via price. The most comfortable competitive structure is one where nobody will gain anything by launching price wars to gain market share, because everyone else is strong enough to counter such attacks. These are often the markets where players make the most money, even after they have stopped growing.

With this we are getting to the point where two key strategic questions meet: the right choice of market and the right extent of growth.

Good strategists choose their market in such a way as to allow them to gain a defendable position. If the market is too big for that, it is advisable to confine oneself to a smaller part of the market where it is still possible. The best strategy for that is narrower specialization.

Markets are not always and only facts of nature; up to a certain degree you have a choice. By far the best principle is to choose the market in such a way that you can achieve a *unique position* in it. The best tool to do that is the *minimum factor focused strategy (German: EKS® Engpasskonzentrierte Strategie—"bottleneck-focused strategy"*). It permits a very precise specialization, based on the principles of natural evolution by which the organism's strengths and the properties of its ecological niche fit together so well that they create enormous synergy effects. For more details on this subject see part VI of this book.

Own Growth

As mentioned several times before, the growth of one's own company (field No. 11) is not a strategic parameter that can be chosen freely, so growth targets must not be used as fixed inputs for strategy planning. The reasons for that will soon become clearer. Growth opportunities and needs do not depend on growth targets alone; they are also subject to the market structure, and targets have to be set accordingly.

The laws of the market and of defendable market share determine how much a business can grow. Sales growth is only healthy as long as it is based on market share improvement—only then will the business be getting stronger rather than simply bigger. Strength, not size must be the strategic goal, and size is not automatically strength.

More size can also mean less strength—for instance, when an increase in sales results from product range extensions or acquisitions which do nothing to improve the company's market position.

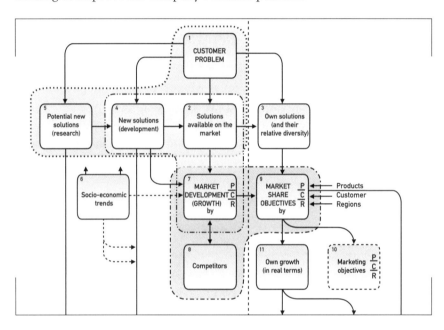

Figure 37: Market shares and growth

What Makes Growth Sustainable? Distinguishing Healthy From Unhealthy Growth

With this in mind, we are now able to define very clearly what the right growth strategy looks like. We have already talked about sustainable growth. Based on the connections and regularities discussed above, we can finally solve the mystery of this term, which has been around for quite some time now yet is still undefined.

It is an essential fact, and obvious from the logic of our navigation system, that growth is not an *original* component of strategy. It is a variable that *depends* on all the higher-level variables discussed here. This is the starting point to distinguish *healthy* from *unhealthy* growth, actually to even identify growth opportunities for a company and, on this basis—via market share targets—determine reasonable growth targets.

It is nearly always wrong to start developing a strategy by setting targets for growth and returns. Yet companies usually do just that, which is one of the main reasons for strategic errors. Growth is the *result* of a useful strategy, its output, not its input. If growth and returns are defined as strategy inputs, it may well be that the company reaches those goals. But it will usually be at the expense of strategic strength. In operational terms, the numbers may look pretty—but the company's strategic position is likely to be weakened.

Whether a company can or must grow, or must not grow any more, is determined at this intersection of market development, competitive dynamics and market share targets. A business must grow as long as it has not gained a defendable position. It may and *should* grow if this helps to strengthen its market position beyond the point of defendability. But a business must not grow any further if this would weaken its market position—for instance if, lured by the temptations of ever more growth, it maneuvered itself into a new market where it could not hold its own and so would be at the mercy of its stronger competitors.

To give you an example: it may well be right—and even *necessary* if the point of defendability has not yet been reached—for a local brewery to grow within the limits of that local market, because this will help the company strengthen its position. However, if this brewery enters the international beer market because of mere growth ambitions, not for reasons of market logic, it will very likely fail—because even if it continued growing, its market position would probably remain marginal.

Apart from this outward logic, there is an inward one: the relationship between growth and productivity I have pointed out in part I.

Marketing Objectives

Marketing objectives (field No. 10) are differentiated by products, buyers, and regions. "Marketing" here means *strategic* marketing. As for the product range, the framework also offers a neat differentiation between *strategic* and *operational* marketing—a differentiation which, although very important in real life, is seldom found in management literature. Strategic marketing is aimed at market share, or the *position in the market*. By contrast, operational marketing is aimed at increasing *sales*.

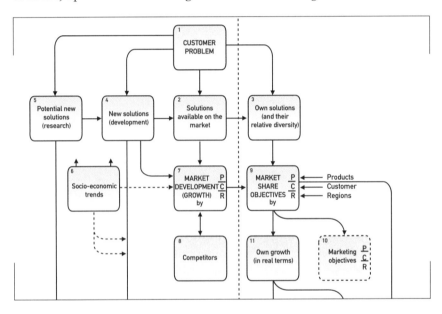

Figure 38: Marketing objectives

Investments and Cost Reduction Potentials

The company's own growth, as derived from the variables discussed before, determines two further pillars of any good strategy: one is *capacity requirements* along with the corresponding investment needs (field No. 12); the other is the *cost reduction potentials* (field No. 13) which also depend on the *experience curve*.

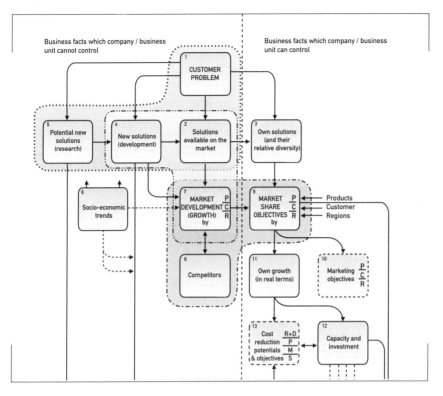

Figure 39: Cost reduction potentials

All these variables are driven by market share targets in the sense of building a defendable market share. Via growth, this market share determines the *bottom cost limit* theoretically achievable, both overall and broken down by functions (R & D, manufacturing, marketing, and sales) as indicated by the letters in field No. 13.

At this point, let me remind you that according to the experience curve and the underlying experience effect, every doubling of cumulative volumes comes with cost reduction potentials in the order of 20 to 30 percent of real value added. This also determines the scope for pricing.

Whether or not these cost reduction potentials are actually exploited depends on the skill and power of cost management. Usually, however, it will not be possible to supply one's services to the market at costs below the bottom limit defined by the experience effect—or if so, it will be owed to factors outside the organization (e.g., government subsidies or faulty internal cost allocation in a group). As a general rule of thumb, companies with smaller market shares have higher costs and will therefore make less money at equal prices than competitors with higher market shares.

The Experience Effect

The experience effect is one of the most frequently misunderstood and wrongly used orientation variables of a successful strategy.

First off, many people deny its existence. With regard to this argument I will say this much: A company with more market share will always have the chance to attain lower costs. As a result, it will be able to survive price wars and stay in the market longer than competitors can. Competitors' ability to utilize their cost advantages must not be underestimated. The premise must be: *Sooner or later, our competitors will manage to take advantage of their market positions to gain cost advantages. Where will that leave us?*

There will come a point in saturated markets when price wars become inevitable. At that point, if not earlier, competitors will begin utilizing their advantages. Often they do it even earlier to prepare for imminent price wars.

Another argument often propounded is that experience effects only exist in the industrial sector, and only in mass production. With regard to this argument, let me point out that it has long been obvious that productivity and cost effects are even more significant outside the industrial sector, specifically in knowledge industries, because it is more difficult to organize knowledge work and knowledge workers in such a way as to achieve experience effects. The economics of some industries are dominated by geographical location (real estate, mining), but even here a high-share company has a better chance of being in the right place at the right time.

Research and Development Objectives

We are now getting to the next field of the Strategy Map—which may seem late to some people but is the perfect point in terms of *logic*: it is the field of *research* and *development* objectives (field No. 14). It hinges on three parameters: not very surprisingly, the first two are new solution technologies, or development (field No. 4), and potential new solution technologies, or research (field No. 5).

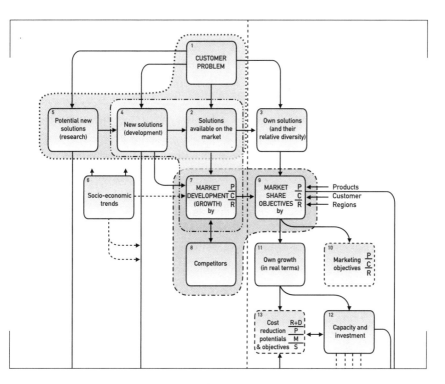

Figure 40: Research and development objectives

The third, possibly less obvious one is field No. 13: cost reduction potentials. A key implication of increasing significance for success is that later cost effects have to be taken into account even in the research and development stage. Or in other words, new products and services have to be developed in such a way that their effect on future costs will be as favorable as possible.

For instance, products such as cars, household devices or computers should be developed in such a way—if at all possible—that they require very little or no maintenance, and that any maintenance that may be needed is quick and easy to perform.

The next two steps take us back to the overall diagram: Results of the strategy are the *organizational* targets and measures (field No. 15) required for strategy implementation, according to the tried and true principle that *structure follows strategy*. This will be the subject of volume 4 of the "Management" series.

Finance and Balance Sheet Variables

In field No. 16 we find the *financial outcome* of all other factors described so far: the *cash flow balance*. It results from the investment needs of the strategy, depreciation and profits, changes in working capital, and—depending on the industry—possible down-payments by customers and respective changes. This is the point where it becomes very clear whether a strategy is even financially feasible throughout the entire period it is supposed to cover.

This also illustrates very well why a management approach chiefly focusing on financial aspects—important as they may be as a foundation for a healthy business—is bound to be strategically blind to all preceding factors that need to be monitored and controlled. Of a total of 18 fields in the Strategy Map, financial factors come in 16th. If this is the point where management realizes that something is very wrong, it is usually too late to take counter-measures.

Another aspect to be taken into account is this: The famous *portfolio analysis*, which became fashionable due to a misconception and is featured in virtually every strategy today—sometimes even confused with it—was originally developed for *liquidity and finance control* purposes. It was never meant to support the development of so-called norm strategies (which are called Stars, Dogs, Cash Cows, and Question Marks) for which it is now used by most authors and consultants and has even become a (misleading) standard topic at business schools.

Portfolio analysis is hardly suitable for strategy design. Its purpose is a different one: making the company's *financial balance* visible and assessable by providing an overall picture of the financial implications of a strategy.

The remaining fields contain the balance sheet tools. So now the process is complete; it has led us from the solution-invariant customer problem to liquidity and the balance sheet.[22]

The next two chapters will describe how each of the elements in the Strategy Map is defined, operationalized, measured, and quantified. It can

---

22 The book form does not convey the dynamics of this complex, but very logical and straightforward process. Please visit our website (www.malik-management.com) for an animated version.

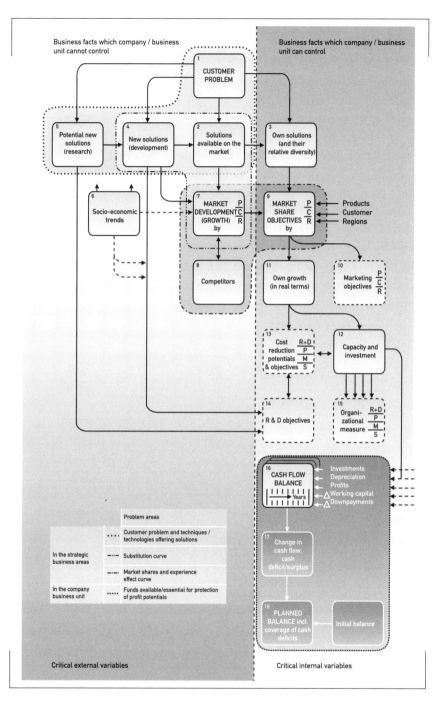

Figure 41: *Strategy Map—overall diagram*

be done reliably, elegantly, and swiftly with our data bases, which cover the data and experience from some 25,000 business years in total.

The MG Navigator and the MG Strategy Map are optimal tools for mastering enormous complexity and business dynamics. You can basically start at any point in the Strategy Map—wherever your interest or need are greatest at the moment—and go through the navigation from there, either very systematically and following the sequential logic or leaping from box to box, whichever your current management situation. No matter how you do it, you will never lose your orientation in the process—and that is a basic prerequisite of reliable navigation.

Finally, allow me this brief comment: True professionals make it their agreeable duty to know both diagrams—the Navigator and the Strategy Map—by heart. This way, they never lose track. They are always able to bind together seemingly unrelated things, keep an integrated perspective and understanding of developments, and are masterly pilots even through demanding challenges.

Part IV:

Following the Change: Success Factors for Your Current Business

"When the history of business strategy is written, the PIMS Program will stand as a landmark. "

Philip Kotler, founder of modern marketing theory

Knowing the What of strategy also includes the knowledge of its empirical evidence. Part IV and V show how strategies are defined and quantified with optimum precision, capitalizing on the breakthrough findings from the PIMS strategy research programs and the Strategy Intelligence Models that are based on these findings. They will be applied to current profit potentials in part IV and to future profit potentials in part V.

Chapter 1

No More Blind Flying: PIMS—
The High Art of Strategy Development

"Evidence based thinking beats wishful thinking."

Keith Roberts, Director of PIMS, London

The Great Transformation21 will bring new opportunities for many companies and their businesses. Managers will be busy gearing up their business strategically, repositioning the company, serving new customer groups, solving new customer problems. This is what I mean by "following change". It will also bring new solutions for corporate structures, cultures, processes, technologies—and, last but not least, for employees. Many of these changes will happen under enormous pressure; there will be no time to make mistakes. One of the solutions to these enormous challenges is the PIMS program, which this section and the next will deal with.

PIMS, short for "Profit Impact of Market Strategy", is the name of the world's largest empirical strategy research program. It was started by General Electric in the late 1960s and, after passing several other stations—including Harvard Business School—in 2004 was acquired by me. I have been operating and refining it since then.

The key question addressed by PIMS is: What are the factors that determine the performance of strategic business units? The usual measure of performance is ROI (return on investment), defined as gross returns (EBIT—earnings before interest and taxes) on the overall capital invested. This ratio, which was invented by GE at the time, was a research breakthrough in itself. Contrary to current usage—or rather: misusage—the ROI was never meant to be a variable for management, or indeed for assessment. It was actually invented to make different businesses in a group comparable to each other. For this purpose, profits had to be determined before interest and taxes, for each of the businesses was financed and taxed in different ways. Of course, if ROI is not the most relevant performance indicator for a particular business (e.g. if investment is zero or negative, or if the business needs to focus on a particular factor such as avoiding competitor entry or achieving a viable market share) then PIMS has the relevant data to benchmark other performance indicators.

Knowing where you stand at any time, being able to precisely define your goals and the way to get there, especially under complex conditions—these are some of the many invaluable benefits of PIMS for business strategies. What used to be a mixture of individual experience, intuition, extrapolating the past, consulting, and copying competitors, is raised to another level of insight by PIMS research.[23]

Just like satellite-based GPS helps reliably navigate ships and airplanes—and now also cars, of course—even through terrible weather, the largest knowledge and database worldwide helps guide corporate strategies through the megachange I call the Great Transformation. As part of our Malik Strategy Intelligence Program (MSIP), the knowledge from PIMS is one of the most effective tools for mastering complexity, as it enables us to answer even the most complex strategic questions quickly and reliably. Especially the highest-risk entrepreneurial decisions are backed up to unprecedented degrees, thanks to PIMS evidence, which often enables companies to gain unique competitive advantages.

Strategic Leadership

PIMS is invaluable for excellent and competitive strategic leadership—even more under the current conditions of complexity than at the time the project was launched. The insights from PIMS enable top management to enhance the accuracy of strategy planning by several orders of magnitude, thus increasing the certainty of decisions in particular on difficult strategic questions. The result is an enormous increase in speed, so more precious time can be dedicated to the most delicate strategic maneuvers—such as mergers and acquisitions, innovation decisions, entry in new markets,

---

23 *Roberts, Keith: "Getting the right business metrics", Malik online letter, 2010.*

product launches, investment and disinvestment decisions, and potential assessment.

With PIMS, managers create a solid foundation for their personal and managerial leadership by taking the right strategic decisions and implementing them with great precision—especially if our other tools for New World complexity are applied in parallel: sensitivity modeling for the cybernetic control loops in the system, Syntegration for maximizing the communication intelligence of large groups, the Viable Systems Model® for implementing "neurophysiology" in the company, and Logical System Analysis for capturing growth dynamics and technological substitution processes (see part VI). Using PIMS does not imply that an entrepreneurial sense of proportion, experience, vision, and intuition will become less important in the future. Quite to the contrary, they will gain even more importance than before: now they can be based on the foundation of facts from PIMS research, which has continuously scanned and analyzed the global strategy universe for over 30 years now.

Epochs of megachange require strategies meeting three key criteria: They have to be right, precise, and fast, because often there is no time for lengthy studies and analyses, and mistakes are not permissible. A strategy like this—based on the data and facts from PIMS—enables companies to remain largely unaffected by crises: not only will they survive them, but they can even prosper when times get difficult. The knowledge and toolkit needed are described in this chapter and the next.

First, in this present chapter I will show what PIMS outcomes mean for the *current* business; specifically for current profit potentials. I entitled this section "Following change" because many businesses today can remain robust and stable, provided they manage to keep adapting flexibly. The next chapter will deal with the core element of every strategy, *customer value*, and how it is analyzed and shaped with PIMS. The chapter after that will explain how PIMS is used to build future profit potentials and what start-up and innovation strategies are best suited for that.

The PIMS Revolution

PIMS was first designed and launched by General Electric.[24] Once again, as in many other areas, the company did pioneer work for strategic management. Back in the late 1960s, GE top management realized that at the degree of diversification that the company had reached—with more than 200 diverse businesses at that point—rational decisions about things like investments or marketing had become virtually impossible. Nobody was able to gain an overview the business as a whole, let alone understand it. So, top management started wondering whether it would not be possible, since there was such a thing as balance sheet ratios, to develop similar variables for strategy.

In addition, the company had made a very costly strategic mistake by trying to take on IBM in the computer business: their analysis had shown that this was a large, growing, profitable market with technological windows for new companies to enter, and as GE itself was a major IT user it felt like an obvious diversification. As a scientific company, GE was intrigued to see if there was any evidence on when entering large, growing, profitable markets was a good or bad idea.

With the company's balance sheet ratios, which were already quite advanced, management was able to compare and assess the company's numerous subsidiaries as far as legal relations were concerned. It was not so certain about the strategy pursued by each division—which was partly due to the fact that these divisions were less and less comparable in terms of legal and balance sheet structures. *Sidney Schoeffler*, the ingenious head of Corporate Planning and Development, was put in charge of this matter. The result was the first large-scale empirical research program entitled "PIMS—Profit Impact of Market Strategy", as management's interest primarily focused on market issues. Soon, however, research was extended to capital structure, value-added chain, productivity, and many more areas that proved to be necessary for thoroughly quantified strategy work. The name PIMS was retained.

In the 1970s, the GE's internal database was extended to include 450 additional businesses, including numerous Fortune 500 companies. A

---

24 See Buzzell, Robert D. und Gale, Bradley T.: *The PIMS Principles. Linking Strategy to Performance*, New York 1987. Also Ceccarelli, Piercarlo and Roberts, Keith: I Nuovi Principi PIMS, Mailand 2002.

phase of internationalization ensued, making PIMS the biggest and longest strategy research project ever conducted worldwide.

The PIMS databases, the results achieved and the creative analysis and modeling tools are unique on a global basis, and from its very beginning the project took the lead for innovation in strategy development. Today, a total of 25,000 data years in business experience from over 4,500 business units are just a mouse-click away for PIMS users.

Strategy at the Strategic Business Unit Level

A major step forward was that, from the very start, PIMS captured data at the level of *business units*. This term, which later was to become a global standard, was invented by PIMS members for data collection purposes. To this date, PIMS is unique in that sense, as most data available from other sources are usually taken from other levels and therefore of limited use.

Business unit data are indispensable because a business unit is the only place where

- business meets customer—or the economic reality where buying decisions are made,
- investment and marketing decisions have to pass the reality test,
- operational performance and value added for the customer are delivered,
- customer value is definitely created or destroyed.

Discovery of the "Laws of the Market Place"

PIMS discovered no less than the universal "Laws of the Market Place". Most people would not doubt the fact that there are basic economic laws, such as prices being driven by supply and demand (although there is much disagreement on the details). But many find it hard to believe that there should also be such a thing as basic laws of strategic management.

Anyone familiar with the PIMS findings on these laws may have an unassailable lead over those lacking that knowledge.

In terms of their characteristics, PIMS strategy laws are similar to laws of nature and always valid in a competitive economy, irrespective of time, place, and type of business. Among other things, they explain how the profitability and growth of a business depends on its competitiveness, market attractiveness, and value chain.

They also show why lots of money can be made in one business but only little in another, how much one can earn at all in a given business, where investments have to be directed to achieve better results in the long run, and conversely, where not to invest even if the target seems attractive by conventional standards.

When it comes to business performance, it is the strategic PIMS profile that counts—not the perceived special circumstances which are often justified by saying, "*Our situation is very different ....*" Still, it is precisely by observing the Laws of the Market Place that every business can become unique in its very own way, provided it applies the PIMS findings correctly. So, just as all human beings are subject to the same laws of biology, all business results are subject to the laws of PIMS. And just like an individual may achieve a unique position due to his biological characteristics, a business can achieve an unassailable position of strength in the market by applying the PIMS laws.

The special PIMS strategy models, which I will describe in this chapter and the next—such as the Par ROI Model, the Look-Alike Model, the Customer Value Map, and the Start-up Strategy Model—are unparalleled in their precision and significance. PIMS allows you to take even high-risk decisions on difficult strategic questions with the certainty provided by a solid fact base, and therefore in minimum time and with unparalleled speed. Things that would take weeks or even months with conventional methods can often be accomplished in a matter of days with PIMS, thanks to its models and the highly organized evidence base.

With PIMS, the competitive uniqueness of a business is carved out with surgical precision and the entire potential of the business is exploited.

A Brilliant Research Idea: Profits Are Driven by Structure, not the Industry

The immense wealth of knowledge and insight that PIMS quarried is rooted in the brilliant notion of comparing businesses based on their *structural configuration* rather than their *industry characteristics* (as is usually done). Industry characteristics remain significant for certain purposes, but for business strategy the concept of structural configuration opens entirely new dimensions of information for strategy planning, which are not included in industry information but essential for the success of a strategy.

What is a structural configuration? It is the set of variables that every business has, without exception and irrespective of the industry. For instance, every business has its variables for sales, profitability, cash flow, market share, value added, productivity, investment intensity, market performance and a market growth rate. According to PIMS, factors like these determine the structure of a business, and the most important are those that determine its profitability.

PIMS provided the breakthrough insight that the structural constellation of these factors correlates much more strongly with the profitability and growth of a business than industry characteristics do. This means that businesses in related industries but with different structural characteristics can generate very different profits, while structurally similar businesses, though operating in different industries, will have similar profits.

Correlation		Industries	
	same	different	
Structure same	HIGH		HIGH
Structure different	LOW		LOW

Figure 42: Structure matters more than industry

In other words, PIMS provides evidence that performance depends, not so much on industry similarity but on similarities in structural configurations. This means that, in addition to industry-specific aspects, significant comparisons and learning effects become possible which could not be achieved within the industry context, due to limited comparability. Take, for instance, a small player which is up against a much larger competitor: While both have to compare themselves against each other as far as the industry context goes, in terms of strategy there is nothing the smaller player can learn from its stronger rival. But it can probably learn from similar situations in other industries which also have small players competing against bigger ones. The concept of structural configuration is closely related to biology and medicine. Every individual, irrespective of gender, nationality, occupation, and ethnicity, has a blood pressure, a pulse, a blood count including cholesterol, uric acid, sugar, calcium, and iron levels, as well as various enzymes and many other components. Such variables are used to determine a person's health and fitness. Other variables such as education, occupation, and ethnicity are not very helpful for that purpose. It is the exact same thing with PIMS. For the first time, strategy research is placed into the same league as the natural sciences, and pulled out of the haze of individual experience, tradition, and folklore.

New Benchmarking Based on the Biological Pattern

These insights are important not only for strategy work in the narrower sense but also for benchmarking, which, while having turned into one of the most frequently used methods over the past 20 years, sometimes produces down-right absurd results. PIMS and its structural data allow a new kind of bench-marking, in which comparisons are made in analogy to morphological biology.

For instance, it would obviously make little sense to compare an ant with an elephant just because the elephant is big and the ant, willing to grow, wants to know just how big an animal can get. With only minimal exaggeration, this is the logic that traditional benchmarking follows. No wonder there are people that try to combine the size of an elephant with the speed of a cheetah, or with the water storage capacity of a camel...

That is why the ant—to stay in this metaphor—needs to compare with other insects; that is, with structurally similar forms of life.

With the PIMS benchmarking toolkit, in particular the so-called *look-alike* analysis, global benchmarking projects provided companies with completely new insights on their *"look-alike peers"* which are much more helpful to them than any of the industry characteristics could ever be.[25]

The PIMS Database Suites

As mentioned before, PIMS is not only the world's largest strategy research program; it also has spanned the longest period so far. From 1972 to this date, the program has continually been maintained and expanded several times, and is still being carried on.

Meanwhile, it comprises over 25,000 business years of experience in the form of data from currently around 4,500 business units from virtually all major industries, countries and types of business. This data has been organized with meticulous care from the very beginning, to be able to use it appropriately, efficiently, and creatively, for there is a continuous stream of new research questions arising. For all these and more reasons, some of the world's preeminent strategic minds, including Michael Porter, Peter Drucker, Philip Kotler, and others, have worked with this database.

As the renowned U.S. best-selling management author Tom Peters put it, *"PIMS has the world's most extensive strategic information database … [It] provides compelling quantitative evidence as to which business strategies work and don't work … [It is] an unparalleled database."*

Figure 43 shows the structural composition of the PIMS database, as well as the statistical spread of business units based on their ROI. It ranges from 25 percent all the way to 85 percent. Businesses that generate less do not exist; they have either been turned around or divested.

PIMS researchers were the first to find out how much money is actually made in business, as shown on the left-hand side of the diagram. This information alone puts users into a superior position, for most practitioners do not know that. I have gathered empirical evidence of this in over 30 years of conducting executive trainings. Even most of my colleagues in university-level business economics have not been able to provide these figures, except for the few among them who are sufficiently familiar with PIMS. University students had no idea, and they cannot be blamed for

---

25 Roberts, Keith: "Good benchmarking versus bad benchmarking", *Malik Online letter*, 2010.

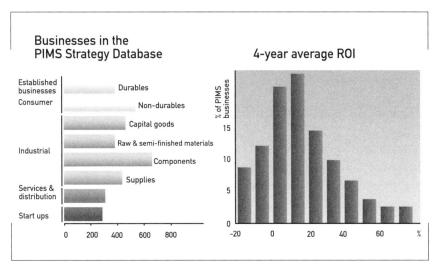

Figure 43: Composition of the PIMS database

that. It comes as no surprise, then, that there are all kinds of tales and rumors floating around about financial markets and the returns achieved in them. The average ROI is 18 percent, the median is 16 percent. Note that PIMS values are gross ROIs, i.e. before interest and taxes.

There are also businesses achieving close to 100 percent in returns, although with rapidly decreasing frequency. Among stock-exchange listed companies these goldmines are a rarity. Usually they are large family-owned businesses which are managed entrepreneurially and free from the constraints of the financial markets. I call them EMEs: entrepreneurially managed enterprises.

A particularly intriguing question was why you can earn 30 percent in one line of business but only 10 percent in another. These and a number of other interesting questions provided the most significant insights on strategy ever.

Due to the enormous masses of data that PIMS unearthed, appropriate methods for knowledge organization were developed at an early stage. In addition to the master database, a number of sub-databases emerged which permit special areas to be analyzed so perfectly that hardly a relevant strategic question is left unsolved.

Below them, there are databases at business unit level for

- start-up strategies for new business and anything to do with innovation strategy,
- brands, brand products and brand innovation,
- sales, sales organization and sales teams,
- the typical business overhead parameters of businesses,
- functional areas such as Human Resources, IT, sourcing, finance.

As mentioned before, and contrary to other databases available, PIMS data are collected at business unit level. In other words, they are captured at the very place of strategic action, where the company competes for customers, where buying decisions for or against its products or services are made, and where value is created and money made. All these things do not happen at the stock exchange but where the customer is and the bill is paid—and if that customer is satisfied, the bill will be paid when it is due, without any deductions.

Universally Valid Factors Determine Seventy-five Percent of Profits

One of the key results of PIMS which emerged quite early was that profits and profit differences depend on a relatively small number of consistent factors. Today it is certain that in any industry and any business worldwide, 75 percent of the differences in profits are due to about a dozen factors and their reciprocal effects. Of these factors, companies have control of all but one, and can shape them so as to ensure success for their strategies. All these factors are measurable, as are their effects on profits. Eight are particularly important.

These insights are at the core of successful strategic management. Anyone who knows and uses PIMS factors has a maximum likelihood of making the right strategic decisions. Hardly anything else is as important for the leadership of companies and their management boards.

It is these strategic variables that have to be kept in control at all cost, if the company is to prosper in the long run. If all is well here, the business will be robust enough strategically to cope with deficits in other areas. Conversely, deficits in these key factors cannot be compensated by strengths in other areas, no matter how great. Figure 44 shows the factors that jointly drive 75 percent of the ROI. They are divided into three

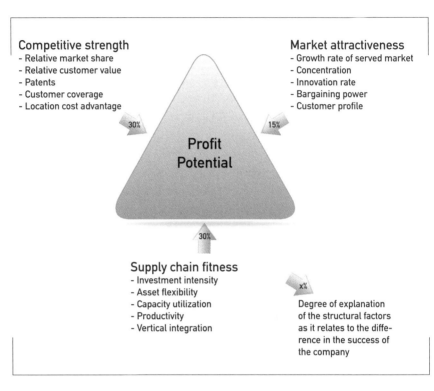

Competitive strength
- Relative market share
- Relative customer value
- Patents
- Customer coverage
- Location cost advantage

30%

Market attractiveness
- Growth rate of served market
- Concentration
- Innovation rate
- Bargaining power
- Customer profile

15%

Profit Potential

30%

Supply chain fitness
- Investment intensity
- Asset flexibility
- Capacity utilization
- Productivity
- Vertical integration

x%

Degree of explanation of the structural factors as it relates to the difference in the success of the company

Figure 44: Key PIMS structural factors for business success

groups: 30 percent are driven by the five factors grouped under "competitive strength". Another 30 percent depend on the five factors grouped under "capital and cost structure", and 15 percent are driven by the factors in the "market environment" categories. The remaining 25 percent depend on a number of additional factors, operational efficiency, and an indefinite degree of luck and coincidence.

Each of these factors is precisely defined, quantified, and its effect on profitability is known. Before PIMS, most of them were completely unknown.

Answering Key Questions of Strategy

Thanks to these insights, for the first time in history we are able to identify precise, reliable, quick, and fact-based answers to the key strategic questions crucial for business success[26]—such as these:

1. What are the *true key strategic factors* influencing the profit of a company, and how can they be defined and measured? How do these factors affect the level and stability of ROI (Return on Investment), ROCE (Return on Capital Employed), ROS (Return on Sales) as well as growth? How quickly will changes made to individual factors become effective?
2. How are these factors connected to each other, and how can they be changed by companies, and used for strategy planning?
3. How do winning strategies differ from losing ones? How can differences be determined and measured?
4. How big are profit potentials based on the particular factors driving a business, compared to current profits, and how can they be exploited?
5. How high can/must strategic innovation rates be in a company's different business areas?
6. How do *diversification and innovation projects* ("start-ups") have to be designed to maximize their chances for success? What quantifiable strategic conditions have to be created in order to do so, and how long does it take for these projects to yield a return?
7. How can make-or-buy decisions be validated empirically?
8. What is the profit potential of *acquisition targets*, what are quantifiable synergy effects and what would be an appropriate acquisition price? What is the best strategy for integrating the acquired company?
9. How high can/should expenses for strategic marketing, research and development, sales, and other functions be, relative to turnover and market size?
10. What would be appropriate target figures for value added, vertical integration, productivity, and capital intensity, to ensure sustainable and long-term viability for a company?

These and more strategic questions, which I will deal with in this chapter, can be answered correctly and precisely thanks to the PIMS research results. There is no other way to get the right answers.

---

26 See also Roberts, Keith: "Nine basic findings on business strategy", *Malik online letter*, 2010.

Eight Key Factors for Success

Figure 45 shows the most important factors and their impact on profitability.

Factor	Definition	Effect
1. Relative market share	Own market share in relation to the sum of market shares of 3 largest competitors	High relative market share is always good. It is particularly important when marketing and/or R&D intensity is high and/or in a downturn
2. Productivity	Value added per employee	High productivity is always good; it is indispensable if investment intensity is high
3. Investment intensity	Investment over value added	High investment intensity affects the company's profitability disastrously
4. Relative customer value	Product, service and image quality offered, relative to competitor, combined with relative price position	Positive for all financial data – indispensable if market share is small
5. Innovation rate	Share of sales revenues generated with products up to 3 years old	Above a certain share of revenues, innovation will affect ROI negatively
6. Growth rate of market served	(Value) growth of market served in percent	High growth rates are positive for absolute profits; neutral with regard to relative profit, negative for cash flow
7. Degree of customer concentration	No. of direct customers contributing 50 percent of sales revenues	An extremely small number of customers is favorable (although this depends on industry characteristics); otherwise a broad customer base is better
8. Vertical integration (real net output ratio)	Value added over sales revenues (value added = revenue-related services)	Particularly good in mature, stable markets

Decreasing importance for / effect on long-term profitability

Figure 45: The eight most important drivers of profitability

From these key factors, I will select a few particularly important ones as examples, demonstrating how they are related to the ROI and how they are linked to each other.

Chapter 2

Strategic Core Knowledge: A Cornucopia of Insights

Market Position

The greater a company's market share, the higher its ROI. Both the absolute and the relative market share strongly and consistently correlate with the ROI, and, as mentioned several times before, they do so across industries, countries, and technologies. This was one of the early PIMS results, which proved universally valid against all doubts and objections.

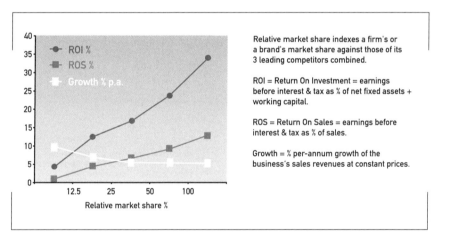

Figure 46: Relative market share enhances profitability, but not growth

There is no empirical evidence to support the frequently heard claim that there was a U-shaped correlation between market shares and ROI. The only way it can be U-shaped is when the definition of the relevant market is disregarded—but that would make any kind of strategic statement pointless because the point of reference would be missing. The alleged U-shaped correlation between market share and ROI has often been put forward using the examples of Mercedes and Toyota saying that Mercedes was generating high ROIs due to its small market shares and that Toyota's high ROIs were due to its large market shares, while the least money could be made in the medium range. Although this "Stuck in the Middle" theory became rather popular, there is no evidence supporting it, since there is hardly any correlation between Mercedes and Toyota. Moreover, Mercedes's market share is actually not small but rather large in the company's *relevant* market.

But the graph contains even more information, which is the correlation between relative market share and *ROS (return on sales)* and the impact of market share on the *growth rate* of a business.

Stability of Results Over Time

Figure 47 reveals something of a sensation: it is the stability of correlations between market share and profitability over time, or to be more precise, over not less than the four decades that have elapsed since PIMS was launched.

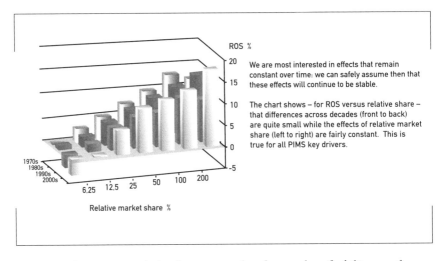

Figure 47: Constant correlation between market share and profitability over four decades

From left to right, we see the relative market shares on the horizontal axis; on the vertical axis we see the (gross) return on sales (ROS). Take, for instance, the columns in front: if the relative market share is 200, the business will usually generate an ROS between 15 and 20 percent. This correlation is shown in four rows of columns for the four decades covered, with the decade starting in 2000 in the forefront of the graph and the decades beginning in 1990, 1980, and 1970 located further to the back. As we can see, there are differences in absolute values but the correlation as such has remained the same over 40 years: the greater the relative market share, the higher the earnings ratios, ROI and ROS.

This finding is truly significant because so much has changed in business over the past 40 years that one would expect anything but invariance in this correlation. Demography, technology, materials, manufacturing methods, distribution systems, customer needs, quality standards, competition, prices, costs, legislation, monetary conditions, interest rates, inflation, and many more things that could be taken into account are different today compared to past periods. A much more useful question therefore is: What has actually remained unchanged? And one of the answers is: *the PIMS relationship between market share and return on investment.*

A Seeming Anomaly Triggers Discovery of a New Factor

The analysis did reveal an apparent anomaly, as approximately 25 percent of businesses with small market shares were found to have a high ROI. How could that be explained? Had PIMS not identified a universal law after all? Detailed analyses of this specific segment revealed, as often happens in quality research, an intervening factor previously unknown which turned out to be one of the most significant PIMS findings.

It is the paramount importance of the quality of market performance and, in a broader sense, of the *customer preference* resulting from it. So, even businesses with small market shares can achieve high ROIs, provided they offer superior quality.

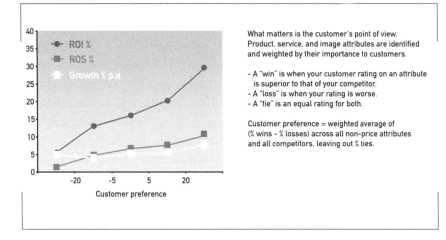

The chart on the left shows:
- ROI %
- ROS %
- Growth % p.a.

plotted against Customer preference (x-axis: -20, -5, 5, 20).

What matters is the customer's point of view. Product, service, and image attributes are identified and weighted by their importance to customers.

- A "win" is when your customer rating on an attribute is superior to that of your competitor.
- A "loss" is when your rating is worse.
- A "tie" is an equal rating for both.

Customer preference = weighted average of (% wins - % losses) across all non-price attributes and all competitors, leaving out % ties.

Figure 48: Customer preference drives profitability and growth

Is Innovating a Good Thing?

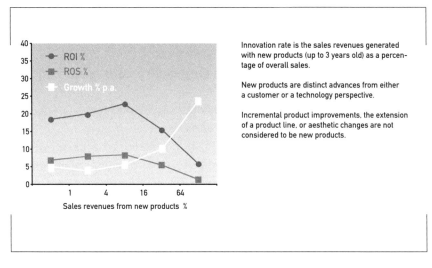

The chart on the left shows:
- ROI %
- ROS %
- Growth % p.a.

plotted against Sales revenues from new products % (x-axis: 1, 4, 16, 64).

Innovation rate is the sales revenues generated with new products (up to 3 years old) as a percentage of overall sales.

New products are distinct advances from either a customer or a technology perspective.

Incremental product improvements, the extension of a product line, or aesthetic changes are not considered to be new products.

Figure 49: Moderate innovation is best for profitability, high innovation is best for growth

What does PIMS evidence tell us about innovating? Change requires and is based on innovation. What impact does innovation activity have on earnings ratios and growth? Even defining the innovation rate (horizontal axis) was a major achievement: it is the share of revenues that is generated with products less than three years old. This definition may be more or less appropriate for different industries, and can be varied for concrete applications.

Again, the general PIMS findings are very clear: The innovation rate has an optimal value, which is around 12 percent, after which its impact on ROI and ROS is negative—because innovating costs a lot of money. On the other hand, the innovation rate is a growth driver of the first order, and it helps to build market share. Against this background, in the chapter following the next I will show what the best innovation strategies look like and how markets can quickly be conquered.

Where Many Businesses Lose Earning Power Without Even Noticing

Many managers are not even aware of one of the most important drivers of supply chains, manufacturing, capital expenditure, and productivity. So massively does it influence these and other factors it can stall even the best market opportunities, all unnoticed because it is hardly apparent from the controlling reports.[27] It is investment intensity—the ratio of capital invested to operational value added. The key question here is: How many dollars do you need to invest in order to get one dollar in value added?

Note that this is contrary to mainstream economic theory, which says that a rational investor will increase his investments in businesses with high capital productivity and decrease them when capital productivity is low. According to that theory, the curve of ROI against investment intensity would remain flat while the ROS would increase along with investment intensity. Existing evidence shows, however, that the competition among businesses does not work this way: with high investment intensity, you have to sell what you can make—not vice versa—so pricing will become mutually destructive, and thus suicidal, as competitors will all try to fill their capacities. What makes it worse is that banks are just too willing to lend money to investment-intensive businesses because all they see is ex-

---

27 Roberts, Keith: "Hard working capital?", *Malik online letter*, 2008.

tensive tangible assets on the balance sheet. What they fail to see is the limited potential for future cash flows.

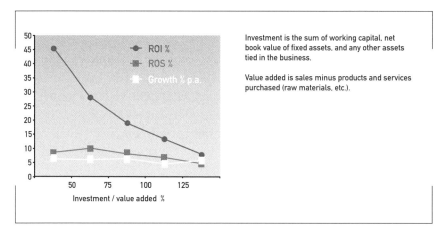

Investment is the sum of working capital, net book value of fixed assets, and any other assets tied in the business.

Value added is sales minus products and services purchased (raw materials, etc.).

Figure 50: Investment intensity is one of the strongest ROI drivers

How Important Is Market Growth?

A counterintuitive finding is the relationship between market growth and the three ratios. Managers' perhaps most frequent excuse for unsatisfactory business results is insufficient or completely lacking market growth, which is usually accepted by everyone because it sounds plausible. PIMS findings teach us otherwise: *Businesses can be managed profitably irrespective of whether markets are growing or shrinking.*[28]

The chart shows the empirical relationship of real market growth with ROI, ROS, and inflation-adjusted growth in sales. Not surprisingly, a growing market will also drive growth in sales. Conversely, a shrinking market will cause business growth to slow down, but to a much lesser extent, provided the remaining strategic drivers are at good levels. This finding gives PIMS major importance for deflationary markets and times of crisis, as must be expected for the coming years.

---

28 See also Ceccarelli, Piercarlo; Ferri, Andrea und Martelli, Carlo: *La crescita sostenibile nei mercati maturi*, Milan/Rome 2008 (*Sustainable Growth in Mature Markets*, so far published in Italian language only).

Even a market decline by over 15 percent, with all other economic conditions unchanged, will lead to a sales decline of only 10 percent.

It is both surprising and counterintuitive that for all other parameters, market growth is far less important than is currently assumed. Even in rapidly shrinking markets the ROI is almost 15 percent, and it rises to just over 20 percent at a market growth rate of 20 percent. It is similar with the return on sales.

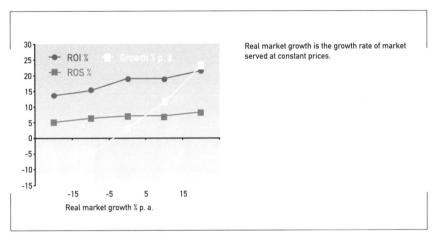

Figure 51: A growing market will moderately drive profitability, and strongly drive sales

This means that even in stagnating markets it is possible to do business and make good money, which many managers vehemently deny when they are first confronted with these insights. Justifying poor performance with lack of market growth is no longer credible in the light of PIMS findings.

Systemic Interconnectedness of PIMS factors

These are just a few of the PIMS findings which are of importance for navigation. The PIMS databases contain many more gems of insight for masterly strategies.

The mere knowledge about each individual factor's correlation with the ROI is a key competitive advantage in strategy planning. A whole new dimension is added with the information on the *interaction* between several factors and how it is connected to the ROI.

The following diagram shows the connection between two of the most important strategic factors, *relative quality from the customers' perspective and relative market share*, as well as their joint impact on profitability.

The fields of the table contain the ROI values resulting from both factors combined. As we can see here, the *highest ROI*—38 percent on average—results from the combination of *top quality* and *high market shares*. Businesses with *small* market shares and superior quality achieve ROIs around 17 percent. If the market share is high, even inferior quality on average gets you an ROI around 30 percent.

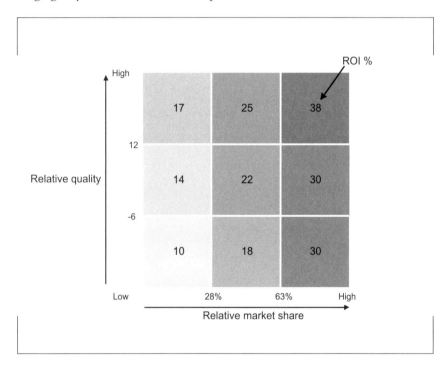

Figure 52: Combined effects of relative market share and relative quality

This is one of the most important PIMS findings, and it is anything but obvious. It implies hope and strategic options for many *small and mid-sized companies*. With a well-planned quality strategy, they can achieve an average ROI of 17 percent despite their small market shares. By contrast, things are almost hopeless for businesses where small market shares meet with inferior quality. They can hope to attain 10 percent before taxes, which means that after deduction of capital cost there will be little or nothing left.

The following diagram provides similar insights. It shows the relation between *relative market share* and *investment intensity* (investment per value added—an enormously important factor), again with its impact on ROI. High investment intensity combined with small market shares will cause returns to collapse.

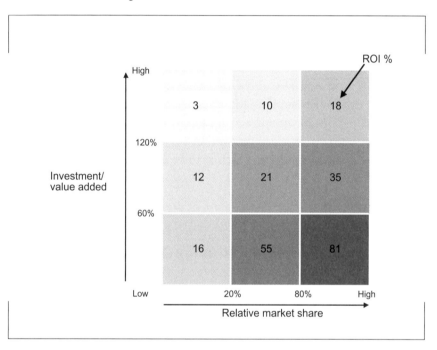

Figure 53: A weak market position plus high investment intensity are disastrous for profits

In much the same way, other *interdependencies* are used to precisely determine and quantify strategic measures, such as those between market shares and marketing expenditure, between quality and R & D expenditure, between value added and productivity, or between productivity and liquid assets.

PIMS and the Six Central Performance Controls (CPC)

All PIMS factors interact with each other and influence each other, in line with economic reality. The dynamic interconnectedness of numerous inter-acting factors is one of the principal sources of complexity. In view of what PIMS has given us, any strategy work that relies on gut feel and common sense and accepts the enormous risks associated with that approach is just as outdated as it would be to take a medicine without considering its side-and after-effects. In part VI I will show how our cybernetic sensitivity model helps to turn this very complexity into a competitive advantage.

An additional enormous advantage of the model is that its variables permit integrating the CPC complex with PIMS results.

In part I, I have briefly introduced the Central Performance Controls (CPC) and their position in my Management System. With PIMS, we now know what factors are important in each of the performance fields, specifically for market position, innovation performance, and productivity. In addition, PIMS permits these factors to be quantified and put on a safe empirical basis.

The Cybernetics of PIMS Strategy Development

As has become shown at several points before, the PIMS program was by design enormously systemic and cybernetic. This also encouraged the application of research methods similar to those used in the life sciences, such as the analysis of structural configurations, which permitted the exploration of patterns or "gestalts". It goes without saying that dynamic models were used from the very start, permitting the differentiation between strategies that work and strategies that don't.

Figure 54 shows some of the systemic-cybernetic relationships which we have to picture in their dynamic interaction.

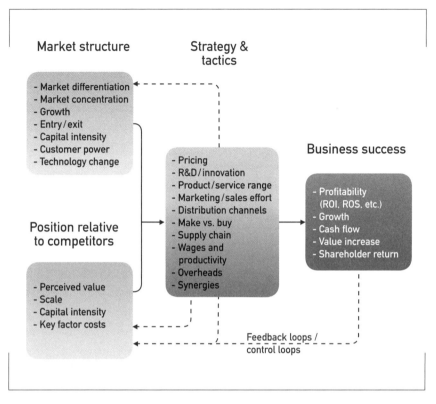

Market structure

- Market differentiation
- Market concentration
- Growth
- Entry / exit
- Capital intensity
- Customer power
- Technology change

Strategy & tactics

- Pricing
- R&D / innovation
- Product / service range
- Marketing / sales effort
- Distribution channels
- Make vs. buy
- Supply chain
- Wages and productivity
- Overheads
- Synergies

Business success

- Profitability (ROI, ROS, etc.)
- Growth
- Cash flow
- Value increase
- Shareholder return

Position relative to competitors

- Perceived value
- Scale
- Capital intensity
- Key factor costs

Feedback loops / control loops

Figure 54: PIMS provides measurable evidence for strategies that work

Overview: Benefits of PIMS Findings for Top Management

1. The strategically relevant factors, whose effects on current and future financial performance (return on investment and cash flow) could only be vaguely estimated before, can now be quantified quite reliably. As a result, it is possible to validate one's strategic deliberations empirically.
2. The outcome is better knowledge of what is feasible and what is not. There is now a much better foundation for formulating realistic strategic and operational objectives than there was in the past.
3. PIMS permits systematic learning from the experience and mistakes of other companies with similar structural characteristics and in similar competitive situations.

4. It enables companies to simulate the effects of their strategies and actions and select the optimal strategy variant.
5. In addition, they can quantify their relevant competitors' strategic options and the implications for their own business.
6. Potential targets for acquisitions or mergers and potential cooperation partners can be analyzed with regard to their current strategic position and future prospects. By using cybernetically grounded planning and facilitation techniques, particularly in combination with the Syntegration methods (part VI), a maximum of knowledge and skill can be activated. In the process of identifying the right strategy, executives and experts on several organizational levels are selectively involved, as appropriate. This way, strategic thinking is firmly anchored in the corporate culture.
7. Effective control of these problem-solving processes permits to deal with change resistance in a constructive manner and to build consensus, understanding, and commitment as prerequisites for effective strategy implementation.

Criticism of the PIMS Program

The methods and outcomes of PIMS have long been exposed to various kinds of criticism from proponents and opponents alike. This was a desired effect, as many PIMS findings ran contrary to positions that had so far remained undisputed in business economics and business administration. Sincere criticism was therefore highly welcome since it helped to revisit and clarify things and raised new research questions. Consequently, PIMS was quite generous and open in permitting access to data material, provided an underlying research interest was credibly communicated. Many of these critics made valuable contributions to the further progress of PIMS. Strategy experts with access to PIMS data-bases included Michael Porter, Peter Drucker, Philip Kotler, and many more.

To this date, the key findings of PIMS have not been refuted. There have been rumors to that effect, but they have never been substantiated. Some common points of critique that have repeatedly been made in literature are mere presumptions which could be refuted.

A major share of the negative criticism results from a lack of knowledge about PIMS itself or the statistical methods used. For instance, people frequently express the—unsubstantiated—view that the program (an international research effort which dates back over 40 years and where renowned scientists have been involved) has essentially been conducted by statistical amateurs. If that was true it would also imply that all the companies that have been contributing to the PIMS database and applying its findings for many years—among them several Fortune 500 companies—would have tolerated or overlooked such major flaw. This kind of criticism obviously bears little weight, even if it is copied unchecked over and over again.

Most of the criticism comes from academia, its authors demanding a degree of precision that would be meaningless for the practice of strategic business management. Quite tellingly, to this date none of these critics have been able to offer suitable alternatives.

Notwithstanding all this, the PIMS professionals themselves would agree there are two cases where the methodology needs to be applied with caution: businesses dependent on location-specific assets (such as real estate or mining) and where performance depends essentially on the quality of the asset, and regulated monopolies (such as water supply/distribution or railways), where performance is constrained by the decisions of the regulator.

What Remains Valid in Business When Everything Changes

Just as the laws of nature remain constant, there are strategic regularities that remain valid even in times of change, and which guide organizations through that change. The greater and more turbulent the changes of the Great Transformation are, the more important it will be to know about the constants in change—the regularities that will remain valid through the change period and beyond—because they will provide the necessary orientation for taking the high-risk decisions required.

Thanks to PIMS, strategic regularities and invariants both for the businesses of today and for those of the future, that is, the innovative business, are discovered and utilized.

As such, PIMS also confirms one of my former propositions, which is that right management is essentially the same everywhere and that all *business organizations* need *the same factors* to function well. The much-heard position that there are profound differences between the U.S. and Europe has also been examined and refuted in all aspects. Another point that has been disproved is that different business sectors, such as capital goods and consumer goods, had to be treated differently in this context: it has been proved beyond doubt that the strategic parameters of both are identical in terms of their underlying structure. Even the enormously increased significance of knowledge as a resource, a production tool, and even a product has yet to cause any appreciable change to the insights provided by PIMS.

Chapter 3

Breaking Strategic Barriers:
Three Pioneering Models From PIMS

PIMS has a rich track record of innovation and advanced insight. It began with the invention of terms that had not existed before but were needed for progress. Among the PIMS discoveries are highly efficient models which broke new ground in strategy planning. I will introduce three of them here: The Par Model for determining business potential, the Loo—Alike Model as a superior tool for making comparisons, and the Customer Value Model for optimizing customer value.

Knowing the Potential of a Business:
The PIMS Par Model

Par is a term taken from golf: it indicates the average number of hits that a golf pro will need to hole the ball. In other words, it provides golfers with a benchmark to measure against. In principle, the PIMS par ROI does the same for businesses.

Reliably determining the actual ROI is a routine task for accounting. However, its significance—just like that of other financial ratios—is very limited, as it is purely operational and often misleading for strategic purposes. One of the things that are usually missing is the most important benchmark to compare against: the profit potential of the business.

With its Par Model, PIMS can provide this information with great precision, reliably and quickly. On the other hand, if the potential is not known, strategic decisions on things like profitability targets, investments, the staffing of strategic business units, or bonus systems will have to be taken rather arbitrarily. Many of the past years' failed strategies would not have been accepted if this information had been available.

With the PIMS Par Model, problems can be solved elegantly, exploring a whole new dimension of strategic options in the process. The par ROI is the return that can be achieved if all opportunities of a business are really exploited. It can be below or above the actual ROI, as I will explain on the next page. So the PIMS Par Model measures the returns potential of a business, thus answering the question as to whether the business is managed as well as it could be and whether all the potential available is actually tapped. In addition, it identifies the strengths that can help to achieve par, as well as the deficits that keep management from doing that.

I refrain from describing the methodology at this point. Instead I will single out just a few practical implications, because par ROI can shed new light on strategic management. Let me just say this much about methodology: determining the PIMS par ROI is similar to determining a person's life expectancy, taking into account his or her predispositions and lifestyle.

The PIMS par ROI creates a completely new, enormously solid basis for assessing strategies and business plans, as well as for setting operational and strategic objectives. It also provides a new basis for the performance appraisal of managers with profit responsibility. Only with par is it possible to decide whether a business can be improved with operational measures or whether strategic changes are required.

Performance Assessment, Bonuses, Staffing Decisions, and Corporate Culture

Suppose we have three business managers named A, B, and C whose business units are generating ROIs of 10, 25, and 30 percent. How good is each manager's performance? Which one should get the highest bonus? And which is likely to become CEO some day? By conventional criteria, the answer is obvious: C is the winner. But the fact is that it is impossible to decide based on these figures. To make an appropriate decision, you have to know the potentials of each of the businesses, or their PIMS par ROIs.

If these are, say, 10 for A, 15 for B, and 45 for C, then A is the best manager and he should get the highest bonus and be promoted—despite having achieved the lowest financial result. A is managing a bad business which probably should be discontinued, but he is getting the most out of it, which translates into excellent management performance.

By contrast, B is achieving a return that is more than twice as high, but all at the expense of the future. He is exploiting the business far beyond its true potential. These results will not be sustainable, for actual returns have a tendency to slide towards par when par is lower. Businesses like these often collapse overnight, because they have long been brittle on the inside without their operational figures showing it. B may have cut down development costs, or expenses for staff training, or saved on quality, or set prices too high. That may work for a while, but not forever.

The true problem, however, is manager C. This individual presents the best return and by conventional standards he will be rewarded accordingly, probably even appointed CEO some day. You may already see him strutting through the office with a smug attitude. In fact he is a bad manager, for he leaves one third of the potential untapped and his efficiency is at a meager 66 percent. He was given a goldmine but he failed to exploit it. Instead, he basks in the spotlight of a high return which, if measured against the potential, is mediocre at best. You don't have to be a genius to get 30 percent out of a business that could generate 45 percent.

If par ROIs are used instead of actual ones, instant benefits include bonus justice, appropriate human resources policies, and excellent performance—for manager A would then be put in charge of business C. The companies' employees would reward that step with high motivation and culture, for they have probably long understood that A is the true performer.

How Looks Can Deceive: Which Business Units Needs What Strategy?

Figure 55 shows the logic of the Par Model. The actual return as provided by accounting is placed on the vertical axis, the *potential* return according to the PIMS Par Model on the horizontal axis. The diagonal line is where actual and par ROIs coincide, or the actual result is identical to the potential one, which in this case is true of business C.

For business A, the actual ROI is higher than the par. That, however, cannot be sustained in the long run. Unless counter-measures are taken, such businesses tend to float to the bottom because their actual performance has no strategic support. So this business needs improvement in its strategic factors. Alternative ways of doing this can be evaluated with the

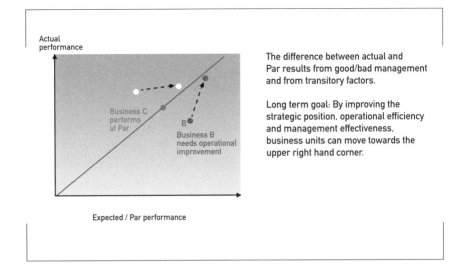

Actual
performance

Business C
performs
at Par

B

Business B
needs operational
improvement

Expected / Par performance

The difference between actual and
Par results from good/bad management
and from transitory factors.

Long term goal: By improving the
strategic position, operational efficiency
and management effectiveness,
business units can move towards the
upper right hand corner.

Figure 55: Potential-based measures

Par Model. The opposite is true of business B: its actual ROI is clearly below par, so this business has considerable potential. It needs operational measures for profit improvement—and again, the Par Model helps identify them.

Learning From Winners: The PIMS Look-Alike Model

The PIMS Look-Alike Model is one of the most powerful tools of strategic management, as it is the first to permit useful comparisons between different businesses. It therefore also helps identify the optimum strategy for a business, and the tactics required to get there. In sum, it represents two of the most significant strategy innovations in one.

This exemplifies the uniqueness of PIMS databases, and the power of the idea of organizing businesses by their structural parameters, not only by conventional plausibility or industry criteria.

In a first step, you determine your *look-alikes*. In a sense, they are your "strategy peers". They are all the businesses in the database which most resemble your own business in terms of their entire parameter profile. In other words, you look for business units most similar to your own in terms

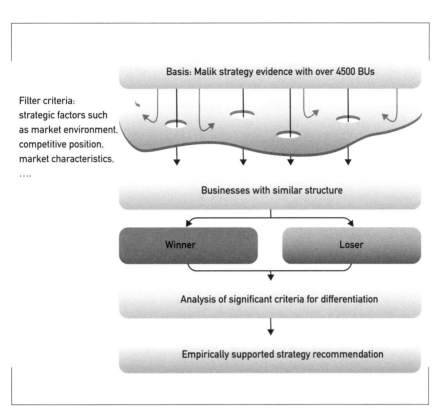

Figure 56: Look-alike filter and separation of winners and losers

of market share, innovation rate, customer preference, investment intensity, and so on—and hence a similar par ROI.

In a second step, you divide up these look-alikes by winners and losers—businesses that improve significantly over time versus those that get worse. For businesses in need of operational improvement, that means an increase in actual ROI; for businesses in need of strategic improvement, that means an increase in par ROI.

Learning From Winners

Winners are all those look-alikes which, starting from a comparable position, have reached a far better combination of actual and par ROI over a certain period of time than other, comparable businesses. In figure 57, the look-alike winners (shown in the top quartile) were able to improve their starting position from a 26 percent Par ROI in 2004 to almost 40 percent in 2007. During the same period, the look-alike losers reduced their Par ROI to 21 percent, the mediocre field improved from 26 to only 29 percent.

The diagram also shows what has distinguished winners from losers in this specific case. This opens very interesting possibilities for planning your own business area strategy. Having seen proof that such achievements are possible even starting from similar positions and that they can be attained through clever strategic moves, rather than being exotic exceptions, you can now think about which of these success elements can be transferred to your own business.

The key differences between winning and losing strategies almost always result from the interaction of several factors which need to be balanced. The solution seldom lies in individual measures, as they could probably have been found by the other peers as well.

In this case, it was a set of measures:

- *Focusing on customers who value good service*
- *Massive support to, but restrictive expansion of the sales force in order to drive growth*
- *Improving service quality and simplifying offerings*
- *Reducing procurement costs, even though manufacturing costs were slightly increased as a result*
- *Increasing buying power through larger contracts with suppliers, which made them more dependent*
- *Keeping sales growth higher than sales force growth (4 percent vs. 2 percent).*

Once again it is obvious that for truly effective management, the former, mono-causal way of thinking no longer works. Everywhere we can see systemic interconnectedness and interaction, as well as the careful fine-adjustment and orchestration of measures. In part VI of this book I will show how to use the sensitivity model for that purpose. As every business is different from the next, such analyses and strategy designs would be very time-consuming if done with traditional means. The New World tools, however, often reduce the time required to about one-tenth.

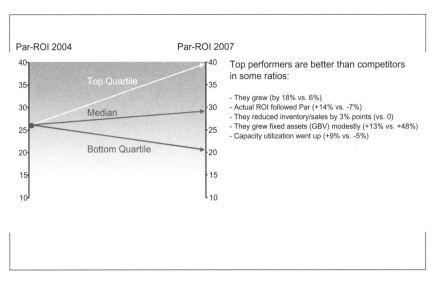

Figure 57: Even top performers can get better

How Everything Fits Together: MG Navigator and PIMS Par Model

The following diagram shows the logic of how the components described in this book fit together. The control variable *profit* in the MG Navigator drives the actual ROI position on the vertical axis in the performance charts of the PIMS Par Model. The level directly above, *profit potential*, is calculated with the Par Model and placed on the chart's horizontal axis. From that we can derive the steps of the Look-Alike analysis, as described above.

Both models, the Par and the Look-Alike Model, are tools offering unbeatable effectiveness, precisions, and speed, to be used for acquisitions, mergers, strategic repositioning, and redimensioning efforts. They provide faster, more precise and better results than any other method I know.

The PIMS Par Concept also revolutionizes investment banking and the private equity business. Pedram Farschtschian has managed to prove this point quite accurately in his book on the private equity business and the challenges it faces in the 21st century. Farschtschian describes the integration of the MG Navigator with PIMS in a logically stringent manner, including its connection with the Par Model. He also points out how apply-

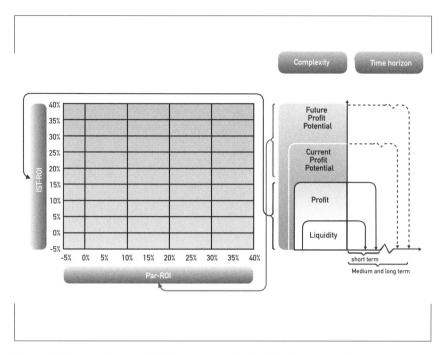

Figure 58: Integrating the MG Navigator with the PIMS Par Model

ing PIMS fundamentally changes the private equity business, as the value of an equity interest can be determined much faster and more effectively with PIMS than with the assessment criteria commonly applied in the industry. So far, the industry has relied on actual performance figures and rough estimates. Now that the par values (or potential values) are known there will be dramatic changes regarding objectives, negotiation tactics, investment sums, and the later management of investment targets, as well as regarding investors' exit strategies.[29]

29 Farschtschian, Pedram: *Private Equity für die Herausforderungen der neuen Zeit. Strategische Innovation für das Funktionieren von Private Equity im 21. Jahrhundert*, Frankfurt/New York, 2010.

The Customer Value Map: Using Customer Value and Competitiveness as Reliable Guiding Stars

"The purpose of a business is to create a customer."

Peter F. Drucker, 1954

This PIMS model requires a little more space than the other two have taken.[30] Here, I remind you of my two postulates regarding corporate purpose (part II):

customer value instead of shareholder value

and

competitiveness instead of value increase.

A broad range of things have been described here, spanning from corporate purpose to business mission and Central Performance Controls, to the MG Navigator and the Strategy Map with its Archimedean point and the solution-invariant customer problem, all the way to here, where I will now show how to determine customer value in practice.[31] Two variables are objective for the purposes of strategy: customers and competition. Hence there are two reliable points of orientation for the overall management of a company and its strategy: customer value and competitiveness. And while it is true that both are moving targets, as long as the person at the helm keeps his gaze fixed on these guiding stars, he will be able to keep the corporate ship on a straight course, no matter what the changes around it.

So, the first strategic goal must always be to serve customers better than any competitor can. To satisfy customers, however, it is not necessary to give away one's market performance for free, as is sometimes claimed—for "serving better" is not necessarily "serving cheaper". Customer value does not only have a price dimension, but a quality dimension as well, which is much more important in an increasing number of cases; besides, competitors are also interested in making good deals. Giving away things is simply

---

30 Gale, Bradley T.: *Managing Customer Value*, London, 1994. Bradley Gale was a close associate of Sidney Schoeffler, the "father" of PIMS at GE, and then for many years headed the Strategic Planning Institute in Boston, which was driving the PIMS research effort at the time.

31 Roberts, Keith und Chussil, Mark: "The meaning and value of customer value", *Malik Online letter*, 2008.

not an option in a market economy, as customers usually prefer a supplier economically sound enough to still be there next year.

The Customer Value Map: Relativity Theory of Customer Value

The solution to this challenge is the *Customer Value Model* from the PIMS program. It leads to the *relativity theory* of customer value, which helps to master numerous strategic issues with ease.

Customer value has two dimensions: one is the quality of market performance and the other is its price. Both dimensions have to be put in relation to competitive offerings, so it is a matter of *relative* quality of market performance and of relative price. So, in a manner of speaking, customer value incorporates the twofold relativity theory of strategic management: value relative to the customer and relative to the competition.

When depicting it graphically we get the strategic *Customer Value Map*. It expresses what value we offer the *customer* as compared to our

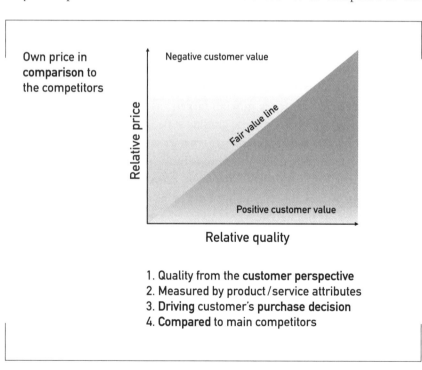

Figure 59: The Customer Value Map

competitors. The diagonal line is the place of consistent customer value— the *Fair Value Line.* It does not always run diagonally, though; the value line can also be steeper or flatter. It is steeper for *quality-sensitive* market performance, where even small quality improvements may permit disproportionate price increases. Conversely, the line will be flatter than average for commodities where price is hardly sensitive to quality improvements. Let us skip all intermediate steps and look at the outcome: By placing the business in the Value Map, we see the customer-value-driven strategic relation between our own company and our rivals, as related to the customer's "world view". It is the survey map of relative success and failure in the competition for the customer, from the customer's perspective. There is hardly anything of greater strategic importance, which is why this analysis leads to the most significant managerial conclusions and measures.

It becomes obvious now why the term "relativity theory" is correct in a double sense: The information contained in the Value Map is both relative to the customer and relative to the competition. Moreover, it is relative in two further dimensions: relative to quality attributes and relative to price. Figure 60 shows a practical example.

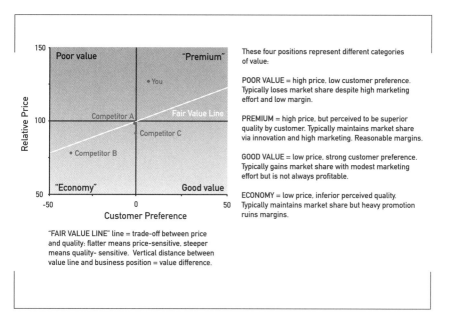

Figure 60: Integrated customer and competitive analysis—example: The Customer Value Map

The Value Map is a *universal tool* because it provides more key information than any other tool. Key questions and the corresponding answers are integrated in one concept and one diagram which should be read as follows:

- Here we have an example of a price-sensitive business, where even a major improvement to relative quality, or customer preference, only permits a disproportionately small price increase. The Fair Value Line runs flatter than diagonal.
- All businesses below the Fair Value Line (or to its right) have a positive price-performance ratio, that is, superior customer value. These businesses will gain market share over two to five years on average, as proved by PIMS.
- Business placed above (to the left of) the Fair Value Line have an inferior customer value relative to their competitors. These businesses will lose market share, and despite their higher prices they will also lose ROI because their marketing and promotion expenses have to be disproportionately high to keep their position.
- Value Analysis also leads us to further, extremely important strategic questions in terms of game theory, such as how competitors will act and react, both of their own accord and as a response to our strategic moves, and which competitors will be easier to attack than others.

These are enough reasons to make Customer Value Analysis a primary tool of strategic management, to never leave customer value unguarded but to monitor it constantly, and to train all employees how to think in customer value categories.

First Dimension: Double Relative Quality Triggers Customer Preference

Let me stress this once again: the better the quality, the higher the earning power of a business. "Quality", however, is a complex concept that needs to be understood correctly to avoid mistakes, which can easily become expensive especially in this area.

"Quality" should never refer to product quality only—the term has to encompass the quality of a business's entire *market performance*. The latter comprises the characteristics of a *product*—technical specifications, performance parameters, material properties, design, workmanship, and so on—but also the associated *service components* such as punctual delivery, availability, user-friendliness, after-sales service, general reliability, financial engineering, and more.

These service components are gaining importance as products become increasingly similar, despite all the efforts made for differentiation. Nowadays all suppliers are able to deliver technical quality; otherwise they would hardly ever get to submit a bid. So in many industries, not the product features are decisive for buying decisions but the services included in suppliers' market performance.

How Customers See the World

The second important point is that value-based quality is almost never what R & D or other technical/scientific functions think: it is always and exclusively the quality *perceived* by customers. In other words, "quality" must always be understood as *customer-perceived quality*. There are no exceptions to this rule. And so it also defines the objectives and purposes of communication, promotion, and advertising efforts.

Customer perception is often light years away from economist rationality. In economics there is only one kind of *objectivity*: it is *customers' subjectivity*. No matter how irrational the customers' behavior may seem to a technician, a physicist, or a computer scientist—it is their rationality. All that matters is how customers see things. A customer is defined as *a person who can say no.*

The subjectivity factor is a bit less important in B2B relations, where buyers are also "pros"—that is, customers' sourcing and procurement people. In cases like these, the rationality factor is easier to anticipate and to assess for a supplier.

As mentioned before, quality is not only relative to the customer's view but also relative to the competition. In business, as in most sports, it is not enough to be good in absolute terms—to win you have to be better than your rivals. The question has to be, "are we superior or inferior to our competitors?" It is particularly important for very technically focused companies. Many engineers have a tendency to do what is technically possible, irrespective of what customers want and competitors offer. Over-engineering has probably done more damage and incurred higher cost than, for instance, financing or staffing errors.

And the last key point is this: For quality assessment, price has to be left out of account, for it is a second, separate dimension. Much too often, competitive price is considered a component of quality. That is wrong. There are of course a few luxury goods markets where the opposite—uncompetitive price—is seen as desirable, but even here the attributes desired by the customer are exclusivity and prestige rather than an extortionate price per se.

Second Dimension: Relative Price

Relative price is the second coordinate of the Value Map. It is a supplier's own price in relation to that of its most important rivals. It is therefore best expressed as an index, With 100 meaning "We are just as expensive as our competitors", and 110 meaning "We are 10 percent more expensive", while 90 means "We are 10 percent cheaper".

From the combination of these two dimensions—relative quality and relative price—we can derive *the double relative price-performance ratio* which best corresponds to the complex concept of customer value.

Fourfold Value Analysis: Self-Image and Public Image, Customers and Non-Customers

Our customer value analysis is always *fourfold*: it is done for customers and non-customers, and for the company's self-image (developed by teams of employees) and its public image, determined by customers.

Here, the logic of the business mission as explained in part II comes into play again.

Employees usually have difficulties exploring and assessing quality from the customer's perspective. Besides, they are partial in several respects: for instance, engineers see quality differently from marketing people, and sales and distribution experts will have yet other viewpoints. A major barrier to quality assessment is employees' potential identification with the product, sometimes to the point of being in love with their own achievements, which, unfortunately, means they are no longer able to see the world with others' eyes.

It is therefore necessary to ask the customers themselves in order to come closer to their reality—which, ultimately, is what drives buying decisions. And even this is turning out to be insufficient in an increasing number of cases, as customers are often unable to say why they buy this product and not that. The conclusion is that we need to watch customers making their purchases, wherever possible, and study their buying and application situations. Best results are achieved by observing customers while they use the products.

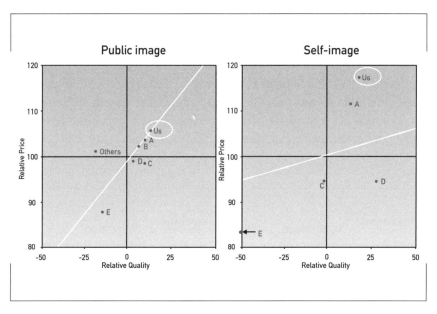

Figure 61: Self-image and public image in a typical customer value analysis

When existing customers are sufficiently known, it is also necessary to look at "not-yet customers", which requires another level of intensity. But it makes sense and it is fun, because it provides so many new insights through such a simple approach.

Figure 61 speaks for itself, and when an analysis like this is performed for your business I recommend studying it very closely. It is at least as meaningful as the cartographic material used by a well-managed army, showing both its own positions and those of the enemy with all relevant details.

The outcomes of self-image and public image analyses do not always differ this much. Still, among thousands of cases analyzed there were only a few with over 70 percent congruence. In other words, 30 percent of the key buying factors were regularly overlooked. The costs of this failure are tremendous, but now there is an opportunity to better understand and eliminate these discrepancies.

What Drives the Buying Decision?

Customer value analysis is performed using a PIMS tool, the Attributes Chart, which contains the value criteria that are supposed to drive buying decisions. These are rated by importance and degree of fulfillment, always in relation to customers and competitors. It turns out in the process that not only are individual attributes rated very differently—often, there is even disagreement on whether something is or isn't an attribute of customer value.

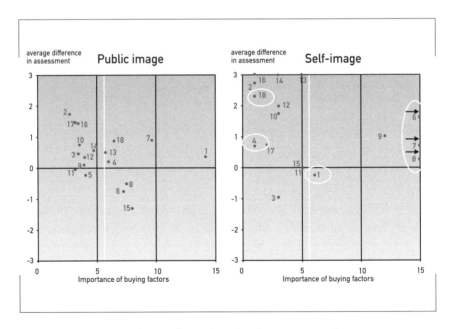

Figure 62: Customer value attributes chart for the same example

Describing each attribute in detail would require a whole case study. Each figure stands for a quality attribute of market performance which is supposed to drive buying decisions, both in the self- and the public image. Without digging any deeper here, it is obvious how far apart some of these ratings are.

Customer value analyses like these are among the most valuable tools for strategy design. Such analyses and their results present fantastic opportunities to learn more about one's own business. Each time, exploring the reasons for different perceptions is like making an expedition into the unfamiliar world of customers and competitors. Also, there is hardly another way to learn so much about oneself.

Feedback Process until the Value is Right

Based on the analyses described, a process of twofold adjustment is launched: for quality *assessment* and for *quality as such*, until all contradictions are eliminated and the self-image is congruent with the public one.

This process generally covers everything from the redesign of market performance to changes in market communications. This way, the "cost gap" resulting from "wasted quality" is eliminated without leaving a "quality gap" for competitors to fill. In addition, the quality of market

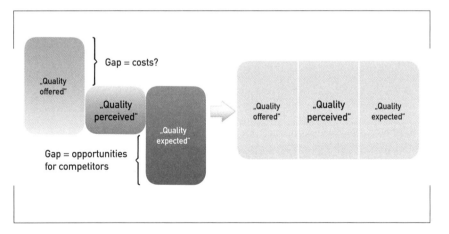

Figure 63: Constant adjustment of expected, offered, and perceived value

performance can be adjusted to match customer perception, or customer perception can be changed through communication, or both.

These efforts to manage customer value pay off extremely well. Leverage effects both on the cost and the price dimension of performance are enormous, often enabling companies to increase their margins by several percentage points. Neglecting customer value management—for instance, for the sake of shareholder value—equates to putting the company's existence at risk, which will eventually cause losses for shareholders, too.

Part V:

Ahead of Change: Success Factors for Your New Business

"We don't believe in progress,
we practice innovation."

Peter F. Drucker

Part V shows how to keep ahead of change strategically, how to actively trigger change, and how to use PIMS findings to set up your start-up strategies for success.

Chapter 1

Constants in the Currents of Change

Does change simply happen, or is it made? The answer is: both. Neither is change pure chaos and coincidence, nor is it completely planned and fabricated. Rather, both dimensions interact in constantly changing proportions and degrees. Social systems belong in the (still insufficiently understood) category of so-called *spontaneous orders* which have their own dynamics and keep restructuring themselves. For more on this subject, please refer to my book *Corporate Policy and Governance*.

Clearly, systems of such complexity cannot really be understood—they remain Black Boxes. The astonishing part is that, irrespective of all that, change does have its systemic pattern and dynamic order. They have emerged from the hypercomplex interaction of an astronomic number of factors and influences, and they can be identified using certain elements of dynamic system analysis. The approach very much resembles the exploration of a new continent, which one might call the knowledge continent of complex systems. This is what the present chapter is about.

The subject of this chapter is among the most important and also the most intriguing that exists for our time and for the Great Transformation21. The chapter centers around the most complex fields of the Strategy Map, to be used for the mega-changes that are either in full swing or yet to come, as well as for the forces that trigger them and the patterns they will assume.

It is about the systemic relationships between the solution-invariant customer problem and the innovation and substitution processes shown in figure 64, fields Nos. 2, 3, 4, 5, and 7.

Whoever manages to peek behind the surface of events and to identify the constants in the current of perpetual change will have immense advantages in the struggle for best positions, or even for survival. Only with this knowledge is it possible to recognize viable solutions. It provides both the lifebuoys and the tools required for building one's new position in the New World. It enables entrepreneurs and top-level executives not only to get better orientation but even to take advantage of the complexity of change that may seem forever impenetrable for those not in the know. Equipped with this knowledge, the understanding of this complexity and its background will quickly become the launch pad, the engine, and the accelerator for new solutions—all at once.

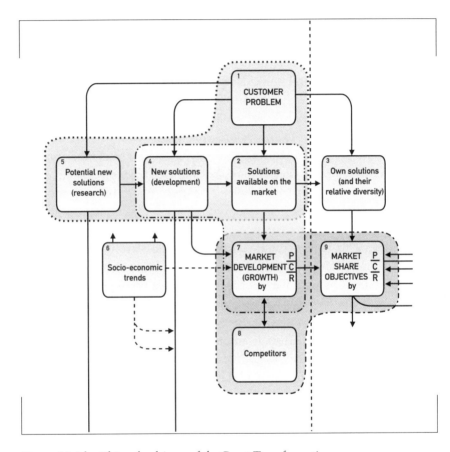

Figure 64: Identifying the drivers of the Great Transformation

I have often discussed the highly complex issues of innovation management and the right strategies for fundamental change with *Peter F. Drucker*.

He was one of the very few people with whom I could talk about the interaction between technology and science, inventions and innovations, and their successful marketing: it requires a broad knowledge of history which is hard to find, as the transformation of initial ideas into useful technologies can only be appreciated by someone familiar with their historical connections.

The Magic of Patterns that Connect

By sheer coincidence, I happened to come across the groundbreaking work of the Italian physicist *Cesare Marchetti* quite early. Marchetti has performed system-analytical research of the S-Curve pattern of technological and societal change. I instantly realized the outstanding relevance that his findings and his approach to analyzing complex systems had for major strategy decisions.

I was predisposed for that due to my interest in connections between cultural and technological history, from early high cultures via Rome and China to the present day. It stretches from the irrigation technologies of ancient cultures, their grand construction sites and their military organization across the system approach of modern research labs and on to the revolutionary social technology of Syntegration for problem-solving, decision-making, and the management of mega-change (and I will get to that in part VI).

Cesare Marchetti was just as competent in these matters as *Peter Drucker* was. Several times I invited him to give speeches and seminars, and the discussions with him were absolutely electrifying for both the audience and me. Today, he lives in Tuscany and, in his ingenious way, studies the life and work of Leonardo da Vinci.

With the utmost elegance, Marchetti had managed to carve out the progress pattern and dynamic order of even the most complex change processes. Many of the change processes of the more than 3,000 cases he studied spanned several centuries, yet they do have a perfect rhythm. They are like a symphony directed by a hidden maestro, or a "hidden control system" driving the entire process of *invention, innovation, substitution, and exploitation*, from the idea to its economic exploitation in the market, but also its later substitution by new solutions.

I instantly realized that the Archimedean crystallization point of such change and restructuring processes has to be the original, solution-invariant user problem, as pointed out earlier, and that anyone with this knowledge can surf the currents of change, since he will be able to see the pattern connecting all systems and their subsystems. Even in things formerly unconnected he will begin to see logical coherence and thus be able to navigate safely.

I was now able to give the concept of the "solution-invariant original user problem" a whole new dimension, as the Archimedean point was not only the user problem of a defined individual or target group, but it could be extended across the entire social universe. It became very clear to me that the original challenges of entire societies can be placed at the center of deliberations—such as *survival, evolutionary adaptation, viability, and functioning.*

We, too, Will Be Replaced: Creative Destruction

One of the greatest challenges to any organization is its transition from one type of solution to its original problems to another solution type. This, precisely, is the true nature of profound transformation. Viewed over historical periods of time, not one single solution to any given problem has ever endured. All solutions are *transient*, that is, of *limited duration*, and only temporarily important. In the same way, not a single product is truly significant to the market, for there is always a replacement.

Consequently, one of the axioms that strategic thinking is based on is this:

"Whatever exists today will change—even if we cannot begin to imagine in which ways."

This is one meaning of the term "self-restructuring" systems. From this first axiom follows a second, a basic strategic premise:

"We, too, will be replaced, although we currently do not know by what and when.

These assumptions are all the more important, the farther away a product is from the *original* user problem: remember that each solution derived from another shares its fate; that is, it will perish sooner or later.

These axioms incorporate one of the most important ideas of change: the notion of *creative destruction*, as the Austrian-American *economist Joseph Schumpeter* so aptly put it. He was the first and only economist so far to recognize how enormously important the process of renewal and replacement is in the world of business. This insight formed the core piece of his economic theory. In other economic theories, the enterprise as a productive subsystem of society and the entrepreneur as a functional cell are hardly ever mentioned at all. Economic theories are about prices and costs, of goods and of money—but never about the people who take risks to innovate and invest, and who take out loans to finance their plans, thus keeping all business activity alive.

This shifts the focus onto the dynamics of change and its *progression pattern*: non-linearity and complex interaction relationships, which almost always follow the basic pattern of an S-shaped curve, the parameters of which can be determined—though not always, but often and early enough to put the most significant and long-term strategic decisions on a solid foundation. There is no other method for achieving that.

Figure 65 shows two overlapping S-Curves for current and future profit potentials. They solve the same original problem, albeit in different ways. From Marchetti's analyses we can conclude that business and society are two "learning systems" because they keep replacing the old with the new, continually adapting and renewing themselves, and acquiring and integrating ever new behaviors, knowledge, tools, and methods in the process. S-shaped curves are the typical progression patterns not of growth but of learning processes. Vivid examples can be found, to name but two, in biology and behavioral science. These transformation processes describe the way in which ideas—represented by inventions and innovations, and ultimately by products and services—find their way into human behavior, through the markets, and afterwards disappear again from society.

Such processes are the master controls by which societal systems structure and control themselves over longer periods of time. They are sufficiently stable to serve as orientation aids. That is why even the deepest and most profound changes do not really come as a surprise. They are only surprising to those who do not know how to read the signs, and who are not familiar enough with the tidal currents of ongoing restructuring processes.

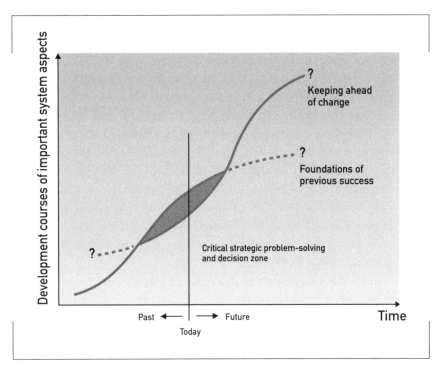

Figure 65: Pattern of transformational change in two waves

Change also comes as a surprise to those who would presumably deny it, claiming they have everything under control, instead of accepting that they themselves and their decisions are part of larger and more comprehensive systems with their own laws. The S-Curves are among the basic principles which allowed me to discover the Great Transformation21 from the Old World to the New World at an early stage.

Symphony of S-Curves: Seeing the Future Clearly

In the course of his scientific career, Cesare Marchetti examined over 3,000 cases, some of them highly complex, by system-analytical means. In almost all of these cases he discovered the same striking patterns and coherences.

For this chapter, I will select from his repertoire a small number of representative cases from very different areas, adding a few examples from our own practice to make the underlying patterns clearer and demonstrate their universal applicability. This will give the reader an impression of the regularities that can be found in the dynamics of change processes in complex, self-restructuring systems. As far as the methodological questions of system analysis are concerned, I will leave those aside.

Marchetti's studies span an enormous range of system analyses covering such different areas as the automotive industry, traffic and transportation infrastructures, power supply systems, the dynamics of urban development, the process of intellectual creation for artists and scientists, demographic and ecological systems, climate issues, and the dynamics of invention and innovation waves.

The S-shaped curve type, sometimes also referred to as *logistic* curve or function, is the basic pattern of *healthy* natural growth. At the beginning it progresses slowly, followed by exponential acceleration until it reaches the turning point, after which it flattens out and evens off at the system's saturation level. Healthy growth is S-shaped growth. Any other kind of growth is unhealthy.

This insight permits another, almost magical vision of the future, which is very different from traditional forecasting methods, as I pointed out in part I of this book. Rather than individual variables, this forecast specifies patterns, which then makes it possible to determine individual pattern factors. In other words, it is a shift from the usual linear extrapolations to the *exploration of patterns* in the behavior of complex systems.[32]

Simple Growth Processes

The first example comes from nature: it is the way sunflowers grow. They take about 85 days to grow, reaching a total height of more than eight feet. Depending on the form of life, the duration and the parameters of growth

---

32 Friedrich von Hayek, known to most people as an economist only, wrote his more important works on the theory of complex phenomena and spontaneous orders. I used it in my 1976 habilitation treatise *Strategie komplexer Systeme* ["*Strategy of the Management of Complex Systems*"] which essentially lays the theoretical foundations for my management theory. Hayek addressed the topics of pattern explanation and pattern prediction in his essay "Degrees of Explanation", in *Studies in Philosophy, Politics and Economics*, Chicago, 1967.

can be very different in detail, but the *pattern of healthy growth* is always the same. No matter whether we are dealing with a bacteria colony in a Petri dish or with sunflowers: the pattern is S-shaped (see figure 66).

Hence, it is possible to forecast growth processes. Even with just a few data points, we can predict three things more or less accurately, the importance of which for business strategies cannot be emphasized enough: first, at what absolute volume level growth will come to a stop; second, where the turning point will be on the S-Curve, which is key to determining the growth rate; and third, how long the whole process will take. In other words, based on the growth pattern we can estimate for a business strategy what the market and sales volumes will be, as well as the growth rates for market and sales volumes, and how long it will take for these points to be reached.

These reference points are invaluable for strategy decisions. The statistical precision with which these parameters can be determined is often amazing. Yet for practical application purposes this is not as important as some may think, when trying to prove all the things the S-Curve can*not* achieve. No doubt this methodical tool has its limitations, too. Being aware of them is just as important as knowing what the benefits are of this kind of pattern exploration.

Statistical precision, as long it remains within reasonable limits, is not as important as the system pattern itself. It is not necessary, for instance,

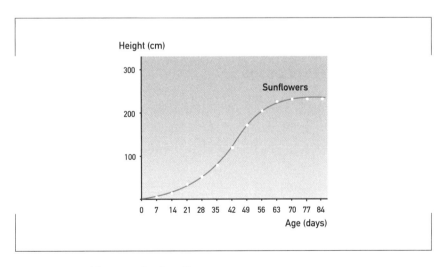

Figure 66: Healthy growth of sunflowers

to begin by taking the critical decisions that will become important several decades later, such as on manufacturing capacity at saturation level. The smart approach is to grow with and into the market and to take high-risk decisions as late as possible, rather than at the earliest possible stage. The further that progress leads us on the curve, the more precise individual data points will be. Or perhaps we will realize that the pattern does not remain stable but shifts in another direction. Both are leads providing orientation, where one would usually be in the dark and have to take high-risk decisions arbitrarily—including the de-facto decision to do nothing, which is usually the one that involves the highest risk.

The same growth pattern is also found in social-technological systems. According to the pattern, for example, the absolute quantity of automobiles in Italy and other countries grew between 1950 and 1990 (figure 67, top left), and so has the share of cell phones in the Austrian telephone

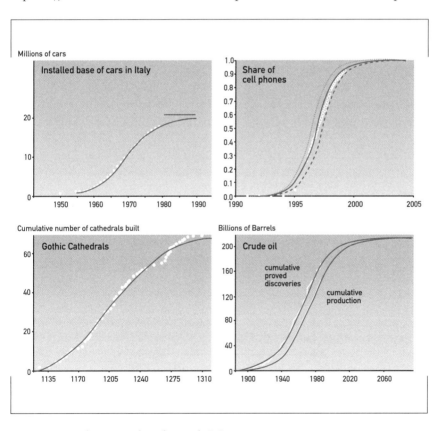

Figure 67: Further examples of growth S-Curves

market between 1900 and 2000 (top right-hand corner). If you look at the data material with the S-Curve in mind, you will quickly recognize the pattern, or be able to look out for it.

Now some may object that these are *ex post* examples and one always knows better with the benefit of hindsight. That is certainly true. But since these patterns occur so frequently, almost without exception, they have to be predictable ex ante. So the question is, at what point in time can we draw what conclusion from exploring the data material? Every little bit of information is valuable in complex situations.

In the bottom left-hand corner we see the pattern in which, over a period of about 200 years, gothic cathedrals have emerged in Europe. The measuring variable here is the cumulative number of foundation stones of all those cathedrals that were considered to be finished at that particular point in time. Another example (bottom right-hand corner) which has yet to be confirmed is the discovery and exploration of oil fields, which are presently running in parallel, following an S-shape. Both curves start around 1900, with the first data going all the way back to 1850, thus spanning a period of almost 200 years. The saturation of both cumulative exploration and production should be reached around 2020 or 2030.

The last example traces Mozart's creative life, expressed in terms of the cumulative number of his works. This curve also follows the same logistic

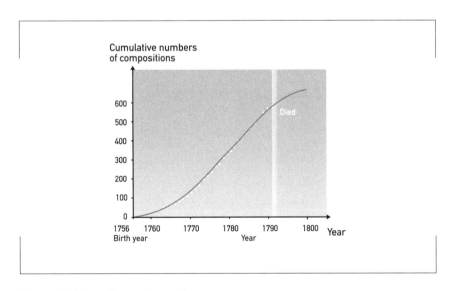

Figure 68: Mozart's creative work

progression pattern, as do, incidentally, the creations of many other artists and scientists analyzed by Marchetti. This pattern is rather thought-provoking, when you think of the conclusions to be drawn—which, however, are not the subject of this book on strategy. The important point here is that we have shown the range of phenomena captured by the S-Curve, and what it teaches us in terms of strategy work.

From Growth to Substitution

From the simple growth processes we are now getting to the more complex substitution processes. It is the same pattern according to which, from 1900 to 1930, the horse was replaced by the car as a means of transportation in the U.S.[33] In Europe, street cars (trams or trolleys) made some progress as a technological solution to the invariant customer problem "transportation", but for a long time they were still horse-drawn. In the U.S., the horse was still the dominant means of transportation in 1900, with almost 100 percent market share.

At that time, the car was gradually entering the global traffic scene. Conquering the market along an S-Curve development, it had gained about half of it in 1915 and by 1930 had replaced the horse in urban traffic. That does not mean that there were no more horses in the U.S. On the contrary, there were more than before, but they now solved different user problems.

The substitution of analog by digital photography (see right-hand side of the diagram) also follows the S-Curve. Remember the story I mentioned earlier, about the attendees at one of my strategy seminars in 1995, people from the analog photography industry, who found the notion absurd that digital technology could possibly replace the analog one. Based on the data material on market shares, and relying on conventional thinking approaches, it was impossible at the time to state with certainty that a total substitution was imminent, that the whole industry would practically vanish, and that everything would be over in a little over ten years—too short a period for major corporations to respond adequately.

---

33 Nakicenovic, Nebojsa: *Transportation and Energy Systems in the United States*, Laxenburg (Austria), 1986.

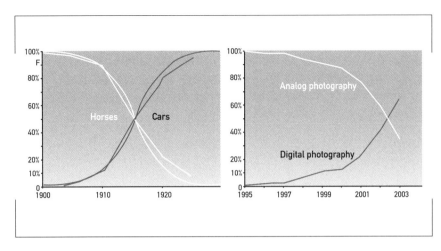

Figure 69: Old Worlds Being Replaced by New Worlds

By contrast, anyone familiar with the innovation cycles described here could be certain even then that disaster was looming. Since the technology as such was quite developed, but not yet present in the market, a strategy scenario would have to cover this potential substitution by asking: *How would our company fare if this substitution really happened?*

The total market dominance of analog photography could not prevent it from being replaced by a new solution technology. The current profit potential of analog photography was bound to vanish because the future profit potential was already a virtual reality. The Old World of analog photography had to perish because the New World of digital photography had already emerged.

These examples show very clearly that the New World does not emerge because the Old World no longer works, but because the new solutions are better by far. The car was not invented because horse-drawn carriages had become worse—rather, the horse carriage had to give way because the car was entering the scene. The same is true of the Great Transformation21.

When Several Systems Compete for Existence

Particularly exciting are the cases of multiple substitution. One breathtaking example is the succession of transportation infrastructures in the

U.S.—from waterways to railways to paved roads to airlines. The future may bring high-performance Maglev (magnetic levitation) trains which, having originally been developed in Germany, are now put to use in China. There are some initial ideas to build a train of this kind from, say, China to Europe. Or it may be something else, like telepresence and 3D reprographics, which meet the same invariant need (being in a different place) without physically moving people or objects.

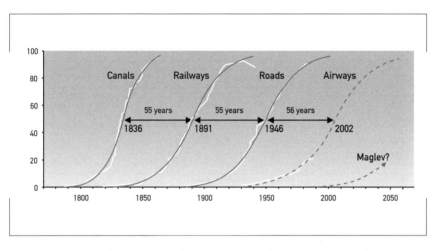

Figure 70: Historical succession of transportation infrastructures in the U.S.

The regularity of intervals between successive mega-transportation infrastructures are truly striking: their so-called half-lives—from one central point to the next—span around 55 years each time. This leads me to mention the name of yet another pioneer: *Nikolai Kondratieff*, about whom I will tell you more shortly. If this basic pattern continues, the next technology will reach its central point by late 2050: by that time the infrastructures will be prospering, and a whole industry will have been built around them. Here, we have the example of an extremely complex process which spans more than 200 years, yet can be captured very clearly in its logic and dynamics by means of logistic system analysis. Behind myriads of details which nobody can survey, an orderly universe is beginning to show.

Another example is the substitution of primary energy sources in the U.S. which, when depicted as market shares on a logarithmical scale, displays a striking pattern. With incredible regularity, one energy surge follows the other, from wood to coal, on to oil and gas, followed by nu-

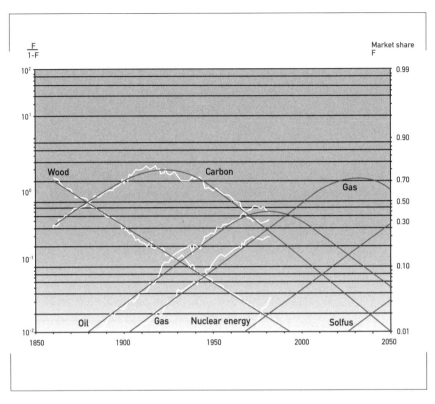

Figure 71: Primary energy substitution in the U.S.

clear power and its likely replacement by a green energy source such as "solfus"—a solar hydrogen energy whose further development is still difficult to predict.

Discovering the Secret Driver of Epochal Change

We are now about to get to the climax of the symphony of magical S-Curves, and of what seems to be the hidden driver of major economic and social transformations: the succession of invention and innovation waves.

As a preliminary stage before the comprehensive, long-term progression analysis of innovation waves, in figure 72 we see the batch-wise development of *basic innovations* as meticulously identified by Gerhard Mensch in the 1970s. A first accumulation appears around 1770, followed by the

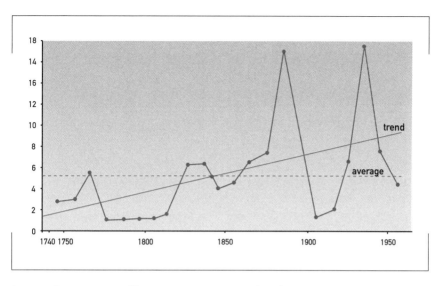

Figure 72: Frequency of basic innovations in 22 decades (1740—1960)[34]

next in 1830, then another in 1850 and finally that of the 1930s. Basic innovations obviously occur in distinctive waves over time. Each time, these technological surges have triggered profound changes in business and society. Again, their peaks show consistent intervals of around 55 years— which gives us a first idea of how things go together.

From this observation, Marchetti inferred four successive technological waves, which follow one another with surprising regularity and determine mega-change over the 400-year period from 1700 to 2100.[35]

When looking at the following diagrams, please note that their vertical axes are logarithmic scales, by which S-shaped curves are transformed into straight lines. In other words, all straight lines in these diagrams would be S-Curves when depicted in a normal coordinate system, in the previous diagrams.

---

34 Mensch, Gerhard: *Das technologische Patt*, Frankfurt, 1977.

35 Marchetti, Cesare: "Society as a Learning System—Discovery, Invention and Innovation Cycles Revisited", in: *Technological Forecasting and Social Change*, Vol. 18, 1980. Marchetti, Cesare: *Pervasive long waves: is human society cyclotymic?* Prepared for the Conference "Offensiv zu Arbeitsplätzen", Cologne: Weltmärkte 2010, September 14–15, 1996.

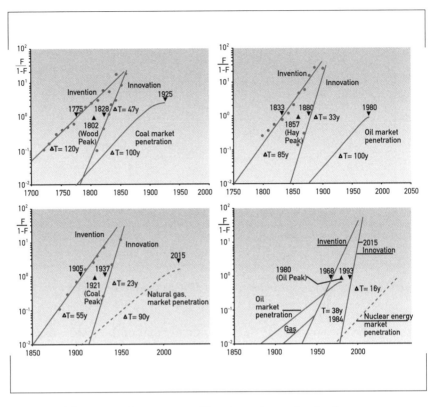

Figure 73: The progression patterns of four invention and technology waves

Centennial Cycles: Invention—Innovation—Substitution—Exploitation

To understand the Great Transformation21 and the strategy issues raised by it, we should now address the striking regularities and time constants of four innovation waves, three of them complete and one still ongoing. Marchetti has studied them based on Mensch's work. The remarkably co-ordinated and synchronized order of many economically relevant events is intriguing enough to warrant a closer look.

The three historical surges have their central points in 1802, 1857, and 1920, the current one in 1980. The surges, or waves, are distributed over the course of time with surprising regularity. In a sense, they pulse in a common rhythm, as a living system would.

Marchetti was able to reconstruct the course of the S-shaped invention wave which preceded the current innovations. As long as the way human beings innovate and absorb new things does not change fundamentally, this fourth wave looks set to continue on the course depicted here. The beginning of the invention wave goes back to the time before the Second World War. Its central point fell on the year 1968. The *innovation wave* begins in the 1970s, having reached about 10 percent by 1984. Its central point is 1993, by which point about half of all innovations of this wave would have been made. The second half of the innovation occurs in the 1990s, to reach the 90 percent mark in 2002. The "T" refers to the time required to get from 10 to 90 percent. The central date of the overall wave comprising both the invention and the innovation wave—the mid-point between the two 50-percent points—is 1980.

As early as in the 1970s, Marchetti predicted that from that point on the market share of oil as a primary energy source would decline and oil would increasingly be replaced by natural gas. This has certainly come true: in absolute terms, we are still consuming more oil, but other primary energy sources are gaining increasing shares in total consumption. The innovations of this 1980s wave will cause another *economic upturn*, although with a considerable time lag. The time until then will be the critical phase of the Great Transformation21, with turbulences, economic difficulties, business collapses, but also enormous innovation activity—marking the transition from the Old World to the New World, from the previous order to another, new global order.

Marchetti had the courage to sketch out—hypothetically—two further waves that would stretch beyond the year 2100. According to him, around the year 2040 natural gas will reach its zenith point in terms of market share among the primary energy sources, to be replaced by nuclear energy as the dominant energy source, which would reach its peak around 2090. According to Marchetti, that would be the point by which the solar fusion energy mentioned above should have become mature enough to take over.

The dotted lines in figure 74 indicate the S-shaped invention waves, the dashed-and-dotted lines indicate the development of related innovations. The lines get steeper and steeper, which means that developments within each wave are accelerating. Nevertheless, each wave follows the previous one at the same interval of approximately 55 years, which is also

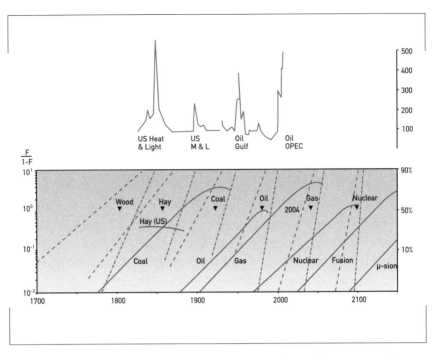

Figure 74: Pattern of the 400-year transformation, made up of invention and innovation

the length of a Kondratieff cycle. The solid lines represent the rise, market share maximum, and decline of the primary energy source associated with the particular wave (wood, hay, coal, oil, gas, nuclear). The maximum market shares of each energy type coincide with the mid-point of an invention-innovation wave.

In the top part of the diagram, we see the development of energy prices of the corresponding waves. According to these, energy prices in constant dollars would have to have dropped after 1980. Viewed superficially and in nominal dollars, the opposite seems to have happened. An additional factor is that outliers like the 2008/09 hedge fund peak of the oil price are short-lived by nature. An oil price below 20 dollars is a realistic scenario for the future. Under conditions of stress, such as a global financial crisis or a war, hyper-complex systems may respond erratically over their full fluctuation range. Looking at the overall picture, it is possible to understand these outliers because they can be viewed in context. Looking at the detail level, it is easy to lose orientation.

The basis of these processes seems to be the way in which human beings *gain* knowledge (researching), *spread* it (teaching/learning), use it for practical purposes (innovating) and finally *exploit* these innovations economically.

Looking at the individual diagrams we can see that the invention and innovation curves get steeper. Every 100 years or so the speed of progression doubles. The astonishing point is that so far, each major wave followed the other in the same interval of about 55 years. This equals the duration of a Kondratieff Cycle, which leads us to the next chapter and the long economic waves identified by the Russian economist Nikolai Kondratieff.

Was Kondratieff Right?
The Rhythm of Long Economic Cycles

To assess the situation and navigate correctly, it is necessary to know a little bit about the so-called Kondratieff Cycles, or *long economic cycles*. Most economists today are hardly aware of them or do not think much of them, as these cycles are difficult to integrate with the mathematical equations they use. They do, however, match the natural insight that there is no such thing as eternal, consistent growth, but a pattern of regular change comparable to that of the seasons.

When from the mid-1980s I would talk about Marchetti and Kondratieff in my seminars and speeches, about a third of the managers and entrepreneurs present would be struck by a realization: all of a sudden, they were able to "see" what they had long been sensing. Another third thought that it was all nonsense, and believed in man's almighty power to shape things after his will. The last third had become pensive and usually wanted more material to read. In my June 1993 Management Letter I published a rather comprehensive analysis of the Kondratieff waves, including their succession in the real economy and the financial word and, above all, the psychological and mass-psychological shifts they cause. My colleague Dr. Linda Pelzmann, a psychology professor, is one of the few experts world-wide in this field. She has taught at the universities of Vienna and Klagenfurt, Austria, as well as at Harvard, and regularly publishes articles in my Management Letters.[36]

In the 1920s, the Russian economist Nicolai Kondratieff, having closely studied price fluctuations, postulated that there was another pattern behind the short-term cyclical fluctuations observed in business: a long wave or economic cycle that stretches over a total of around 57 years. There are certain statistical issues involved, which I will not address here because they do not make a difference for the basic idea.

Kondratieff's findings are enormously valuable for complex and risky strategy decisions, when it comes to identifying *points of orientation* and *underlying patterns* in the whirlpool of everyday events and the turbulences of change. Four historic cycles have been researched quite well:

1722–1784	62 years
1784–1842	58 years
1842–1896	54 years
1896–1949	53 years

It is quite stunning how they correspond with Marchetti's invention-innovation waves. It appears that the Kondratieff Cycles are the economic consequences of these underlying drivers of ideas, inventions, technology, innovation, and commercial exploitation.

Should history repeat itself in that manner, which in my system scenarios I assume to be one of the most probable options, then the current *Kondratieff Cycle* began in 1949 and reached its peak around 1980. It was in its plateau around 2000, and has basically been on the downward move since then, which will go on until around 2013 or 2015.

Depending on whether you take the historically shortest or longest K-wave durations, you will end up with different end dates for the current one—which, however, is not really relevant for the practice of strategy development because the end of a "calendar" K-wave does not necessarily have to be followed by an immediate growth surge. The *Kondratieff Cy-*

36 Pelzmann, Linda: "The Triumph of Mass Manufactured Will—Circumstances and Rules", Malik Letter (previously M.o.M®-Letter) (11/02), and Pelzmann, Linda: "Collective Panic", *Malik Letter* (02/03). Linda Pelzmann teaches at the universities of Vienna and Klagenfurt, Austria, as well as in Harvard and regularly publishes in my Management Letters.

cles have long valleys, so it can take many years until an upturn is strong enough actually to be felt by the population.

In previous comparable situations, this has been due to human psychology and the general mood. There are, however, new methods—in particular the Syntegration method introduced in part VI—which can help trigger positive mood changes within a short period of time. Previous users of this approach have referred to the effect as "miraculous". The across-the-board application of this revolutionary and innovative approach may not instantly change economic facts, but it would surely change people's attitude. In this point, at least, history would not have to repeat itself.

Self-Destructing and Self-Creating Systems

One common feature of *all* previous Kondratieff Cycles was that each of them was linked to distinct, prolonged bull markets at the stock exchanges, which would regularly occur during the plateau phase and end with *extreme bear markets and crashes* in the downturn phase. After the peak, stock prices dropped 70 percent during the first Kondratieff Cycle, 80 percent during the second, 50 percent during the third, and 90 percent during the fourth K-wave. Usually these price slumps would occur in the last fifth or sixth of the K-wave—out of the blue, it seemed, as the economy was doing well and prosperity was rising. In reality, change had long been progressing deep within the system. Its undercurrents had not been visible on the surface of economic data, or had not been read correctly and in the appropriate context.

It is part of the tragedy of our existing market economy system, and of some of its poorly understood components, that the *financial excesses* have always been far greater than the fluctuations in the *real economy*. So recessions turned into depressions, irrespective of what the respective governments and their institutions—such as central banks or treasuries—were doing. In the course of a K-wave, the financial sector tends to drift away further and further from the real economy (the producing sector) and take on its own momentum, with financial figures exceeding several hundreds or thousands of times the real needs of businesses in terms of investment and trade financing.

More and more it becomes obvious that *financial markets*—contrary to popular opinion and economic theory—are not really markets at all, in the true sense of the word, because the laws of supply and demand to not apply here. The more the price of a share goes up, the more it gets sold, and the deeper its price plunges, the harder people try to sell it. In real markets it is the other way round. The more expensive cars or tomatoes become, the fewer are sold, and vice versa. While in the real part of the economy things self-regulate, in the finance sector they continue to escalate to the point of self-destruction.

One underlying mechanism is the build-up of excessive debt which no longer fulfills any productive purpose but creates bubbles in the financial system. Loans can no longer generate their own interest and repayments, but can only be reduced through deflation, which regularly leads to mass bankruptcies of businesses and states, and often to decades of economic deadlock.

To this day we do not know why Kondratieff's cycles and Marchetti's waves always last around 55 years. One of the reasons probably lies in the succession of generations, and how people learn, teach, and forget.

Then again, this time constant seems to be related to mass-psychological[37] and social moods. They are now addressed by a new branch of research, socionomics[38], which I find enormously interesting. The results so far are truly fascinating and have broad implications, so we can expect this discipline to generate revolutionary results. At the heart of socionomics is nothing less than the insight that the causality in social systems needs to be reversed.

It is not external events that cause or trigger people's actions, the theory goes, but, on the contrary, the causes of people's actions lie in themselves: in their mass-psychological moods which determine their behavior irrespective of external developments. It is the endogenous change of collective optimism to pessimism, and vice versa.

According to analyses, endogenous moods and mood swings also determine the way people assess their perception of events.

---

37 See, e.g., Pelzmann, Linda in various issues of the Malik Letter (previously M.o.M®-Letter), as well as Malik, Constantin: *Ahead of Change. How Crowd Psychology and Cybernetics Transform the Way We Govern*, Frankfurt/New York 2010.

38 Prechter, Robert Jr.: *The Wave Principle of Human Social Behaviour and the New Science of Socionomics*, Gainesville, 1999; Casti, John F.: Mood Matters. *From Rising Skirt Lengths to the Collapse of World Powers*, New York, 2010.

This means that actions differ depending on whether people see the same event in a positive or a negative light. What we have here is a typical cybernetic feedback loop with opposite signs, so to speak, compared to what one might expect according to classical physicist thinking.

Chapter 2

Innovating for the Great Transformation21: How to Preprogram Success

In this arena of major change processes in self-organizing and self-restructuring systems—processes that sometimes span several centuries—the act of innovation meets its greatest challenges in history and society. All organizations at all levels and in all segments of society have to innovate in order to survive and prosper, and they have to make their key decisions precisely in those phases in which change is turning everything upside down. Hardly anything will be as meaningless as experience, as valuable as it may have been in other phases. What use are the experiences of horse carriage drivers when it comes to dealing with automobiles? In these times of change, the most reliable navigation aids are our insights concerning the factors that, by law of nature, remain constant amid the dynamics of complex systems.

Everything changes: the stage on which everything takes place, the play that is performed, and the role each organization plays. A phase of upturn within a Kondratieff Cycle, such as that beginning in 1949, provides a completely different backdrop for strategy design compared to the turbulent phase of a beginning or ongoing downturn, or the transition from an expiring K-wave to a new one. That is the reason why even strategy concepts which have long worked extraordinarily well—so well, in fact, that they were believed to be universally valid—will fail, as the foundation of their success is eroding. The better a strategy used to work during the upturn phase of a K-wave, the less useful it will be in the downturn phase, with its large-scale austerity programs, its deflation and financial collapses.

Thanks to our wholistic approach, which is based on system theory foundations, we are able to survey the entire scene and the invariances that all phases have in common. We have the navigation systems for all conceivable phases of development—upturn, downturn, and transition phases alike. They allow us to navigate safely through the Great Transformation, taking advantage of the complete toolset:

- The wholistic Malik Management Systems (MMS),
- the Malik-Gälweiler Navigation System,
- the Strategy Map for navigation,
- the PIMS research findings,
- the other PIMS tools: Customer Value Analysis and Customer Value Map,
- the crucial findings about mega-change processes driven by basic inventions and basic innovations,
- and their effects on the economy: the Kondratieff Cycles.

Before we get to the strategies for a new era, there is one last step that is missing: avoiding the errors that have been passed on from the Old World and will continue to dominate the text books and consulting frameworks for some time yet. These errors would massively hinder or even prevent innovation successes under the new conditions of complexity. After that I will address successful start-up strategies and their quantification, as well as the principles to be observed in implementation management.

From the Art to the Craft of Innovation

Innovating is a frequent subject of management literature, but it is seldom put in the right overall context.

In this current K-wave, innovating was "*discovered*" in the late 1970s as a consequence of the recession that was going on. During the 1980s it then *became a fashion* which lasted far into the 1990s. As most management fashions, it involved lots of show and verbiage, culminating in the excess of the New Economy excesses and then vanishing as the bubble burst. That is not the end of innovating, though. What matters now is the implementation of innovations to master change in the Great Transformation21.

This will be the broadest and longest innovation phase in history. So far, the most innovative period was the second third of the 18th century. It was a time of unprecedented change in business and society. New ideas were born and inventions and innovations made nearly every month, and they were implemented more quickly than in other phases. So, this is not the first time an epoch is characterized by rapid and breakthrough change, as many contemporary observers mistakenly believe.

But there is a *major difference* between our time and that period. The innovators of that time ventured into "uninhabited" new territory, both literally in geographic terms and figuratively in terms of business. The main part of the discovery of America and the imperialistic colonization of non-European continents took place in the 19th century. There were hardly any organizations, except for governments and their administrations, which were modest by modern standards, as well as armies and churches and a few stand-out organizations, such as the East India Trading Company.

The economic space was largely unoccupied at the time, whereas today wherever you go you will meet "inhabitants" defending their territory fiercely, sometimes desperately. The discoveries and inventions of that time almost always led to the emergence of entire new industries which were largely without competition. To name just three of many examples: Around 1850, the analgesic effect of salicylic acid was discovered, leading to the rise of today's pharmaceuticals industry. Then there was the first dynamo which led to the emergence of the electrical industry. Finally, the first bank in the modern sense was founded: Crédit Mobilier.

None of these developments was triggered by an *organization*—it was always a person. But that was rarely the inventor or discoverer, it was the *innovator*. For instance, contrary to popular belief it was not Thomas Edison who invented the light bulb: as early as 40 years before Edison's 1882 patent application, *Frederick de Moleyns* obtained the first patent we know of. It was not the light bulb that Edison invented, but the "illuminated city" and the *electricity industry*—all by utilizing and commercially exploiting the light bulb. He was not an *inventor* but an *innovator*. These are two very different functions.

The men at the helms of the gradually emerging organizations were pioneers who were admired for their fame and enormous wealth. This gave rise to the belief that entrepreneurial success and particularly innovation were all about art, special *talents, intuition*, and the like.

This belief still holds, and it has been cultivated and repeatedly renewed by articles and biographies that glorified that type of person. Not only is this notion wrong—it has *disastrous* effects because it causes people to address innovation from the wrong angle and from an *innovation romance* point of view.

Even if one was to accept the idea of there having been special talents in individual cases which helped bring about economic success, it would not help us much today. Today, *every* company and almost *every* manager has to be innovative. We need to turn the *art* into a *craft*. It is the only way we can hope to bring about the numerous enormous innovations we will need.

Incidentally, turning an art into a craft is nothing new, even if some may believe it to be impossible. Mankind's entire progress is owed to the instances in which an art of a *few* people was turned into a craft for *many*. This was the path of development that modern medicine took, as well as architecture, aviation, and, last but not least, modern management.

Misconceptions About Innovation

The first step from art to craft—and from there to professional innovation management—is to eliminate misunderstandings and errors. I will address five of them on the following pages.

Error 1: Innovation is Made in Labs and R & D Departments

There is not a single innovation that was achieved in a research lab, an R & D department or a university. People at these places create something no less important: the *idea*, the *prototype*, the *invention*, and/or the *discovery*. That, however, is something different from innovation. *Fixating on an idea*, and consequently on *creativity*, is one of several *wrong* starting points for innovation, from where all efforts are guided in the wrong direction.

To innovate properly, it is necessary to focus one's gaze *on the market*, strictly and uncompromisingly. The only true definition of innovation is market *success*. Only this starting point and this definition will provide the opportunity to find the right strategies. Only when something new has an impact in the market, should one permit employees to speak of innovation. Everything has to be seen, planned, and judged from there.

One does not necessarily have to control a large share of the market, as this cannot be expected from something new. Even if it is only an embryonic market success for the time being, it is still the key characteristic of incipient success. Only thus can we properly define and judge the individual steps from the idea to market success.

The idea (as new and groundbreaking as it may be) is important, but it is only a *start*. And contrary to popular opinion, it is the easiest, simplest, and cheapest of all. Difficulties and challenges follow after that.

After the idea has been created, one has to explore whether it will work. A *prototype* has to be developed, and key *experiments* have to be designed and carried out. It is much more difficult and expensive, and it takes much longer. After the prototype phase, the next step leads us to *design for mass manufacture*, with yet higher cost and time requirements. Up to this point there has only been expenditure in the company, and revenues are still a faraway thought.

Only after that do we have the *start of marketing*, again with considerably higher costs and more time involved than the idea itself ever required, and with first revenues gradually beginning to trickle. This is the point where innovating begins. Broadly speaking, with each successive step following the idea the expenditure involved will increase tenfold. This gives you an impression of the financial *proportions* to be considered.

Error 2: Creativity is a Key Factor

Because everyone is so fixated on step one, it is a general belief that *creativity* is particularly important. In almost every book on innovation, creativity is a central topic; companies interested in innovation are offered creativity trainings; creativity is claimed to be a prominent characteristic of managers.

No doubt creativity is important. But contrary to widespread opinion, a lack of ideas is hardly ever the problem. It is not ideas that are lacking but ideas that are *implemented*. Even in the most "uncreative" companies we usually find *more* ideas than will ever get implemented. Only ideas that have been implemented can be referred to as innovation, if one does not want to risk getting off the track.

In truly innovative organizations, creativity is seldom an issue. There is no time to talk about creativity because people are busy innovating—that is, they deal with the technical and professional side of innovation management. They concentrate on implementing ideas. This is even true of the fashion industry: it is easier to produce a *creative* collection than to put together a *marketable* one.

Error 3: Innovation is Purely or Largely High-Tech

This misconception came up in the 1990s, along with electronics and the beginning digitalization. Its impact is disastrous. High-tech is important for most companies, but fortunately not for all by far, for innovations in high-tech areas are among the most difficult, risky, and costly. Failure rates are much higher here than in other areas. *High-tech* is not necessarily *high-profit*.

The danger associated with this misconception is that in the search for innovations it pulls attention away from the much more *numerous* possibilities that low-tech and no-tech areas will offer in the future.

For instance, one of the largest, most important and most lucrative areas of the past 30 years is *trade* in its various different forms. In virtually every area we have seen a complete restructuring of sales channels, but it has only been noticed by those in the know. In books and magazines on innovation, little could be found about this phenomenon because most are so fixated on high tech innovations. Innovations in trade have little to do with high-tech per se, although they also play a part there.

And even in the most innovative technologies, innovation is certainly not always restricted to technology as such. Here, too, key innovations often concern changes in the market, the social sphere, or in human behavior. A new technology that fails to have an impact on these things will often get stuck in its development phase.

Other examples of low- and no-tech innovations are fast food, convenience food, and health food. Even snacks and pet food belong in the category, which have become a market success for companies like Mars and Nestlé, while organic food is yet to gain comparable importance. But it does remain a possibility for the future.

The important thing is that one should never be misguided by high-tech products. 70 to 80 percent of our consumption is made up by trivial, often quite unintelligent products, and this is not going to change. The difference is that even these products will be produced and marketed in very non-trivial, highly intelligent ways in the future. Often, this is where innovation is at home. So do not let yourself be blinded and confused. High-tech makes the headlines in the *media* and fascinates *engineers*. But the mere fact that something is fascinating and gets lots of attention does not mean it is most important or promising.

Error 4: Only Small Companies Are Innovative

People keep talking about the sluggishness of major corporations and singing the praise of *small* enterprises. This view is not entirely justified. True, small companies are often *creative* because decision paths are short so decisions can be quick. Often they reach the prototype phase rather quickly. So much for the *advantage* of being small. *Now to the major disadvantages.*

Small companies often have two problems: They are under-financed and under-managed. They have neither the financial means nor the human resources to manage the much more difficult steps of serial production and marketing successfully as well. That is why, in the final analysis, so many small companies are nothing else but interesting *acquisition candidates* for those who do have the means and the professional management know-how. Once the prototype phase has been reached, or perhaps the first small production run, small companies usually lose momentum. They are good *starters*, but *not good finishers*. They like the sprint distance of creative idea generation, and it is what they are good at. Effective innovation, however, is an endurance discipline, a long-distance run, and what matters is what forces you have left in the *second* half.

Nor is it true that *large* companies cannot be innovative. Many major corporations have proved capable of radical innovation. One example is General Electric, but there are many more. These companies—not the small ones—are who can teach us the *craft* of innovation. The New World methods, such as the social "technology" of Syntegration, permit even the largest corporations to be swift on their feet, and push growth barriers further up. More on that will follow in part VI.

Another factor should be kept in mind: Many innovations we will need require immense capital expenditure and staying power. Small companies will have to stand back *from the outset.* This is true, among others, of new energies, of ecological innovations, of aerospace, agriculture, traffic, and many other fields. Only very large companies have a chance to raise the funds required for investments of this size, and in many cases even the largest ones will not be able to do this *alone*, only *in conjunction* with others.

This does not mean, however, that small companies are unable to innovate. *They are, if they do it right.* But even more than the larger companies, they depend on professional craftsmanship for innovating. It is precisely the small companies that cannot afford what the pundits usually emphasize most: pioneer spirit, enthusiasm, and innovation romanticism.

Large companies are able to absorb the occasional mistake—small ones are the first to go under.

Error 5: Innovation Requires a Certain Type of Personality

Back to my critical remarks about so-called *pioneer personalities*. According to a very widespread opinion, innovating takes the *proactive, creative, dynamic, entrepreneurial, risk-loving pioneer type*. Well, these "universal geniuses" are surely in the minority, not only for statistical reasons. We certainly need many more innovators than there will ever be entrepreneurial "universal geniuses" available. Fortunately, however, it is *not necessary* to rely on pioneers. There is a *craft* of innovation, and a sufficient number of people can learn it.

I am not saying that *anybody* can become an innovator. But it is possible for about a third of potential managers, and another third can be enabled at least to make a major *contribution*.

Among the thousands of entrepreneurs and managers I have met over the years, there have been several such pioneer personalities. Some of them, however, were a burden for their organizations just because of their pioneer spirit: they hindered prosperous development by focusing their creativity and initiative on the wrong things. I have met *many more* people, however, who were capable *implementers*, usually very down-to-earth types without the slightest trace of innovation romanticism, who would take one step after the other, meticulously planning and thinking through their innovations and then making them come true with stamina and perseverance.

Another point to consider is that so-called pioneers have often been *put on that pedestal posthumously* by their biographers. Often they were quite unspectacular individuals. If asked to forecast their later success or failure before their achievements became obvious, most people would have given them little chance in view of their not being the pioneer type. Many were even regarded as oddballs and loners by those around them. There was not much about them that reminded of a shining hero. Taking a closer look, however, one will find that a common factor about these people was the way they worked: very systematically, very thoroughly and meticulously. We can learn the craft from them.

So, the key question to be asked must not be: Who were these people? It must be: What did these people *do*, and how did they *go about it*? This way we can turn an apparent art into a craft that can be learned. Even Michelangelo had to deal with the hassles of statics, scaffolding, and mixing paints, which he did with great care and professionalism. Without these manual skills, his works of art would have remained mere ideas and visions.

On the other hand, innovations cannot emerge from craft *alone*. Great and unique things require additional capabilities beyond that. But innovation does not always have to be great and unique. There are innumerable places where we need the smaller, less spectacular kinds of innovation that require *craftsmanship and professionalism*—and that is something we can teach, learn, and practice.

Chapter 3

Mastering Even the Unknown: The PIMS Start-up Strategy

At this point another key strength of PIMS comes into play: thanks to the specific analysis of start-up businesses and the organization of relevant data in a dedicated start-up database, the optimum innovation strategy has been identified. Precisely when top managers face their greatest challenges and the most complex and high-risk decisions, PIMS research provides sound, evidence-based data on how innovation should be designed from the start in order to maximize its chances at success and build a permanently healthy business.

Where they show up	Examples
Competitive advantage	- Non-existent - Inappropriate price positioning - Wrong segmentation - Need for more differentiation on crucial attributes
Competitor reaction	- "Full frontal attack" when "flanking movement" would work better - Aiming for niche which can be wiped out - Underestimating the splash
Share gain potential	- Over- and under-optimistic - Not enough capacity which creates demand for competitors - Stopping marketing too soon - No second wave of innovation
Long term profits	- "Quick returns" mentality - No appreciation of cost/price dynamics

Figure 75: Typical start-up mistakes

Let me start with the typical mistakes regularly found in start-up strategies. Their effects are disastrous, and they are the reason why eight out of ten innovations are bound to fail. The standard problems of innovation, as shown in figure 75, cause enormous cost and bankruptcies by the dozen.

So there are commonalities of failure. *But are there commonalities of success as well?* What are invariant characteristics of successful start-up businesses? The essence of the success strategy for new businesses can be summarized in one sentence[39]: *The most important factors for the success of a start-up business are the scope and the speed of market penetration.*[40]

Start-ups as a Synthesis of Several Arts: The Secrets of Innovation Success

The faster you get ahead in the market and the faster your sales go up, the faster your margins will improve with the right management approach, thanks to the experience effect, and the more the relative marketing and R & D expenditure can be reduced. Once the business approaches maturity, market share is the key prerequisite for stable profitability—with it, profits can hardly be avoided.

After the start-up phase it gets much more difficult to build market share; moreover, rapid market share growth at the very start reduces the initial costs of market entry.

Figure 76 shows all factors that are crucial for the success of the start-up business as a whole. On the left-hand side we see the key factors; on the right we see the respective values for slow and for fast market penetration. There is no better way to meet our requirements for strategy design in the New World—right, precise, fast, and coherent—than with these PIMS findings. This is yet another example of how guesswork is replaced by insight, and how wishful thinking is firmly grounded by means of evidence-based decisions.

With the knowledge about previous successful innovations, which has been quantified and stored in the PIMS databases, even the unknown can

---

39 Dörner, Dietrich: *The Logic of Failure. Recognizing and Avoiding Error in Complex Situations.* New York, 1989, 1997.

40 Roberts, Keith: "Evidence on start up businesses: take off requires full throttle", *Malik Online letter*, 2007.

		slow Penetration	rapid penetration
Marketing stance	served market relative marketing expenditure	low behind	high ahead
Innovation	% new products year 4	None	steady
Uniqueness of offer	Relative customer preference Relative company image Relative price Relative breadth of offer	low poor high / low narrow	high good parity broad
Distribution Channel structure	Number of customers	many	few
Management experience	Familiarity with marketing needs Familiarity with technology	little none	very very
Ability to meet demand	Committed capacity	low	high
Market environment	Real market growth Number of competitors Share competitor A	slow many low	fast few high

Figure 76: Key factors for start-up success

be reliably quantified. Using the logic of the Strategy Map, a special road map can be derived for successful start-up management. That alone is extraordinarily significant because innovation involves enormous risk. Even the smallest piece of information than can increase the probability of success is extremely valuable. PIMS provides the right information, and lots of it. As a reminder for your orientation, below see once again the Strategy Map with the key factors of innovation.

The following key questions can be answered with certainty based on the PIMS findings:

• What competitive advantages do we have?
• How big a market share can we achieve?
• How much money can we make once the business is fully developed?
• How much does a start-up cost to be successful?
• How long will it take to be successful?

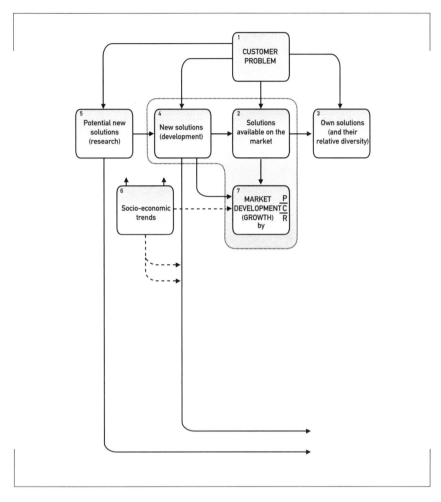

Figure 77: The Strategy Map

- What are the best strategies?
- Which general conditions are favorable, and which are not?

What Makes a Business New?

A first key question for starting on the start-up strategy is: *What makes a business new?*

PIMS gives us a clear and straightforward answer. The following criteria are crucial:

1. A business is new if at least two of three things are new to management: the product, the market, and/or the technology.
2. Furthermore, a business is new if investments are systematically made today in order to make future profits, so current profits are deliberately forgone. Whatever serves the purpose of improving current profits is not new in the start-up strategy sense.
3. A business is new if customers and competitors regard is as being new. A product, for instance, must not simply represent an extension to an existing product line. Adding a new fruit to a range of fruit preserves is not innovating in the start-up logic. By contrast, a low-calorie product line would be something new, and would probably be perceived as new by customers and competitors.

The key is that something is new *for us*—the company producing it. It does not matter whether the product already exists somewhere else, as our own company is at the start of this development and has no access to others' experiences. Like anywhere else in life, everyone has to gain their own experiences. Still, there is much to be learned from others, such as what is offered by the PIMS findings.

Applying these criteria does not have to be treated as a science, as is often done in academia, where entire doctoral theses are built around questions like these. In practice, the problem is simply and pragmatically solved like this: In case of doubt or borderline situations, the business is treated *as though it were new*. It is always better to overestimate a task than to underestimate it. Overestimating something in this sense will hardly have negative effects. The opposite, however, can ruin the business.

How Long Does it Take for a Start-Up to Be Successful?

The stock exchange boom years have made investors impatient. Not only do they want *big* money—they want it *now*. Most innovations, however, take some time to become mature, and they cannot be accelerated at will. Nevertheless, a revolution may take place in the near future, as the Syntegration method permits some time-consuming phases of innovating to be massively accelerated.

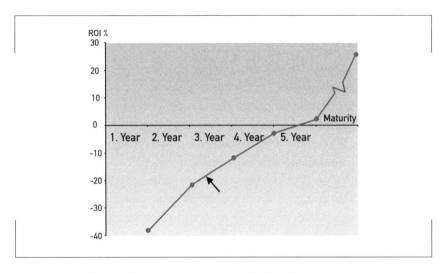

Figure 78: Profits should not be expected over the first few years

The typical start-up business starts off deep in the red at market launch. Both development costs and market launch costs have to be regarded as *sunk cost* strategically, no matter how they are treated by accounting. At the end of business year one, the start-up businesses will have a negative ROI of almost 40 percent, according to the average of all start-ups captured in the PIMS database. It takes around five years until a start-up reaches break-even. Only about a third of all start-ups reach that point in three years, one fourth needs eight years. This insight alone is enough to steer managers' thinking in the right direction. Some of them, however, refuse to accept such insights—they aggressively fight the tried-and-tested research findings, either because they just don't want to believe them or because, having seen their reflection in the mirror, they begin to realize what mistakes they have made. Often they gamble away their greatest opportunities by acting like that.

Based on the PIMS knowledge, many projects which would normally have been tackled with hope and courage are recognized as being futile. This way, PIMS helps avoid wrong decisions which would otherwise incur enormous cost. As a result, strategies for new endeavors are tackled from a totally different perspective, and if they do meet the criteria described below, their success, instead of their failure, may be treated as a foregone conclusion. This is another example of what *right, precise,* and *fast* means when referring to strategy.

How Best to Put New Things on the Market?
The Optimal Start-up Strategy

PIMS actually does provide a sound and unique answer to this challenging question.

On principle, the same structural factors are relevant for the success of start-up businesses as for established businesses, which was addressed in part IV. That is hardly surprising because configuration-related insights apply for all businesses. In addition, there is a very specific point to be observed: in the case of start-up strategies these factors have to be observed, or developed, in a certain *chronological order*, as shown in the following diagram.

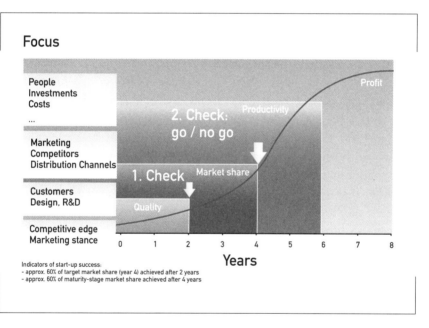

Figure 79: Successful start-up businesses: the way leading to the goal

Four successive phases have to be observed: The first is to secure the *quality and customer value at market launch*, the objective being to build *market share* as quickly as possible. This is required to increase *productivity* and reduce cost in the third phase, in order to achieve a nice, sustainable and almost secure return. In between these phases there are two important checkpoints for Go or No-Go decisions, as shown in figure 79. The horizontal axis of the diagram represents the duration of the strategy; on the vertical axis we see the main fields of action.

Phase 1

The key to market entry for an innovation is the *quality of market performance*. That is why it is sometimes preferable if the head of finance is not present at start-up meetings. Financial considerations regarding the calculation of profits, cash flows, returns, and finally the stock prices and shareholder value absolutely have to stand back: there is *not a single innovation* that from the beginning on pays off by *financial standards*, to the extent expected by investors.

At the beginning, key maxims are:

"Quality is more important than cash flow."
"Market share is more important than profit."

The starting point absolutely has to be *customer value*; there can be no compromise here. The new solution for the user problem must be better than previous solutions. This follows from the logic of the Strategy Map. Consequently, differentiation from competitors and superiority over previous solutions are at the heart of the strategy. The fields of action required differ slightly, depending on the specific kind of innovation; typically, however, they are research and development, design, market position, and competitive advantages. In the case of innovations, customer value chiefly arises from solution quality, understood in a very comprehensive and systemic way, and not so much from price, as we will see later.

Logically, this is where the Customer Value Map described in part IV is used, as well as a tool called Attribute Analysis, to carefully identify the key buying factors. At this point it becomes quite clear how the circles close over and over again, and the tools so far discussed complement and enhance each other in many ways. Our methods are not sequential and stand-alone. They form a synergetic overall system, an orderly universe of tools, as it were, which can unfold much greater effectiveness than stand-alone tools. This is a consequence of transitioning from sequentiality to synchronicity, as will become even clearer in part VI. It also plays a part in modern physics, when totally new cosmic properties are discovered.

Phase 2

Quality, customer preference and customer value help to build the market strength that is needed for the final game. Market position is the key to sustainable success, so start-ups need to build market share fast.

So this is the situation in which fast growth has to be the primary goal for a business, in order for it to achieve—remember?—a *defendable* market share. In this phase, focal areas are marketing, customer service, sales channels, and competitive intelligence.

How much market share and how fast? Two years later, the market position will first be reviewed to see whether the business is heading in the right direction. If so, it is continued—if not, it is better to discontinue it because initial losses are the smallest. After four years comes another point for deciding whether to continue or give up. This is one of the toughest decisions, as the investments and expenses accumulated are usually enormous and often even life-threatening, if the target has been missed. Decisions are made with an eye on finance, but the crucial part is the market position gained over the past years.

In situations like these, their emotions often urge managers to keep on, to "hang in there", and radiate optimism. But true professionals know when to stop in order to ensure that they get another opportunity in the future.

Phase 3

As pointed out in parts III and IV, market share is the key prerequisite for achieving superior *productivity*, above all by accumulating experiences along the learning curve. This is particularly important and urgent in the case of innovations. At the start of phase 3, key areas to focus on are controlling and finance, productivity increases, rationalization, optimization of effectiveness and efficiency. It is important to ensure, however, that any action taken will not be at the expense of customer value, development, and marketing.

Phase 4

If the productivity issue can be solved as well, there is usually no reason to worry about *profits*. Of course there can be unfavorable economic developments, such as price peaks in important raw materials, exchange rate issues, or simply an economic downturn. Risks like will these always exist, irrespective of one's strategy. But the strategies described here will help build the potential that enables companies to operate from a *position of strength* even when times are bad. This means they are more likely than others not only to survive but even to prosper, due to their rivals' weak-ness.

True Professionalism in Start-Up Management

Successful innovation is an *endurance discipline*, not a sprint. Being part of the game in the beginning is a piece of cake—*enduring* is what matters, or the ability to cope with crises and setbacks.

Innovations involve plenty of risk and a small chance at success. The much-demanded courage, pioneer spirit, and appetite cannot compensate for the risk itself. And while risk lovers get lots of attention because they are interesting to the media, they often go bankrupt shortly afterwards. After all, there is also the kind of courage that is based on sheer naïveté and ignorance, and it is a bad guide for taking on risk.

As the time and financial resources required are almost always overestimated, a host of mistakes is programmed from the outset. As a result, there is no strategic option left, and the only thing left to do is respond to imperatives.

So, the remarkable detail here is not the failure of so many innovation projects, but the belief that existing knowledge can be ignored.

Maximizing Start-Ups' Chances of Success

Having obtained an overall picture of innovation strategy, let us look at some questions in detail. For a successful start-up business, PIMS research has identified a series of highly relevant factors to maximize success chances. A start-up strategy that does not include the following elements, at the very least, is unprofessional and probably wrong. So if this minimum cannot be fulfilled, it is better to forgo the new endeavor because it will surely lead into disaster.

There are two groups of factors relevant for innovation success. The first entails general conditions in the outside world, the second comprises the factors influencing the strategy as such.

The Right Environment for Start-up Businesses

What are good conditions for innovation? PIMS tells us: figure 80 lists the individual factors in vertical order, and the parameters in the table field show us what properties are negative and what are positive for strategy success.

The first table shows environment or general conditions which, figuratively speaking, make up the stage design. Seven factors drive success and failures.

General conditions	Value	bad	Positioning (Average of PIMS database)	good
Market growth		slow		fast
Phase in life-cycle		phasing out		recently launched
Type of market entry		late successor		inventor
No. of competitors		many		few
Importance of market for main competitors		high		low
Market shares of three largest competitors		small		big
No. of direct customers		many		few

Figure 80: Key factors of a favorable innovation environment

I will pick two of them, market growth and customer structure, to illustrate the nature of PIMS findings.

Strong Growth Makes Innovation Successful

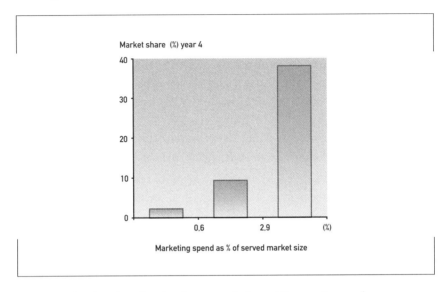

Figure 81: Market share is gained most easily in rapidly growing markets

In figure 81, we can see the enormous significance of market growth for innovation success. A key finding is that very different standards apply for innovation than for mature businesses. For instance, a growth rate of 4 to 5 percent is quite respectable for established businesses. For a *start-up business* it would be much too low. To make innovations successful, we need growth rates around 25 percent and higher. Times of change are times of growth, because they are times of substitution. The opportunities offered by the Great Transformation21 will be enormous, but only for true masters of their trade.

Innovating is Easier in Markets With Few Customers

Figure 82 shows the importance of customer structure for the success of innovation. While a majority of managers believes markets with lots of customers to be better for innovation, research findings show otherwise. A highly concentrated market gets you almost double as much market share as a market with lots of customers. Only PIMS can tell you what high concentration means: it means less than 100 customers. If you have only 20, even better. A small number of identifiable customers makes it much easier to customize your approach and meet their requirements than a large, more or less anonymous mass.

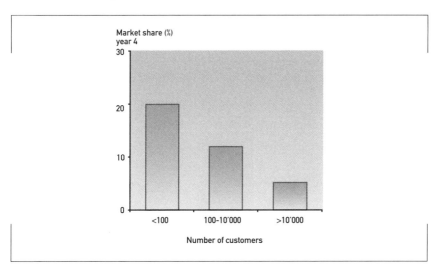

Figure 82: Markets with few customers are much more favorable

Choosing the Right Strategy in the Right Environment: Knowing, Not Guessing

The following figure 83 provides an overview of the factors that *directly* influence the start-up strategy.

In my over 30 years of working with middle and top managers, only a minority of them was aware of these things. These people were enormously successful innovators. A majority did not know that information of the kind provided by PIMS even existed.

In view of the risks involved in innovation, the value of this knowledge cannot be rated highly enough. Hence the question is not what it costs to gain this knowledge but what it *costs not* to have or to use it.

Thanks to PIMS research, all the factors listed in the table have been quantified, so you can evaluate your own situation against the PIMS findings. This will enable you to determine the right strategy for your business with maximum precision and, thanks to the database support, within a very short time. This is the way to implement properly, precisely, perfectly, and quickly. I will single out three examples here which I consider to be particularly important.

General conditions	Value	bad	Positioning (Average of PIMS database)	good
General management experience		little		much
R&D experience		little		much
Relative no. of customers		smaller		larger
Relative diversity of customer groups		lesser		greater
Relative size of customers		smaller		larger
Degree of product innovation		lower		higher
Capacity		low		high

Figure 83: Key factors for the right start-up strategy

Aggressive Marketing is Key

Start-up success calls for marketing. Of course, high marketing costs increase an enterprise's initial losses, but they bring a much more important advantages: rapid market share gains. "Think big" is a tried-and-tested rule of thumb for successful strategists, including military ones. The difference in success is as much as 100 percent, as figure 84 shows. The vertical axis shows the market share typically achieved in the fourth year after market launch—relative to marketing expenses, which are located on the horizontal axis and denominated in percent—mind you, of the total market, not the company's own sales. These are enormous sums, but they are effective.

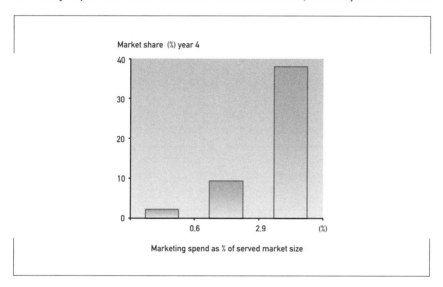

Figure 84: Aggressive marketing is key for rapid market share gains

Maximizing Customer Value

Since two results have been combined in one chart here, the vertical axes are shorter, which is why the scales should be studied closely. Innovations have to be recognized as such by the target customers, and they have to convince them by offering superior customer value. Prices are less important, as will become clearer in the following section. Particularly at market launch, the differentiation with regard to other solutions is crucial. Good solutions are replaced by better ones, so there is no reason to save on quality and utility. A particularly important tool here is the Value Map with its key buying factors. Quality also includes "irrational" attributes like design, perception, and emotion—such as what has consistently been communicated for the Apple products, and with enormous success. For many economists, these things are hard to understand because they do not fit their rational criteria.

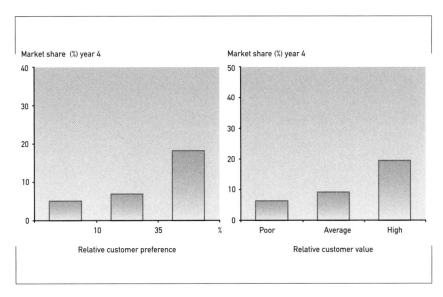

Figure 85: Relative customer preference and customer value drive market share

Pricing is Less Critical

Prices should be set at about the same level as competing products. Lower prices do not provide an innovation advantage.

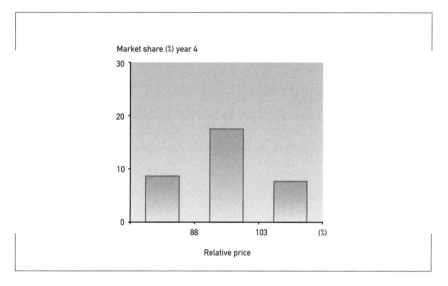

Figure 86: Set the same prices as your competition—unless you have significant, sustainable cost advantages

Getting Prepared for a Second Take-off

After market launch, it would be a mistake to rest on one's laurels. Rather, you should get prepared for a second wave of "attacks". Figure 87 shows how considerable market shares can be gained with 20 to 100 percent of sales generated in the second wave.

To achieve that, the start-up business needs permanent research and development. Figure 88 shows R & D expenditure over sales in the first four start-up years, as compared to R & D expenditure for a mature business.

The important point is that the differences between these results are robust. This is not about decimal points but about considerable orders of magnitude. The accuracy of data material is usually not that important; identifying the approximately correct values is the key.

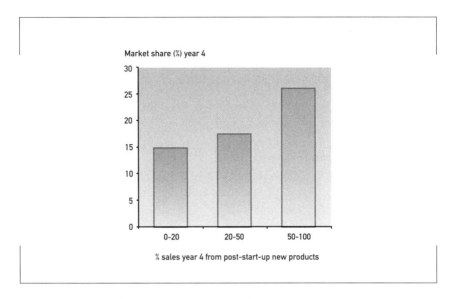

Figure 87: A second innovation wave pays off

In total there are about twelve factors determining the success or failure of a start-up strategy. Some are plausible when explained, others are counter-intuitive and will set off light bulb moments of agreement—or conflicts of faith.

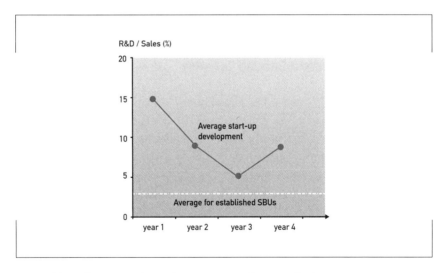

Figure 88: R & D expenditure for start-ups and mature businesses

Such "conflicts of faith" can be resolved very easily through effective guidance: A strategy that ignores or deviates from PIMS findings will have to be substantiated very well, for it stands against the entire, well-organized evidence of PIMS research. Of course, I cannot absolutely rule out that in the glittering world of strategy and business there might be striking exceptions turning PIMS results upside down. But one thing is certain: the often-heard killer argument that "our situation is altogether different" won't do. Quite on the contrary, it indicates a need to dig deeper into strategy knowledge.

Chapter 4

Implementing Start-up Strategies: Basic Rules for Effective Innovation

By itself, the right start-up strategy would not suffice to ensure business success. The specific challenges new endeavors pose also require a special touch in *managing* start-ups.

My management systems are also useful for managing a new discipline explicitly featured in the "Management Wheel®". This is a key advantage of my concept of treating management like a profession.

"Right and good management" as visualized in the Management Wheel remains valid in all its aspects: tasks, tools, principles, communication, and responsibility. Managing the fundamentally new is not "a different kind of management"; it continues to be "right and good management", although applying it to something yet unknown will be more difficult and demanding than applying it to something familiar. The differentiation between the management of "known" and "new" things as shown in the Management Wheel is crucial for executives' effectiveness in practicing their profession. This differentiation does not refer to content but to the difficulty of application. In many instances, managing the Great Transformation21 will involve changing *everything*. No stone will be left unturned, the—often underestimated—reason being that any adjustments made on one lever will usually result in necessary changes in all other levers as well.

For implementation in new situations, the following basic rules for top management are the key to success. They protect managers from making numerous unnecessary mistakes which could ruin the success of the innovation at the last minute—even if the strategy as such is perfect. They belong to the heuristic Master Controls of innovating. More details on the subject can be found in my book *Corporate Policy and Governance*.[41]

---

41 See Vol. 2 of this book series. Malik, Fredmund: *Corporate Policy and Governance. How Organizations Self-Organize*, Frankfurt/New York, 2011.

1. Go for the Top:
Market Leadership and Distinct Changes

Anyone planning to introduce a product-market innovation should aim for *market leadership*. For all other kinds of innovation, as in technology, organization, processes, information sciences, and behavior, the goal has to be to make distinct changes which are *visible* to everybody and really *make a difference*.

This will not always be possible. Even if you go for goals of this kind, the results may sometimes be second- or third-rate, or even completely useless. But only if you are determined to win can you mobilize the forces and resources which at least offer a chance of reaching the goal. If you content yourself with just any goal, or simply a plausible or even a small one, you will get according results.

This is true for sports and it is true for innovations. The only way to tackle something with the care and thoroughness required, and to seriously deal with suitable methods and approaches, is to aim for the top.

An additional aspect to be considered here is that small changes often meet with the same resistance as major ones. In change processes, you will have to be prepared for people fiercely defending each and every vested right; so you will have the hassle either way. If that is so, at least the result should be worthwhile. The Syntegration method is particularly effective here, as it unleashes social energies and implementation power in completely new ways.

2. Make Room for New Things

Innovation has to be started by *systematically letting go* of the old; otherwise there wouldn't be any room for the new. It would be buried in the "waste" of what was previously adhered to. Consequently, *systematic "waste disposal"* is the order of the day. The Management Wheel contains a special tool for that purpose[42], which is the key to success in major

---

42 Malik, Fredmund: *Managing, Performing, Living. Effective Management for a New Era.* Frankfurt/New York, 2006.

change. The fastest, most radical, and—by comparison—simplest way to achieve innovation and change success is to stop doing the wrong things.

3. Separate the Old From the New

This principle complements rule No. 2. If the old and previously valid cannot be fully eliminated, at least it has to be *separated* from the new wherever possible.

The new has and usually requires a different logic compared to the old. This is a consequence of the overlaying S-Curves, as shown in chapter 1 of part V. There must be different rules, different methods and approaches applied, different standards observed, different strategies pursued. Almost everything is different with new endeavors, and so they have to be handled differently. This can only be done with the necessary firmness—or at least it will help immensely—if things are strictly separated. Amidst the megachange of the Great Transformation, this principle is enormously important.

Some aspects warrant particular emphasis:

a) Different Yardsticks

A growth rate of less than 5 percent is usually excellent for *mature* products in *mature* markets. These days, you can be glad if a business like that grows at all; many will shrink or vanish completely during the 21st century deflation phase. *New businesses, however, will have the chance of achieving two-digit growth rates, and they will need them, as PIMS results show.* The same is true for productivity increases. For long-standing operations, a 2 to 3-percent productivity increase is not bad. But if new processes and systems fail to achieve much more and to range in the two-digit area, the cost of innovation usually will not pay off. Again, the Syntegration method described in the next part offers the necessary impact enhancement by, e.g. by accelerating even the most complex decisions up to 100-fold.

b) Different Budgets

Managing innovations requires *two* budgets: one for the current, familiar business and another one for the new operations. While the budget for the known business can be based on experience values, the new one cannot. Known businesses can be budgeted rather precisely and at a high level of detail; new businesses can only be depicted in outline and incompletely, which is why error tolerance levels must be high and adequate reserves in terms of time, cost, personal resources, etc. have to be planned. While the old is based on experience, the new can only be based on *assumptions*.

If these important differences are mixed in one budget or plan, the tools will lose all their meaning. Neither the old nor the new can then be judged and managed properly.

c) Different Schedules

The time a manager will have to dedicate to known and familiar activities can often be predicted and estimated quite well. He will also know *when* to set aside some time for these things. Not so with new activities: the only thing that is certain here is that you will have to spend much more time on the management of innovation and change, and that you can never know when exactly you will need it. An innovation manager is on stand-by 24 hours a day.

d) Different Reporting

Known activities can be controlled quite well based on numbers and their variations. Of course, good managers never rely on numbers alone; they also want to be informed of qualitative aspects and things like moods and opinions. Still, the numbers on familiar businesses are meaningful because they permit comparisons, for instance, with past periods or similar operations. For new things, and in times of fundamental change, there are hardly any experience values available.

e) Go and See for Yourself

Numbers about new activities are *always* unreliable. It is always better, therefore, to go to the place of action and get a first-hand impression of how things are going. Listen to those responsible and watch them, let them think out loud, accept that they will also utter presumptions, hopes and fears. Often, they will say, *"we don't know yet; impossible to say right now; we believe...; could be that....; we think that ..."* and so on.

But it takes "weak" signs like these to at least squeeze a little bit of information out of a jumble of assumptions—to "catch the scent", so to speak. Managers who are only out for "hard facts", who want everything to be "black or white", should not be given responsibility for innovations.

All of the above speaks in favor of a clear separation between the new and the old, wherever feasible.

4. Look for Opportunities in Problems

A considerable share of managers' work is dedicated to solving problems. But if you *only* focus on problems you may *overlook opportunities and chances*. This is where innovation potentials typically lie. To put it bluntly, even when all problems are solved not a single opportunity has been tapped. This makes a business mediocre, not good. To be successful, you have to identify and exploit *opportunities*. This is a fundamental idea I have addressed earlier in this book, when I talked about business missions.

The most excellent and effective managers are distinguished by a certain way of thinking: They keep asking, *"what are the opportunities inherent even in this problem?"* As devastating as a situation may be, they keep looking for the positive side, the chances and opportunities. That is what makes them potential innovators.

So persistent is their approach that it may sometimes seem compulsive and naïve. But these managers are anything but gullible optimists. They call things by their names, refusing to gloss over the facts, and judge situations soberly and realistically. And yet they know that at the end of the day, executives are not paid to solve problems but to identify and tap opportunities.

5. Ask Controllers for a Second "First Page"

This fifth rule reinforces the fourth and translates the general way of thinking described above into a practical controlling approach.

What does a *good* controller do? Apart from writing a report and presenting the numbers, a good controller will thoroughly list all negative deviations from plan on the first page of his report, marked in red, to ensure that management simply *cannot overlook* them.

So what about an *excellent* controller? An excellent controller will additionally list all positive deviations, marked in green, on the second "first page" of his report, so they, too, cannot escape management's attention.

This is much more than a gimmick. It focuses managers' attention on the signals that often indicate hidden opportunities. Where are we doing better than we had anticipated and budgeted? Where are we progressing faster than we had planned? Positive deviations must also have their *reasons*, just like negative ones. These reasons have to be clearly identified so they can be explored further.

Usually they are concealing a special strength or *opportunity* that so far has gone unnoticed. In these areas, even small, but very deliberate additional *efforts* will often generate considerable additional *results*. So resources should be directed there.

When there is no information on positive deviations, management boards will inevitably focus on problems only, or on negative deviations. They will have to look at them anyway, but the important thing is also to make use of chances and opportunities, which is why the related information has to be compiled and presented accordingly.

6. Write Down Your Expectations

The written form is a key principle of innovation. I have met executives who, as innovation managers, keep a careful and meticulous record of everything relevant.

Human memory is not only patchy but, above all, very *"elastic"*. It does not work like a computer. Rather than storing information as-is, it works on it and keeps shaping and reshaping it.

That is why good innovation managers write down their expectations regarding the future course of the innovation process. They, too, are unable to draw up a precise budget—but they are very clear about how they want things to develop. They make notes of their talks with employees and their observations. They will not let their memory play tricks on them because they know about its limitations.

7. Determine Cut-off Points

One point is particularly important to effective innovation managers: They know *when to stop*. They have precisely defined marginal conditions for their innovation endeavor by answering the following question: *"What are the circumstances which, if and when they occur, will cause me to accept that I have been mistaken and that something fundamental has to be wrong?"*

They take special care to write down these conditions, and they keep checking reality against them. Their thinking goes something like this: "If in this project we have not reached such-and-such within three months, something is very wrong." They define this cut-off point in advance to prevent good money from being thrown after bad.

The two most important go/no go points for market position have been clearly defined in the PIMS start-up strategy.

8. Make Sure You Have the Best People

This has to be a basic principle: The best people to have for start-ups will be dedicated to the project *full-time*, wherever possible.

Not only do you need the best people—you also need people with *credibility* in the organization. Now what gives a person credibility? It is neither rank nor status, neither position nor title. There is only one reason for credibility, and only one path that leads there: *visible, presentable, convincing results*. Anyone who has yet to produce results is not credible. He may be a *hope* but he will not be able to get people's *trust*.

The implications of this principle are serious, as precisely those groups of people are least suitable who are *most frequently* put in charge of innovation efforts:

- Young people, because they have yet to produce results.
- Staffers, most of whom will have achieved results before which, however, are not visible to others. The worst option is a combination of the first two: *young staffers*. It is different if staff functions are manned with people who have gained operational experience in earlier stages of their career, and therefore have been able to prove what they are capable of.
- People in organizational or HR development, for the same reasons.

9. Run Tests

Effective innovation managers abhor a certain kind of innovation: the kind that, due to the nature of the problem, has to be rolled out across the *whole* organization or the *whole* market. In the normal course of business, cases like this are rare. During the Great Transformation, however, they will be quite frequent.

Still, one should try out the new, if and as possible, before launching it all across the system. Even the best plans and concepts have their flaws. So two or three serious test runs should be carried out. A serious test is one that makes people say: *"Well, if it works under these conditions there must be something right about it…"*

Good managers use tests to track down and eliminate mistakes, and for something *even more important: to invalidate potential later excuses right from the start.* The time spent on testing pays off several times through faster implementation—once the new has been shown to work.

10. Strictly Focus on a Few Things

As every major innovation requires *full attention* and the *best people*, and involves high risk even then, experienced innovators focus on a very *small number* of innovation projects. They never give in to the temptation to dissipate their energies.

This way, they create a situation where the effort will either become a breakthrough success, or, if it fails, they can say with fullest conviction: "*We have done everything this organization is capable of. We have made no mistakes or false compromises. The fact that we failed in spite of that means that this is definitely out of our league, so we will give up with our heads held high and with limited losses, and look for a completely different solution.*"

These basic rules will also remain valid in the New World. With the new and partly revolutionary methods I will describe in the following part, they can be applied even better and more effectively.

Part VI:

Revolutionizing Management Methods: Strategic Approaches Without Time or Space Limits

*"…discoveries are hard to communicate…
one has to lift one's eyes to see a new horizon."*

Stafford Beer, founder of management cybernetics

Part I has explained the Why and parts II through V the What and With What of mastering complexity and change. Now this last part describes the How: the methodology for the right strategy and strategic management to master the challenges of the Great Transformation21.

Chapter 1

Direttissima: Taking the Most Direct Path to the Right Strategy

If we knew everything we need to know in order to act the right way, we could explore new paths in terms of methodology. Many of the steps required when using traditional methods would become superfluous. This would reduce the time normally required for strategy development by up to 90 %.

This is one of the basic ideas, which has guided me from the beginning, in creating the methods I will present in this part of the book. Today, these methods and tools are highly developed and have stood the test of time in numerous real-life applications. So now the time has come for them to demonstrate their rapid and full impact in securing companies' success and occasionally even preventing their demise.

"Direttissima" is what I call the approach of following the most direct path to the right strategy. The term itself is derived from my free time passion, mountaineering, where it refers to the "most direct" (Italian: direttissima) route to the mountain top. In modern mountaineering, a direttissima is the most direct natural trail—as opposed to the "drop", the geometrically most direct route from the top to the foot of the rock. The earlier direttissime were very popular in the 1950s and 60s, and the only way to climb them was by using artificial aids, ultimately bolts. Back then, these were daredevil actions that only the cream of the crop were able to accomplish.

For more and more young alpinists, however, this approach was incompatible with the ethics of "fair means climbing". They started looking for natural direttissime, where they would not need all those artificial means.

As a result, progress in alpinism took a new direction which differed greatly from what most people would have imagined. It was the very rejection of artificial aids and pegs which ushered in a new era of enormous advancement and almost limitless achievements. My own alpinistic skills were much more limited, but I was fascinated by the idea of a natural direttissima, both in alpinism and—as an analogy—in one of my professional specialties, corporate strategy.

As early as in 1977, when I headed what was then the Management Centre St. Gallen Foundation, I developed, together with two members of my team, a special workshop methodology for top management teams,. In the spring of 1978 we applied it for the first time, working with the general management of a leading Swiss insurance company (a team of eight) to interactively develop the organization's processes for objective-setting and performance assessment. The effectiveness of the methodology surpassed our expectations: after only one and a half days we had basically worked out the joint result.

The scientific foundation for this approach had been laid between 1972 and 1976 in my doctoral and professorial theses, where I developed a comprehensive method for shaping complex sociotechnical systems in the context of a national research project. I simply referred to that method as "System Methodology".[43]

A formative trial of the method, which I would later finalize and call the "Direttissima of Strategy", took place over dinner with a successful entrepreneur in the early 1980s, in a popular restaurant in Vienna, Austria. In the course of our conversation, I jotted down one of my best strategies on the back of the menu, which over the following two years enabled him to gain world market leadership in one of his business areas. He had originally invited me to dinner because he intended to find out what corporate strategy actually was. A few months before, one of his senior executives had graduated from business school and was now urging him to design a strategy for the company, which he believed was currently lacking although the company achieved remarkable financial results.

When we left my host took the menu, on which I had scribbled a rough sketch of the Gälweiler navigation system, explaining it to him in the process. I had also put down an improvised description of the client's problem and, for extra customer value, jotted down a few possible solutions, a draft for a business mission, and a few numbers for market shares, investments, and ROI. When we bid our goodbyes, he said that this had been very helpful for him because it was completely different from what his ex-

---

43 Gomez, Peter; Malik, Fredmund, and Oeller, Karl-Heinz: *Grundlagen einer Methodik zur Erforschung und Gestaltung komplexer soziotechnischer Systeme*, two volumes, Bern/Stuttgart, 1974.

ecutive had brought back from business school. We stayed in touch and our "strategy project" was a step-by-step continuation of our joint "dirett-tissima".

The first systematic trial of my approach followed in 1984, after an almost traumatic experience with a very large strategy project. As was customary then, and in part still is today, strategy development started with a SWOT analysis to determine opportunities and threats. A total of roughly 100 senior executives were involved in the project, organized in eight or ten thematic teams.

In the course of the project, about six folders worth of brilliant analyses of the company's environment were compiled. The different teams' work took up the first quarter of the overall process, which lasted about 15 months in total. This was considered a rather speedy approach at the time, in view of the company's size and complexity, for the executives had to develop the strategy alongside their day-to-day business. On the whole, the project went very well. Its outcomes met with unanimous approval in all corporate bodies, and that marked the beginning of a very successful phase, particularly in terms of the company's globalization.

In retrospect I had to wonder how much of it had actually been necessary and whether there could have been faster and less unwieldy ways to reach the same outcome. Being a mountaineer myself, I thought of the vast difference between the first climbers' expeditions in the Himalayas, which used to involve several hundred people and transportation of material that lasted for weeks, and the later, quicker Alpine-style climbs, with just a small rope.

Another thought I had originated in cybernetics: it was the realization that it is not perception that controls behavior but vice versa—the organism behaves in such a way as to establish a certain perception on its neuronal screen. This notion of "behaviour controlling perception", coined by William T. Powers, follows from the Essential Variables theory of the great pioneer and neuro-cybernetician Ross W. Ashby.[44]

According to this theory, an organism needs to control a certain set of so-called essential variables in order to survive, and, by means of its control systems, to shield them against any external disruptions, including those that were yet to occur.

---

44 Ashby, W. Ross: *An Introduction to Cybernetics*, London, 1956; and Powers, William T.: *Behavior. The Control of Perception*, Chicago 1973.

This fueled my determination to rigorously apply the approach on strategy methodology, for I realized that to develop the strategy we actually needed less than 10 percent of the data compiled. Incidentally, this is also typical of the way the human brain works; it uses just a minute fraction of the data available[45] and transforms it into the information ultimately relevant to our behavior. Unfortunately, back then we were unable to predict just *which* 10 percent of the data this would be, but I was determined to solve this problem sooner or later.

One of the outcomes was the Central Peformance Controls (CPC) concept, which I have introduced in Part II. It summarizes the essential variables of an organization in the six performance controls outlined. As long as these variables were under control, or so I thought, a company would prosper. Consequently, I now had to look for the information that would immediately affect these six performance controls, in line with both the logic of the MG Navigator and the Strategy Map which I was already familiar with and using. This, I assumed, would enormously simplify and accelerate the analytical approach, for once you know what you need to know for a strategy, your search process will become very direct and very efficient.

This made for a crucial part of the direttissima method, which is based on an in-out-in logic. The six essential variables of the Central Performance Controls define the organism's inner world which it has to keep control of. At the same time, they define the information required in order to achieve this.

The CPCs shown in fig. 89, bottom left, are like six windows of a house from which you can look outside in all directions, even up and down, to find the information required to control the six variables. On the right-hand side of fig. 89, the CPC is embedded in a model of the environment. Not only do the CPS define what relevant pieces of information are; they also provide the "vessels" to store and organize that information—or the "knowledge organizers" as I have described them in my book *Corporate Policy and Governance.*

Thanks to this methodological advance, the same analyses that used to take several months could now be accomplished in a matter of days, in the context of a well-managed workshop. An essential prerequisite, however,

---

45 Frederic Vester has depicted this very clearly in his book *The Art of Interconnected Thinking*, Munich, 2007.

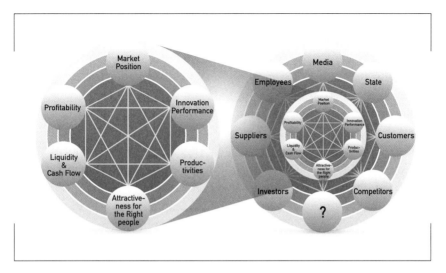

Figure 89: The CPCs define the relevant pieces of environment information and project it back onto themselves

was that the key individuals of a company—those that were really familiar with the business—are part of that process.

Organizing this is not very difficult; you just need a few key people. A further advantage of this approach is that it enables us to determine not only the knowledge available in an organization but also, as a by-product, the lack of knowledge—all in a "painfree", face-saving way. Participants are usually quick to notice this, and for the sake of making quick progress in the discussion, often initiate the necessary research to obtain the information that is lacking.

The next step towards the Direttissima is very natural and almost self-evident, for the state of information often permits immediate decisions, as the persons responsible are present.

This way, the process phases Search—Find—Decide can alternate in a circular-evolutionary process, and complement each other so harmonically that even those top managers who with traditional approaches are hesitant to get involved in strategy development will suddenly turn into enthusiasts.

As for myself, in the course of this work I was able to test continually whether my CPCs were really universal. They soon proved to be. What had been months of hard work with traditional methods could now be reduced to three two-day periods, often on weekends. The problems typically arising when schedules have to be coordinated would suddenly shrink to a minimum. The three two-day workshops required are usually two to three weeks apart, resulting in an overall duration for the entire process of six to nine weeks.

Ideally, the team will comprise top management and, selectively, some of their key experts. Additionally, the team will need the company's controller and sufficient assistant staff to document work results.

In this approach, participants will be aware of the CPC model at all times. This way, you can elegantly leave aside the usual sequential approaches in which you have to follow a certain agenda, item by item, which, of course, disrupts natural systemic coherences and inter-dependencies. A CPC-driven discussion is free to leap this way and that, as long as it stays on one of the CPC-relevant topics. In this process, the CPCs act as both navigational aids and vessels for documenting results. This permits a mode of operation which is highly satisfying, in particular for top managers, as they are allowed to think and discuss in a way that comes natural to them, rather than being restrained by the rigid structure of an agenda.

The first meeting is preceded by a compressed preparation phase. During this time, I have to study the organization thoroughly enough to gather sufficient knowledge of its business in order to not only steer the discussion but also influence it actively, if and as required. For in a Direttissima process, I am not simply a neutral facilitator who confines himself to coaching the process as such—rather, I am an active participant who, interacting with top managers, will bring his knowledge and strategic experience to the discussion. With the MG Navigator and the Strategy Map in the back of my mind, I am always able to safely steer the discussion, because I know what to look for.

As for the mode of discussion itself, I like to refer to it as an "amiable cross-examination". The setting permits immediate cross-referencing of contributions, as everyone concerned is present.

For support I need some assistants—not to record the minutes of the meetings (which will be done by the company's own staff) but to develop, simultaneously with the ongoing discussion, the key models matching the particular issue. It will usually be a sensitivity model which crystallizes from the discussion very naturally: the Integrated Management System IMS from Part II, which is used for improving corporate management processes and later for implementing the results, as well as the Viable System Model for structuring the business.

These were the early origins of what is now the SuperSyntegration method, which will be dealt with in this chapter. In chapter 4, I will then outline the Sensitivity Model and the IMS, while the Viable System Model will be described in the fourth volume of this book series. The Direttissima approach was my field of experimentation, where I first tested my idea of simultaneously applying several tools in the course of an ongoing discussion. It worked, passing the test with flying colors.

The largest group of people with whom I successfully applied the Direttissima was 15, a number just about manageable if you have the experience required and are familiar with the organization in question. The ideal team size for a Direttissima process is, as always, a group of seven plus/minus two. If the group consists of fewer than five people, it will usually lack some of the knowledge required; with more than nine people the group will be increasingly difficult to manage.

Experience has clearly shown that a well-selected group of seven is usually able to assess the business correctly and to take or at least prepare many of the necessary decisions right on the spot.

The Direttissima approach combines two key advantages: On the one hand it is well-structured because it is clear from the start what exactly the group needs to know to devise a strategy. On the other hand, this is precisely why it is also enormously flexible, permitting a considerable degree of improvisation. In other words, the Direttissima enables executives to conduct discussions in a way that comes naturally to them, spontaneously and often even erratically and by association, without losing sight of important topics; at the same time, the approach is rigorous and structured.

The strategies developed that way were always excellent, for participants would usually correct each other very promptly. Under circumstances like these, a wrong strategy would not stand a chance of prevailing.

Moreover, the personal presence of the company's top management is almost a guarantee that decisions taken will be implemented.

For small groups, the Direttissima approach is still the quickest and best method for mastering complex challenges to corporate top management. It does, however, require a substantial degree of factual knowledge and experience in directly dealing with top managers. If these conditions are met, the Direttissima is the optimum approach in terms of content quality, throughput time, and power of decision implementation.

The invention of the syntegrative communication processes[46] in the early 1990s, marked the transition to another development stage: problem-solving approaches which had proved to be highly effective could now be applied in much larger groups. The subsequent refinement of the approach and its integration with our management systems and associated cyber-tools also revolutionized the methods of strategy development, and in general of mastering transformational change. We have reached an unprecedented level of efficiency and speed for making top management decisions, and in particular for their implementation, achieving a degree of impact which until then would have been considered utopian.

I enjoyed long-standing and close ties with Stafford Beer. Together we founded the Cwarel Isaf foundation, named after his place of residence in Wales, with the goal to further develop the afore mentioned syntegration methods.[47]

---

46 Beer, Stafford: *Beyond Dispute. The Invention of Team Syntegrity*, Chichester, 1994.
47 It has been and still is one of my key concern to keep the visionary works of Stafford Beer available to the world. This includes further developing his concepts, as we have been doing with the Syntegration methods mentioned above which now also exist in super and (exponential) hyper formats; cf. following chapters.

Chapter 2

Revolutionizing Change With the Syntegration Method

When I let my mind run free, trying to imagine all the situations in which the Syntegration[48] method could be applied, I find it hard to think of examples where it could not work.

Unless I am very much mistaken, this would mean that the Syntegration method could become the greatest socio-technological innovation, as it revolutionizes the way organizations operate. The approach would be a milestone in the socio-technology of opinion formation, of decision making and of implementation. Already a number of business leaders and politicians have established the Syntegration method in their organizations as a standard tool to master the major challenges they face.

Epoch of New Leadership: Quantum Leap in the Social Technology of Functioning

When I say in this book that we need a new economic miracle, I also mean that this is possible. Under current and future conditions, new solutions cannot simply be found by spending even more money—least of all in the public sector, even if governments had the money. Whether or not organizations function well is not a question of money, but of brains and creativity. What we need is a new mode of operation for most societal organizations, which, in turn, requires large-scale restructuring of their infrastructure. In all probability, this will also lead to a fundamental reform of *democracy* itself. The new methods certainly make it all possible, and once something is possible, it tends to come true.

---

48 The registered *trademark is Malik SuperSyntegration® (MSS®).*

Being ahead of change, even actively driving it and working twice as effectively, even if only half the money is available—these are some of the maxims of the multiple revolution that will make the New World come true. The faster this happens and the more widely it is rolled out, the less painful the transformation will be, and the faster an increasing number of people will become aware of the benefits of the New World.

Change and Innovation—Swift and Effective

The challenges of the Great Transformation21 are so enormous that traditional approaches and ways of thinking will grow less and less effective, and eventually even become entirely useless. And this is regardless of whether the transformation will come with a bang or whimper—whether there will be dramatic crises or a socially compatible mode of change, even a period of fundamental renewal, enabled by innovative tools like the Syntegration method.

No matter which way it will happen: mastering this change will require new solutions and approaches. In an increasing number of cases, change can no longer be managed sequentially and on the micro-level of organizations, as has been the case with traditional change management. It is much more effective to renew the organization *as a whole* and *simultaneously in one major effort.* Previous elements are removed or given new functions; new elements are added. Above all, many employees are given new tasks. One must, however, also be prepared to part with employees or lose them. Between one-third and half of all staff may not be able to cope with change, but would actively block it if they stayed. If the organization cannot keep pace with change, it will be a classic case of being *out of control* as described in cybernetics.

With the Syntegration method, however, such change processes can be accomplished quickly,[49] reliably and with controlled risks.1 In many instances, this will enable a new beginning, outside existing structures, in line with the principle of innovation that I have mentioned before: *separating the new from the old.*

---

49 The capabilities of the Syntegration method have been demonstrated in around 600 applications.

What is the Syntegration Method and What Does it Accomplish?

The term *Syntegration* is the name we found for the most innovative, indeed revolutionary, approach to strategy and change that we have developed so far, based on over 30 years of experience in cybernetic management. It is an extremely fast problem-solving tool delivering groundbreaking results, both in terms of mastering the greatest and most complex challenges and with regard to the key decisions taken at the top management level. The word "Syntegration" itself is a combination of the words "synergy" and "integration".

The method has been developed by integrating three system elements. It comprises:

- an innovative cybernetic communication process which enhances both knowledge and intelligence,
- combined with our Wholistic Management Systems for the reliable functioning of organizations, and
- a menu of cybernetic tools to be applied simultaneously in order to master complexity.

Applications

The Syntegration process is suitable for all complex issues whose solution has to be developed jointly by a number of people.

It is therefore ideal for questions of strategy, to achieve the strongest leverage for large-scale redirections. Applications include:

- Developing a corporate policy and business mission
- Repositioning an entire corporation and/or its business divisions
- Ensuring a smooth post-merger integration
- Exploring new markets
- Realizing complex investments
- Devising strategies for growth and globalization
- Fundamentally restructuring the organization
- Realigning the research and development strategy
- Creating a sense of urgency and fast cultural change

- Launching complex innovation processes
- Initiating and developing new technologies
- Setting up or restructuring complex sales organizations
- Staff development and training.

Increasingly, Syntegration is also applied in the public sector, e.g, in urban development or to solve complicated regional problems, where the usual democratic procedures are increasingly reaching their limits, unable to cope with today's complexity.

With the Syntegration method, there is no need for a host of costly expert opinions and lengthy consulting projects. It also replaces the internal change processes, some of which entail monstrous dimensions, and which often fail due to internal resistance, and even more frequently because they are too sluggish and slow to cope with today's complexity and dynamics. They are overtaken by change itself.

Typical Key Questions for the Syntegration Method

A three and a half day Syntegration process will always begin with a key question. Typical private-sector examples include:

1. How should our Asian strategy be realigned in view of economic turbulences?
2. What can we jointly do to reduce our delivery time by half?
3. What does our U.S. strategy for prescription drugs have to include in view of the new regulations for FDA approval? (FDA = U.S. Food and Drug Administration)
4. How can we save at least another 5 percent of cost of sales, while simultaneously strengthening our competitive position?
5. How can we secure the supply commitments resulting from our strategy, using our existing manufacturing plants?

For NGOs and NPOs, key questions may be these:

1. How can we save our city from imminent insolvency?
2. How should we design our city's IT landscape to create the maximum possible, sustainable benefit for our internal and external clients?

3. How can we actively shape change? (This was a question posed by a large, federal-level ecclesiastical association)
4. How should the management and organization structure, as well as the governance of our research institute be designed so we can expand our leading position in an environment of increasing complexity and dynamics? (This is just a small sample from a large number of potentially relevant questions.)

Simultaneous High-Performance Approach for Solving Complex Questions

Syntegration is the most efficient and the fastest solution approach to those interlinked challenges that concern many or all organization units of a company: the type of challenge where high-quality decisions will require the simultaneous involvement of many capable people across the organization—because their *aggregate* knowledge is required for good solutions—and at the same time the *efficiency of a small team*; and where *top speed* is key to success, both for time and cost considerations.

Change of Mood and Energizing the Organizational Culture

In the brief course of a Syntegration—just three and a half days—participants usually feel a number of positive emotions developing: such as a sense of community, togetherness and solidarity, and an overwhelming urge to implement decisions, which is quite often described as a "fighting spirit" since the method, instead of producing minimal compromises, leads to maximum consensus in the group regarding solutions and required actions.

This is why the Syntegration process often causes a sudden change of mood and attitude within the organization. And because participants develop solutions and measures themselves, using entirely new methods, they are all focused on a common goal and demonstrate an unprecedented momentum for implementation. It comes as no surprise, then, that approximately 70 percent of all necessary actions identified in a Syntegration process are usually implemented within six to twelve months, provided the organization is proficient in performing effective change management.

Syntegration Pays For Itself

In view of the growing money shortage—especially in the public sector—it becomes more and more important that the use of the Syntegration method finances itself directly through its own results. In addition to that, the process usually generates two—to three-digit returns, making it one of the best and most sustainable investments for the future of an organization—in particular of public-sector organizations, where the need for such improvements is greatest.

One reason for that, among others, is the following: the innovative and still unfamiliar social methodology of the Syntegration process is usually employed at a point where all conventional approaches have been tried and all conventional savings potentials exploited. The responsible managers often believe they are at the end of their means when they realize that the saving measures taken are still not sufficient.

Further decisive improvements can therefore only be found through new ways—with the new functioning of the organization. It is exactly this which brings almost without exception the mentioned enormous investment returns, which are therefore also sustainable in the long-term.[50]

Pushing into the Vacuum Between a Small Team And a Large-Scale Conference

The Syntegration approach precisely fills the gap between the small, efficient teams and the large, increasingly ineffective management meetings and conferences. A small team can be highly efficient, as long as it has no more than seven members, ten at maximum. This is an experience shared by almost everyone, and I keep hearing it when we conduct a Direttissima.

Large conferences, by contrast, include many people but are usually unable to cope with highly complex and dynamic matters, which often ends in utter helplessness—not because people lack capabilities but be-

---

50 See the example of the German city of Fürth in: Mieg, Harald A. and Grafe, Fritz-Julius, "City development under the constraintsof complexity and urban development: a case study on the application of systems modeling and Syntegration to the city of Fürth", in *Journal of Uban Regeneration & Renewal 6 (1) 2012/13;* also Mieg, Harald A. and Töpfer, Klaus (eds.), *Institutional and Social Innovation for Sustainable Urban Development,* London 2013.

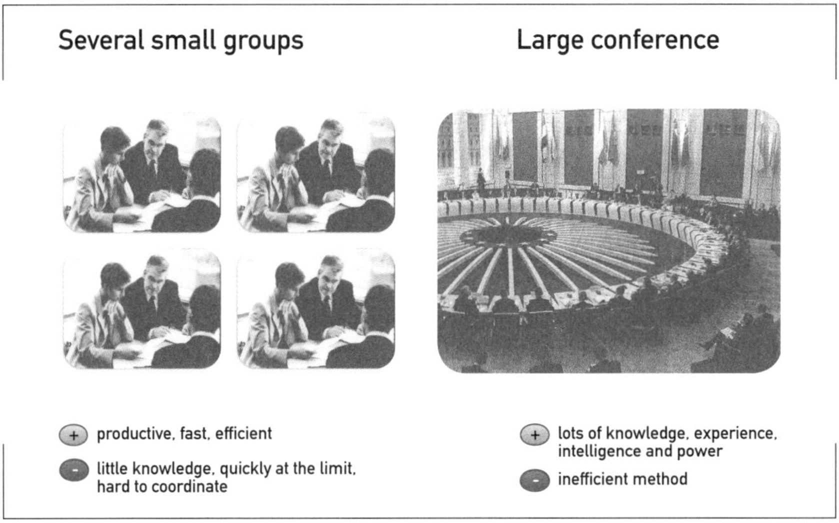

Several small groups	Large conference

+ productive, fast, efficient

− little knowledge, quickly at the limit, hard to coordinate

+ lots of knowledge, experience, intelligence and power

− inefficient method

Figure 90: Small team / large-scale conference

cause they can only resort to approaches that are bound to fail under the circumstances.[51]

Cybernetically self-regulating communication process

These achievements obtained with Syntegration have become possible due to the invention of a new cybernetic communication process, in which participants are interlinked in such a way that they can collaborate as coherently as if they were part of one huge single brain. It is a working mode that they have never experienced before.

Thanks to the communicative network structure and the perfectly synchronized process, all information available flows from each person to the next in a self-regulating manner, and is spread over time and space throughout the entire system of 40 people. Despite sometimes widely varying interests, the approach enables 40 top people in an organization to

---

51 This method is 80 times more efficient than small teams, and up to 100 times faster than traditional decision-making processes. In other words, the efficiency level of a small team is a mere 2 percent compared to Syntegration, and the method usually saves around 90 percent of the time required for problem-solving.

collaborate as precisely and harmoniously as if they were a symphony orchestra.

Non-hierarchical cooperation

For the unparalleled impact of Syntegration to take place, it is imperative, among other things, to ensure that there will be no hierarchy whatsoever in the problem-solving process. Every individual is granted the same chances for participation. In public organizations such as municipalities, this democratic approach is particularly important to make sure all the different parties are duly involved. In the business sector, however, this is more about the fact that non-hierarchical processes manage to tap into much more information and create a better general mood. This is one reason why Syntegration processes, almost without exception, get 90 to 100 percent satisfaction rates. Participation and the resulting high satisfaction is one of the most important prerequisites for a fast and friction-free implementation.

Almost like the light beams in laser technology, the Syntegration process bundles all pieces of information and focuses them on the key question expressing the challenge at hand. All of this happens with a communicative "radiation energy" by which even the strongest thought bunkers are virtually *dissolved*, With the Syntegration method it is not necessary to crack them open—they will open automatically, as if by magic, in the course of the process.

Universally Applicable Without Any Particular Requirements
The Syntegration method is universally applicable. It has been tested and has proved its worth for all cultures and all types of organizations, irrespective of their size and field of work, and for all kinds of problems. The Syntegration method is applied in particular to highly complex problems. For simple questions it is not needed, as conventional team approaches will do. A Syntegration does not require any special preparations, apart from phrasing the key question, selecting and inviting participants, and providing the local infrastructure.

As such, the Syntegration method is by far superior to other approaches. In fact, it is not even comparable to them—just as a state-of-the-art super-computer cannot be compared with the main-frame computers of past decades.

The Whole and Its Parts

The result of assembling all system components into the Syntegration method is, in its own way, just as sensational as assembling the components of a car. As with every real system, what were originally individual components now form a new functional potential, or a *system*, which, as a whole, has new and different properties compared to the individual components. In life sciences, these characteristics are referred to as "emergent properties".

That is the deeper meaning of the phrase, *"The whole is more than and different from the sum of its parts"*.

The volume on *Corporate Policy and Governance* from this book series, as well as my book on the "Strategy for Managing Complex Systems" contain more detailed information on these emergent system phenomena. This whole point can easily be illustrated using the example of water: From our chemistry lessons in school, we all know that water is a combination of hydrogen and oxygen. For our purpose, however, it is more important to stress something not every chemistry teacher will point out to students: the fact that none of the two singular elements has the properties of water—just as the individual components of a car do not have any horsepower.

The "Magic Formula"

I sometimes use the following "formula" to playfully summarize the Syntegration method and provide a memory aid:

$$1/ 40 / 12/ 3 / 40 > C, M, S, D = AP$$

As briefly as possible: For the most complex challenge currently faced, the organization's approximately 40 key people develop solutions for the twelve most important sub-topics within 3 days. To that end, they determine the roughly 40 key measures to be implemented.

This way, participants develop creative solutions (C), maximum consensus (M), the spirit for change (S), and the drive to implement (D) by utilizing, in a self-organizing manner, all the knowledge available, all the creativity and brains, and by unleashing lots of human energy. That, in turn, strengthens the action power of management (AP) exponentially and enables the organization to function perfectly.

While you may smile at the "formula" itself, the effects described are a proven fact. With the Syntegration approach, countless meetings, workshops and appointments that need to be coordinated as well as travelling, and periods of business-related absence are a matter of the past. Everything is accomplished in just three days—and participants, full of enthusiasm and energy for change, have little but the implementation of their joint solutions in mind.

Due to the time compression, Syntegration is also an ideal approach for quick strategy reviews and, if necessary, for changes to the strategic course, which will increasingly become necessary over the next few years as a result of the Great Transformation.

Apart from the large SuperSyntegration approach which involves 30 or 40 people and lasts three days, there are also faster versions if you do not need, or want, so many people involved. These faster and "slimmer" versions are, in a sense, the high-performance sports cars within the Syntegration family.

The Brain of the Firm:
Brain-Like Function Through Cybernetic Interconnection

In a pharma company 2 billion euro in research funds were redirected into new research areas in three and a half Syntegration days. With the same speed, an international high-tech-corporation integrated an acquired company, decided on the new strategy, designed the required organization and fixed the new implementation priorities. Through the Syntegration process new teams were formed from both firms, which set to work all eager for a fresh start. And the IT department of a large Swiss city achieved such substantial improvements with the Syntegration method that in the following two years it received the SAP- and CISCO-innovation awards. There are many more examples.

In a specious analogy, top management is sometimes referred to as the "brain of the organization". As important as the individual people in senior executive bodies may be in the sense of this analogy, what matters most is how they work together, and that depends on their informational interconnection across space and time. The currently used methods of conventional management, however, do not permit interconnection of a large number of people to the extent required for consensus-building and decision-making. Syntegration represents a major breakthrough at precisely this point, enabling certain functions in an organization to actually cooperate in a brain-like fashion.

That is why it is virtually impossible to describe a Syntegration process with precision, just at it is impossible to put a Mozart symphony in words. Yet both are very easy to experience. I will therefore confine myself to describing just one principle of operation of a Syntegration: the interconnection of participants and topics, followed by the overall architecture of a Syntegration.

As mentioned before, the core of the Syntegration process and its "engine", so to speak, is an innovative communication process which originates in brain research and which performs optimal cybernetic self-regulation. The artful syntegrative interconnectivity, mathematically modeled upon the geometry of an icosahedron (see fig. 91), enables up to 42 key

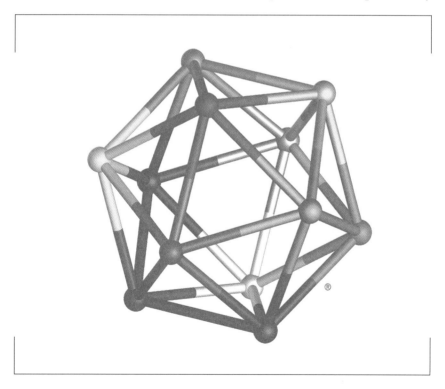

Figure 91: Icosahedron® for syntegrative interconnection

people to work together with the harmony and precision of a symphony orchestra. As a result, their combined knowledge, creativity, and intelligence join together in a self-organized manner to solve twelve sub-issues and their combined capabilities are condensed into solutions borne by a maximum of consensus.

This communication structure is one of the reasons why, as opposed to conventional approaches, there are no blockages with Syntegration; instead there is more highly efficient communication and unrestricted exchange of information, which permits optimal interconnection of the knowledge of everyone involved. The first analyses of this subject date back to the 1940s, including, above all, the groundbreaking experiments carried out by Alex Bavelas.[52]

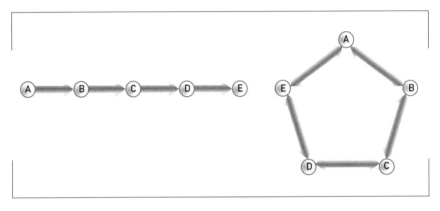

Figure 92: The kind of interconnection defines the communicative performance of the system

If we compare the icosahedron structure with the opposite extreme form of communicating, the linear chain structure depicted in figure 92, most of us will be reminded of the old children's game called "Chinese Whispers". If we connect a group of people in a linear fashion, as shown here, and if A passes a message to B, who passes it on to C, etc., it is quite certain that the message will be totally distorted by the time it reaches the end of the chain. The longer the chain, the higher the likelihood that this will happen.

---

52 See Bavelas, Alex: "Communication Patterns in Problem-Solving Groups", in: Foerster, Heinz von et al. (Eds.): *Cybernetics. Circular causal and feedback mechanisms in biological and social systems.* Transactions of the 8th Conference, Josiah Macy Jr. Foundation, New York 1952.

Now if the linear chain is a vehicle for preventing or distorting communication, producing frustration along the way—irrespective of who exactly is involved—the second way of interconnecting the points—in a circle, as shown in figure 92—will permit very effective communication and thus a high level of satisfaction and positive atmosphere. So, depending on the mode of interconnection, a system with the same people will function in very different ways.

The icosahedron, the three-dimensional shape with twelve vertices, represents the communicative *network structure* for an optimal interconnection of 42 individuals and twelve topics. In addition, we need a protocol stipulating the precise sequence of stepts to take, in order to control the self-regulating communication *process* over time. This way we obtain the results I have outlined in this chapter, embedded in our Wholistic Management Systems. The relevant principles of operation will be the universal laws of cybernetics: Self-organization, self-regulation, and evolution of knowledge, intelligence and creativity.

The Integrated Architecture of Syntegration

But there is even more. Figure 93 shows the integrated overall structure of our Syntegration bouquet of methods that I am going to explain now. In real-life application, all elements unfold their effects simultaneously, just as the different instruments in a symphony orchestra play together harmoniously.

Interestingly, though not surprisingly, there are remarkable structural and functional similarities between SuperSyntegration and modern super computers. For instance, the heart of the Syntegration approach is the core process of communication, which works in a similar way as the *processor* in a computer does.

Next is the blue icon of my General Management System (GMS) which, in terms of its function, corresponds to the computer's *operating system* (e.g. Windows). Arranged around it in circular fashion are the methodological cyber-tools, which in terms of function are comparable to an application soft-ware such as MS Office (Word, Excel, PowerPoint, etc.). In MSS, we have ten cyber-tools, a selection of which are simultaneously applied in the course of the core communication process. In terms of function, it is again comparable to the way every application in Windows is not

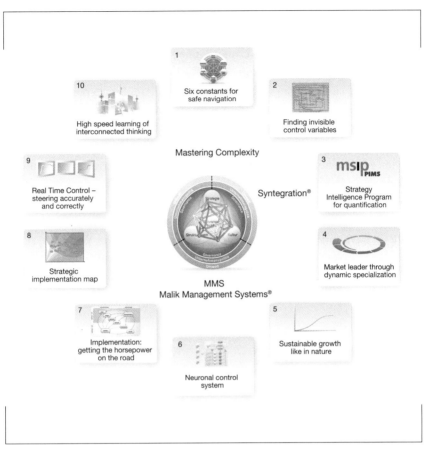

Figure 93: The bouquet of cyber-tools

always needed, but often several of them are being used simultaneously and all have to be available at any time.

The ten cybertools are, clockwise from the top:

1. The complex of Central Performance Controls (CPC) required to control the essential variables for the organization's viability.
2. The sensitivity model for cybernetic control loop interlinkages, for identifying the forces of self-improvement and self-destruction, which are active in the system, and for identifying suitable variables for effective intervention.

3. The Strategy Intelligence Program (MSIP) with PIMS as its centerpiece, for quantifying CPCs and sensitivity models and ensure measurable parameters.
4. The Minimum Factor Focused Strategy for identifying the perfect specialization and establishing a unique position in the market.
5. The bionic S-Curve tool for exploring growth and substitution dynamics in markets and business.
6. The Viable System Model (VSM)® for shaping the organization's "nervous system".
7. The Management System Audit (MSA)® for checking the functionality of the management systems and processes currently in place.
8. The interconnection models to ensure swift and consistent implementation.
9. The Operations Room for real-time information and control.
10. The ECOPOLICY program for learning interconnected thinking.

These cybertools are used simultaneously in the course of a Syntegration process. To ensure optimum results, we have developed a special application method which we call *TIEx—Total Immersion Exploration*®. Together, these tools provide the solutions required for organizations to function perfectly under conditions of dynamic complexity, interconnection, and fundamental change.

SuperSyntegration can perhaps be compared to the smartphone, where a real revolution—both technological and social—occurred within a short period of time, just as it is now going to happen with management methods.

Whereas modern smartphones get handier all the time and offer more and more convenience features—including internet and e-mail access, camera, audio player, video functionality, etc.—some years ago you needed an extra device for each of these functions. You would have to deal with hosts of cables and plugs, carry around CD cases and DVDs, a laptop computer, and so forth. Very much old-world, yet also quite advanced compared to the analog technology before that.

The revolution of management systems and methods that is starting has similar dimensions.

The Right Time for the Great Transformation

In view of the challenges of the Great Transformation, our Syntegration approach, which is one of our greatest *methodological innovations*, has come at just the right time. This is no coincidence. After having perceived and diagnosed the imminent transformation, we developed and tested the approach with this new era in mind. In our consulting practice, together with our strategy experts, I had increasingly realized how difficult it was to answer complex strategic questions, and implement the resulting decisions, using the approaches then available (see my corresponding remarks in the Direttissima chapter).

With the Syntegration approach, a cybernetic high-performance tool, even the greatest and most complex challenges of the Great Transformation21 can be mastered with a degree of efficiency that had been considered utopian previously. One reason for that is that it involves the technology of *simultaneous problem-solving*: twelve sub-issues can simultaneously be addressed using up to ten cyber-tools, while maintaining the interconnected nature of organizational reality and even actively using it to enhance organizational intelligence.

For instance, strategy, structure and culture can simultaneously be taken account of, with all their inherent interconnectivity, within one single Syntegration process. This provides enormous advantages for top management, in terms of the quality and impact of their master control decisions.

In other words, the Syntegration process greatly enhances the power of top management. Moreover, organizations are energized and dynamized to a similar extent, so that Syntegration also initiates a new era which, for lack of a better term, I call the epoch of *New Leadership*. For an increasing number of entrepreneurs and CEOs, MSS has turned into a key tool to enhance their creative drive and leadership dynamics.

The Way to New Prosperity

As mentioned earlier, there is an increasing number of applications for Syntegration in public bodies. Syntegration is even more important there, as public organizations—which hardly have any money as it is—will have even greater burdens to bear once the crisis gets worse. There is no need for cities to degenerate, as experienced experts rightfully fear.

With the Syntegration approach, developments like these can be turned around. Communities in distress can be brought back to prosperity. Corresponding efforts can only succeed, however, if those involved in urban development stop clinging to conventional approaches. Solutions to urban and regional development issues can less frequently be found in more money, even if there was any; rather, as in the industrial sector, they must be sought at a higher level of operation. *Functioning twice as well—at half the cost.*

Particularly when the money is tight, we cannot leave the sick, elderly, and unemployed to their fates. On the contrary, we need to do even more for them in difficult times, to maintain a humane society and prevent radical movements. An organization's ability to function depends much less on the financial means than it does on the right knowledge and methods to cope with the complexity of today's society. Efforts that appear pointless with traditional approaches will become possible with Syntegration, as it replaces money with creativity and intelligence, with the active use of the key persons' combined knowledge, and with the creation of the necessary implementation energy.

Democracy is Reaching the Limits of Complexity

A functional state is a basic prerequisite for successful businesses. Consequently, companies will have the greatest interest in the reliable functioning of public institutions. Even if the state still had enough money or ways to borrow more, problems would still be far from solved. It is the very processes of conventional, democratic governance that are less and less suitable for coping with the complexity of today's society. As exemplary and functional as democracy may have been for many years, in today's world of interconnected, highly complex systems it increasingly reaches its limits even in smaller organizations, such as cities and municipalities.

Interest groups that keep placing obstacles in each other's way, idle coalitions, sluggish opinion-forming and decision-making processes, fragile consensus at the lowest level of possible compromise and an often ineffective implementation of measures are some of the common deficiencies even when there is no immediate financial pressure. This also increases the risk that the increasing paralysis of democratic processes will give rise to new demands for authoritarian approaches.

Chapter 3

The Cyber-Tools

In this chapter, I will explain the third element of the Syntegration: the cyber-tools. Let me start by reminding you of the three-part Syntegration architecture, consisting of

1. the syntegrative communication core process, in analogy to the processor of a computer,
2. the General Management Model, corresponding to the computer's operating system,
3. the cyber-tools, which are comparable to the application programs running on a computer.

I use the term "cyber-tools" when referring to the tools we use to resolve key issues in the course of a Syntegration process. While all of the tools can be applied individually, they have by far the strongest and quickest impact when used in the Syntegration context. Their combined and simultaneous application will soon become standard. At the end of a three-day Syntegration process there are results, which, outside the syntegrative process, would take months to reach, as the key people would have to be interviewed individually or in workshops. So the advantages of the combined application are enormous.

Figure 94: The Cyber-Tools

Some of these tools have been mentioned in previous chapters, such ast he Central Performance Controls (CPC) and the PIMS programs, as well as the bionic system analysis using logistic S-Curves.

Further tools include the Sensitivity Model (SensiMod), the Minimum Factor Focused Strategy (*Engpass-konzentrierte Strategie—EKS*), the Management System Audit (MSA)® and the Implementation Tools with our Real-Time Operations Room (RTO).

The Viable System Model (VSM)® will be the central subject of the fourth volume of this book series, which deals with the structures and processes of a company, in line with our General Management Model.

All of these tools are fully integrated. For instance, when working with the Sensitivity Models we regularly use the CPC and PIMS variables. Likewise, the tools are used in all subsystems of the Integrated Management System. We are yet to find truly powerful terms for this full integration of multidimensional high-performance tools into a condensed pack of tools which simultaneously generate all the necessary results in only three days..

SensiMod: The Sensitivity Model As the Organization's GPS

One of our most effective cybernetic tools both for strategy development and strategy control is the *Sensitivity Model (SensiMod)*.[53] It was pioneered by Prof. Dr. Frederic Vester, with whom I maintained a long cooperation. Today, his long-time team member, Dr. Gabriele Harrer, is heading the competence center "Sensitivity Modeling" at Malik Institute.

The Sensitivity Model (SensiMod) is a tool for the computer-based, wholistic recording and depiction of random parts of reality as interconnected systems, together with their inherent cybernetic control mechanisms.

---

53 Vester, Frederic: *The Art of Interconnected Thinking. Ideas and Tools For Tackling Complexity*, Stuttgart, 1999. Frederic Vester has left us an immense wealth of publications, ranging from his books to TV documentaries to his traveling exhibition "Our world—an interconnected system". It was one of the best sources of its time on complex systems and biocybernetics, and fascinated both the young and the old. For more details on his work, please visit www.malik-management.com.

In a Syntegration process, the Sensitivity Model has two key functions at two very different levels. On the one hand, we use the tool to model the business system at the factual level, where products, customers, competitors, prices, technologies are concerned. On the other hand, we use the tool to model implementation measures as a coherent, interconnected implementation system. I will explain the latter function at the end of this chapter, when I deal with the Operations Room.

Modeling the Company's Business as a Cybernetic System

To develop a successful strategy, a key prerequisite is the principle of real-time control. You have to be familiar with your current and target position at any time in order to be able to adequately control things. That, in turn, requires an overview of the whole system to be controlled. The possibility of knowing at all times where you stand, where you can go and how you will get there, are among the basic prerequisites of any right strategy.

As I have outlined at an earlier point, the associated control and steering tasks have long been solved in aviation and shipping, and are now accomplished just as naturally in automotive traffic, using a satellite-based high-tech navigation system, the GPS (Global Positioning System). Our Sensitivity Model performs the same service for corporate management that GPS does for a car.

Let me start by explaining some the Sensitivity Model itself and its simultaneous application in a Syntegration process.[54]

Discovering the Invisible Cybernetics of the System

Just as we cannot see natural forces, such as gravity, we are also unable to see cybernetic forces such as Control Circuits. Both forces can only be observed from the behavior of, and effects on, objects and variables.

In figure 95 on the left-hand side we see the relevant variables of a system and on the right-hand side the cybernetic interconnections, or control

---

54 The book as a medium involves some limitations here, as it only permits me to explain the static of systems. To learn about the dynamics, I refer the reader to our website www. malik-management.com.

circuits of these factors. What we see here is the model of an industrial corporation which specializes in control engineering on a global scale. People there were instantly intrigued by our approach, as they could see how, with our tools and ways of thinking, we were approaching the core of their own expertise. Management realized that we were applying their existing expertise on the company itself and its functionality, thus raising their own management system to a new and higher level of function, just as they had done before for their customers when they worked on control systems for machines, vehicles, and aircraft.

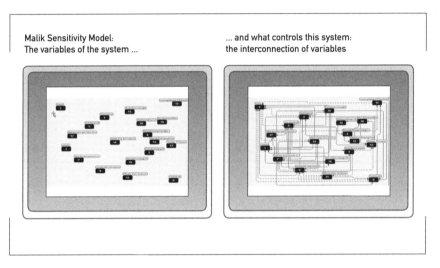

Malik Sensitivity Model:
The variables of the system ...

... and what controls this system:
the interconnection of variables

Figure 95: From a collection of influencing factors to a system

It is the invisible interconnections that turn a set of variables into a dynamic system. And since these are not simply random interconnections but regulating and influencing ones, we have modeled the "cybernetics of the system". Just as one might speak of the "physics of a body" or the "statics of a building", we speak of the "cybernetics of a system", referring to its self-regulating interrelations, which determine its functionality. In short, it is one of the purposes of our Sensitivity Model to make the invisible visible and tangible.

The "Spaghetti Model"

But what do we have to do to achieve such a model? We refer to the manual means required for that as "Spaghetti Model", and it is shown in figure 96. In the syntegrative core process, Syntegration participants automatically generate the information that is relevant for the subject at hand, which we record and map into the SensiMod process. Again, variables are depicted (manually, this time) on the left, and the network of interrelations on the right.

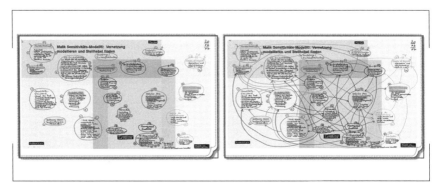

Figure 96: The "Spaghetti Model"

Using special, highly intuitive software, we perform an analysis of the control circuits driving the system, which are usually interlinked across the whole system. It is something almost comparable to the nervous system.

Through this analysis of system cybernetics, we identify the main levers for the direction of the system, namely the system's Master Controls. Note that interventions are always tested with regard to their indirect effects, by way of a simulation, before control measures are actually implemented.

Figure 97 shows a screenshot of the system with first analysis results regarding its control dynamics and control circuits.

The dynamics of the system are then depicted, as shown in figure 98, in the *Sensitivity Risk Map*. This helps to find out which variable will have what effect, i. e., whether a variable is active or passive, whether it acts as a buffer or has critical impact.

Humans lack several natural prerequisites for understanding and steering complex systems. For instance, the human brain can only grasp at any given time a small number of variables to steer its actions. More specifi-

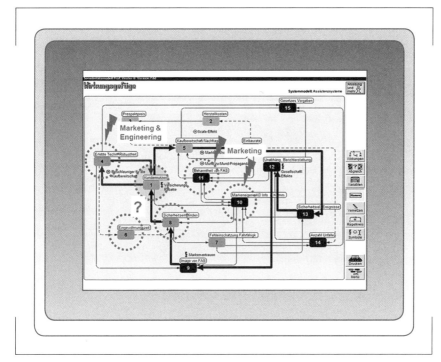

Figure 97: Master Controls and Control Circuits

cally, only seven plus/minus two variables can be observed independently of each other, and even fewer interconnections.[55]

This insight is used, for instance, in the design of aircraft cockpits. With extended training, specialists may be able to increase the number by three to five additional variables, but that is it. This goes to prove that life, based on biological systems, has so far only been able to master a limited extent of complexity and that, if complexity is to develop further, this can only happen in socio-cultural and socio-technical ways, by enhancing adaptation capabilities and intelligence.

So if we need to observe many more variables and their interconnections to really understand the system and be able to steer it, we need special tools—such as our Sensitivity Model. With these computer-based models, top managers now obtain just the kind of information they need

---

55 Miller, George A.: "The magical number seven, plus or minus two: Some limits on our capacity for processing information", *Psychological Review 63 (2)*, 1956, pp. 81—97.

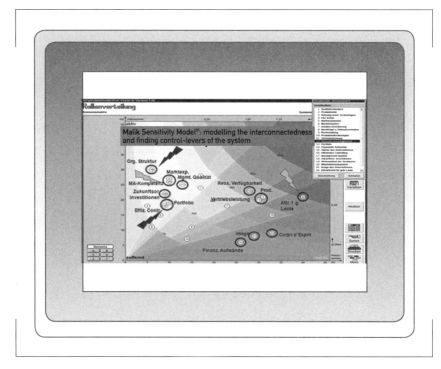

Figure 98: Map of effects and risks

to understand the system and its inherent functional laws, both for the organization as a whole and for individual operational units. With Sensitivity Models for each level of the organization, control intelligence can be implanted down to the capillaries of each business unit, thus reinforcing itself throughout the system to an extent that would be absolutely impossible without cybernetics.

Application of the CPC, Quantification With PIMS and S-Curves

Now there are two obvious next steps: integrating the Central Performance Controls—wherever applicable—into the SensiModels and using the insights gained from PIMS (as described in part IV) to quantify the variables of the SensiModel. The 25,000 data years compiled by PIMS, the PIMS research results and the PIMS models transform the Sensitivity Model into an enormously powerful tool. In addition, the trends of the Great Transformation require installing S-Curve diagnostics into the SensiModels.

The Inner Model of the Outside World

Next, we use the SensiMod to take a crucial further step in the control logic of organizations: we can also use it to implement the cybernetic concept of the *inner model of the outside world*. This is in line with another cybernetic law of control, according to which control of a system cannot be better than the model of the system itself. So, control quality and model quality are directly related. The corresponding theorem by Conant and Ashby goes like this: *Every good controller must be a model of the system*. The following graphs illustrate this basic principle and its real-life implementation with the help of SensiMod.

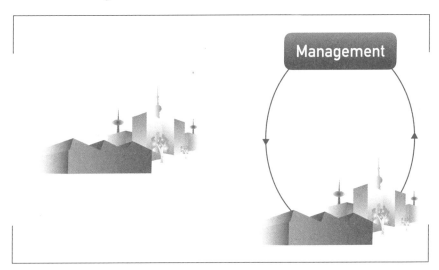

Figure 99: The naïve view of direct control

We are dealing with a reality (left-hand side) which has to be managed (right-hand side). That, however, is impossible without a model of the reality to be managed. Usually, in the absence of modern navigation tools, this "internal model" is limited to the experiences and imagination of CEOs and top management teams.

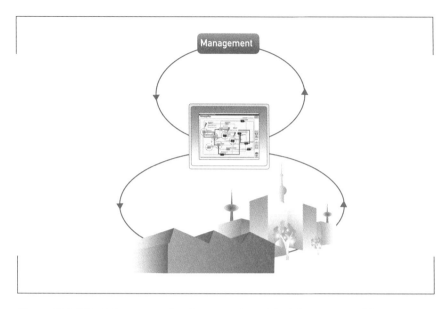

Figure 100: This is how it works: the internal model of the outer world

While these capabilities continue to be important for senior executives, they are now complemented and supported by a SensiMod specifically developed for control purposes, as shown in figure 100. This is the help our systems and tools provide: they enable executives to make optimal use of their capabilities.

This inner model of the outside world is not a static but a dynamic depiction; i.e., the continued changes in the outside world are fed into the model and—as we have come to know from the GPS system in a car—keeps showing us where we are and what our options are.at any given time. It is exactly the same with this application of the SensiMod in organizations.

EKS: Dynamic Specialization

Another cyber-tool to be used in strategy design is the *Minimum Factor-Focused Strategy* (or EKS, from its original German name *Engpass-*

konzentrierte Strategie[56]). It is also applied simultaneously with the Syntegration method. Contrary to its conventional, stand-alone application, which produces outstanding results in its own right, its impact is massively rein-forced by its simultaneous application in the syntegrative context, and the time required is reduced by up to 90 percent.

The EKS approach is the general *heuristic* by which the evolutionary strategy of specialization is transferred to the field of corporate strategy. Wherever it was rigorously applied, which was in tens of thousands of cases, it enabled the establishment of businesses that dominated their markets. It made numerous entrepreneurial dreams come true and helped to build and secure livelihoods. The EKS approach is therefore key to managing the Great Transformation, as the transition from the Old to the New World cannot be the exclusive responsibility of large corporations; rather, we are likely to experience a grass-roots revolution.

First off, what is a heuristic?

It is a searching, or rather: a finding principle. My book *Corporate Policy and Governance* included a chapter on the subject and here, too, the term is again of crucial importance, which I will explain in the chapter following the next.

While an *algorithm* is a program which—correctly applied—helps to *positively* find targets that are *known beforehand, a heuristic* is a program which helps find *unknown* targets with a high degree of *probability*—in particular *moving targets*, as are typical of times of major change.

In the case of the EKS approach, the unknown target is the *best possible specialization* for a business, enabling it to obtain an unassailable and *unique position* in the market. However, as markets permanently change, EKS is also—in line with the natural principle of evolution—a method of *dynamic* specialization[57], i.e., a specialization which keeps challenging itself and which, if applied correctly, will automatically adapt to changing conditions.

Although there were not many who shared my point of view, I realized as early as in 1970 that the cybernetic, self-regulating processes of natural evolution are of enormous significance for the control and management of companies. Shortly thereafter, I learned about Wolfgang Mewes and his

---

56 See related comments in the list of registered trademarks and copyright-protected names
57 Malik, Fredmund; Friedrich, Kerstin, and Seiwert, Lothar: *Das große 1×1 der Erfolgsstrategie. EKS®—Erfolg durch Spezialisierung.* 13th edition, complete revised and amended, Offenbach, 2009.

EKS concept, which intrigued me for precisely this reason. Forty years had to pass by, however, for me and Mewes to meet..

Thanks to the integration of the EKS concept into our cybernetic management systems, combined with our other cyber-tools, it can now unfold its full power for mastering complexity, just in time for the Great Transformation.

Wolfgang Mewes changed the name of the concept several times, to make it clearer what his innovation is capable of accomplishing and to be understood as a pioneer of new thinking in this field. He first named it *Evolutionskonforme Strategie ("Evolution-Compliant strategy"), then Energo-kybernetische Strategie ("Energo-Cybernetic strategy") and finally Engpasskonzentrierte Strategie ("Minimum-Factor Focused Strategy")*. This latter reflects the insight that forces are always applied best and most effectively by focusing on the minimum factor, i.e. the essential key strengths.

Evolutionary Specialization for Every Company

Allow me to spend a few words explaining the scientific background of my early interest in EKS. The phenomena of specialization are among the most exciting topics in evolutionary and behavioral research. *Konrad Lorenz*, the great pioneer of behavioral research and Nobel Prize winner, gives an impressive description of the principles of evolutionary specialization and its fantastic results in a variety of manifestations.

All forms of life are highly specialized, as a result of their strategies for mastering complexity and for maximizing energy efficiency—and the only exception seems to be the human being, who is an all-rounder. But even man is a specialist, according to Konrad Lorenz: a *specialist for non-specialization*—a specialist on a higher level. As a species, this enables humans to adapt to almost any type of circumstance. This, in turn, is one of the most powerful solutions of nature for mastering complexity, as it combines two overlapping ways of tackling complexity.

So, maximizing the ability to adapt through non-adaptation is the principle of evolutionary cybernetics which Mewes also discovered for corporate strategy, and which he made usable for all companies—even the smallest ones—by defining a brilliantly simple sequence of steps.

Then Rupert Riedl, Konrad Lorenz's disciple and colleague, created one of the most comprehensive collections of literary works on evolutionary theory, including his *Order in Living Organisms* and the generally more popular book *The Strategy of Evolution (Strategie der Evolution)*. Lorenz and Riedl's work had already influenced me when I started working on my PhD, and their findings, as well as those of other great exponents of evolutionary research, found their way into my professorial dissertation *Strategy of the Management of Complex Systems.* And so it happened that bionics experts started taking an interest in the subject. Prof. Dr. *Ingo Rechenberg,* one of the German pioneers of bionics, was able to prove that it is not only the outcomes of evolution which have been optimized but also the method that nature used to achieve these outcomes[58], which I also commented in my professoral thesis.

Adaptation and specialization are two of the basic principles and drivers of evolution in all its manifestations, from single-cell organisms to global society structures. Even further, they encompass everything from cosmological structures beyond social systems to the manifestations of informational and communicative structures and systems.

Specialization in business, and in society overall,

- conforms to evolution,
- eases competitive pressure
- enables peak performance,
- leads to better problem solutions,
- is easier to communicate,
- raises expectations with regard to competence, and
- expands the scope for action.

Frequent objections, according to which specialization also has its disadvantages, apply primarily where specialization turns into overspecialization and diminishes the ability to adapt. That is why EKS is about *dynamic* specialization. The advantages of *proper* specialization by far outweigh its disadvantages.

---

58 Malik, Fredmund: *Bionics. Fascination of Nature*, Deutsche Bundesstiftung Umwelt, 2007: Malik, Fredmund (Ed.): *1., 2. und 3. Internationaler Bionik-Kongress ["1st, 2nd, and 3rd International Bionics Congress"]*, Malik Management Zentrum St. Gallen, 2008, 2007, and 2006.

Successful Application Examples

Companies applying EKS include renowned market leaders such as Würth, Kärcher, Logitech and Kieser Training. Much of their entrepreneurial success is owed to the rigorous application of the EKS concept.

In his book *Hidden Champions*, Hermann Simon explained that, while there are many and greatly differing paths to entrepreneurial success, there is one strategy which successful companies apply with remarkable frequency: EKS.[59] Apart from the renowned names mentioned above, there are numerous small and medium-sized companies which have attained market leadership positions based on excellent, often highly creative achievements.

For instance, a simple painting and decorating business based in the federal state of Baden-Württemberg, the kind of which there are thousands in Germany, specialized in floor marking services for sports facilities and became the world market leader in its field. An ordinary bed-and-breakfast in the Bavarian Forest turned into a special, very successful hotel for handicapped people which is always booked to capacity. An optical store in the state of Hesse successfully specialized in sports eyewear. Another successful EKS practitioner in the Munich area teaches athletes the fine art of sprinting. It is not simply "training" they offer—as opposed to many others—but "sprint training" for athletes in all the sports where sprinting is key.

Now, for the transition from the Old to the New World in the context of the Great Transformation, the importance of EKS can hardly be overestimated, for it is one of the quickest ways to bring about another economic miracle—which will have to be based, above all, on major advances in the capillaries of our economic system: in small and medium-sized businesses. Perhaps even more importantly, EKS can enable individuals to specialize successfully, thus boosting their life skills. This will be one of the supreme forms of self-management. More on this subject can be found in the first volume of this series, Management. *The Essence of the Craft.*

---

59 "In the context of specialization and focus, we were able to find that the EKS approach has been applied surprisingly often. This is one of the few secrets we revealed about the 'Hidden Champions'." Hermann Simon *Hidden Champions. Lessons from 500 of the World's Best Unknown Companies*. New York, 1996.

EKS-Based Specialization: One Law of Nature, Four Principles, Seven Steps

Building on the fundamental ideas of biology and evolutionary theory, in particular the natural law of the most effective use of forces, Wolfgang Mewes developed EKS as an approach based on four principles and seven steps.

With brilliant simplicity, it leads to the most strikingly successful forms of specialization, often in niches which may be small but, precisely for that reason, are usually very profitable. These companies just need to be careful not to get carried away seeking growth for growth's sake.

But EKS is also applied in very large markets, Würth and Kärcher being cases in point. The key criterion is not large or small, but whether or not it is a *defendable specialization*. The more "pointed"—i. e., focused—a specialization is, the higher the probability that EKS will enable the company to gain market leadership and ultimately take a unique market position, a de-facto monopoly—based not on governmental protection but on its own superior performance.

The objective of EKS is to become or remain the best problem-solver for a certain target group.

The four *principles* of EKS are:

1. Concentrating one's resources and reinforcing one's strengths
2. Solving bottleneck situations
3. Delivering value rather than reaping profits
4. Non-material values taking precedence over material ones.

The seven methodological *steps* of EKS are:

1. Analyzing the status quo and specific strengths
2. Finding a promising specialty
3. Identifying a promising target group
4. Performing a bottleneck analysis
5. Developing a specialization-innovation strategy
6. Developing a specialization-cooperation strategy
7. Determining the constant basic need in order to secure long-term success

The similarities with the Strategy Map and PIMS principles are obvious, making EKS fit perfectly in our set of tools.

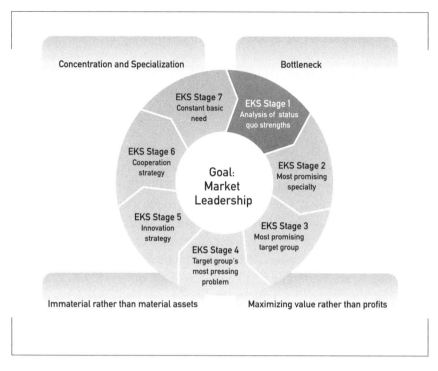

Figure 101: EKS—principles and methodological steps

Figure 101 shows the principles and steps of EKS.

The above-mentioned books by Friedrich, Malik and Seiwert contain further details on the methodology, in particular key checklists and questions, as well as numerous application examples.

The EKS Success Spiral Market Leadership and Unique Position

The rigorous and iterative application of EKS creates an evolutionary success spiral, as shown in figure 102.

It is set in motion by concentrating one's own resources and pursuing a dynamic specialization on certain target groups and market niches. The logic of this success spiral is both simple and compelling: Even the first steps in the focusing process will provide learning gains leading to increases in efficiency and productivity. This, in turn, will improve financial results and enable companies to further enhance their market performance, which will trigger more demand leading to sales and profit increases. At the same time, increasing market shares will expand the entrepreneurial scope of action and reduce economic and financial dependencies.

These *outcomes* of the EKS logic are not new; yet the logic and adherence to its principles and steps are either unknown to many people or not applied with sufficient rigor. It corresponds to a wish that probably most entrepreneurs and executives have: being provided with a magic formula for success.

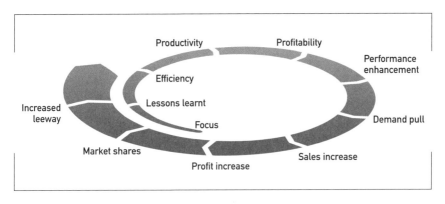

Figure 102: The EKS success spiral for market leadership and unique position

The EKS success spiral also comprises many of the strategy elements I have described in my chapters on the Navigation System, the Strategy Map, and PIMS.

Management System Audit (MSA): New Ways of Functioning and Implementing

The next simultaneous application of Syntegration with "time-lapse" effects is our *Management System Audit*. Years ago, we developed this cyber-tool for diagnosing the status quo of a company's management systems compared to the standard defined by our Integrated Management System (IMS®).

Using Traction Assistance to Produce the Right Results

Here I would like to remind you of the first chapter, where I explained how the IMS originated from the combination of the General Management Model and the Management Wheel and how it is the standard management system *for right and good management*, both of entire organizations and of single operative business units.

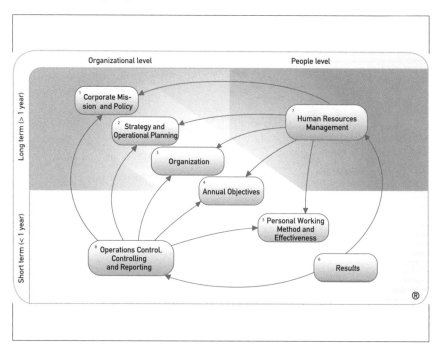

Figure 103: Integrated Management System IMS—overview

This is how the management systems work together to effectively transform purpose, mission, and strategy into results. In a sense, the IMS can be compared to the traction of a car, which brings horsepower on the road and converts it into performance. In modern cars, electronic driver assistants ensure optimal conversion. Based on the way it is built, the IMS corresponds to a high-performance SUV with all optional components, such as four-wheel drive, switchable reduction gearing, downhill control, and traction intelligence. That is why the IMS is suitable for use in any kind of organization. As a reminder, see a depiction of the IMS in figure 103.

In 2008, the Integrated Management System IMS was declared standard by the German organization TÜV[60]. It is now used as a basis for TÜV certification of the quality and reliable functionality of management systems in business organizations.

What the MSA Management System Audit Can Do

The MSA (Management System Audit) approach was created for the implementation of the IMS, which I had developed and published back in 1981[61] and which has become the standard theme of our management training. We have continued to refine and accelerate the implementation of the IMS at client organizations ever since.[62]

The purpose of the MSA is to systematically diagnose the status quo of an organization's management systems in order to determine the measures required for further development and systematic refinement of the IMS and then carry out a program for its implementation. It is important to us that we always base all improvements on the current state of the organization. Only very seldom is it necessary to start from scratch, as there are always some systems already in place. Otherwise, the organization would not exist.

What the Result Looks Like

Figure 104 shows a typical result of an MSA diagnosis performed after a Syntegration. What we see is the development stage of the management systems of a German bank: For compliance reasons it dealt very thoroughly with corporate policy and especially corporate governance (white fields), which is why it had reached a rather advanced stage there. By contrast, the

---

60 The German TÜV ("Technischer Überwachungsverein") is one of the world's largest technical service organizations to define and monitor safety standards, carry out inspections and issue certifications.

61 Malik, Fredmund: Malik, Fredmund, Management-Systeme, in the series "Die Orientierung", Nr. 78, ed. Schweiz. Volksbank, Berne, 1981.

62 Klauser, Marius: *Lenke, was dein Unternehmen lenkt: Management-Prozess-Architektur (MPA) als Quantensprung in der Unternehmens- und Mitarbeiterführung*, Frankfurt/New York 2010. Stöger, Roman: Prozessmanagement. Qualität, Produktivität, Konkurrenzfähigkeit, Stuttgart 2009.

system components colored light blue in the graph were moderately developed at best, and all the dark blue areas were clearly underdeveloped. For "business as usual," the light blue subsystems of the Integrated Management System were acceptable and generated satisfactory results, but they were far from adequate for coping with the turbulences of the years 2008 and 2009 and would have presented a substantial risk for the future management of the company.

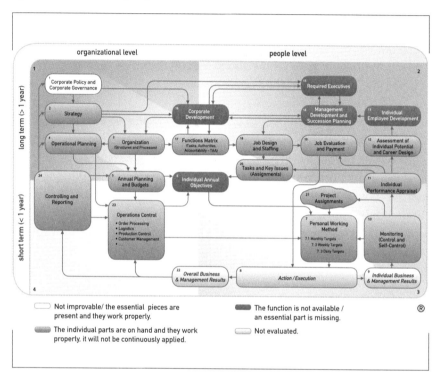

Figure 104: Example of an MSA result

It was particularly unfortunate that the company had fallen short of its personnel development responsibilities and that the management-by-objectives process did not work well enough to allow them to quickly respond to the difficult conditions presented by the acute financial crisis. The implementation of immediate measures through system components 6, 7, 10, 11, 20, and 21 was inadequate and caused a waste of time and money, which was particularly disastrous given the crisis situation. What was missing was a "four-wheel drive", so to speak, to be switched on for added power.

Now these shortcomings did not actually put the company at risk—but it was unable to seize a number of unique opportunities, including a potential acquisition, because it was not quick enough and lacked personnel reserves. By carrying out an improvement program precisely targeted at these neuralgic management system elements, a functional improvement of several areas could be initiated: the immediate introduction of the necessary tools and methods, combined with dedicated training measures, led to fast improvements.

Above all, it was the speedy training of staff in applying the new tools that ultimately turned around the situation and, at the same time, generated an enormous push for staff and executive development overall.

Much of the implementation power of these personnel and organizational development measures was due to the Syntegration process carried out shortly before, since this was what generated the joint insight by 40 top managers that something had to be done about the IMS areas mentioned above. Therefore the necessary readiness for change had already been established. It was no longer a question of If, but of How. The slightly revised MSA diagnosis, which was presented to the board just a few days after the Syntegration process, confirmed the consensus about the poor state of the bank's management systems, so that the measures suggested were easily accepted.

What would have taken several months with classical personnel and management development, considering the sheer size of the bank, could be accomplished within just a few days and immediately implemented, thanks to the simultaneous approach with the Syntegration method. The time compression factor was extremely valuable to the bank, especially in its crisis situation, both in terms of money and with regard to corporate culture and staff motivation.

Full Integration of Management Systems and Tools

Perhaps the reader's mind has wandered a few steps ahead at this point, since in the logic of my management thinking it is a natural next step to build the other cyber-tools and their results into the relevant IMS elements.

For instance, the SensiMod for modeling the business system would belong to the elements corporate policy and strategy. As you may remember, this SensiMod also includes the PIMS and CPC quantifications as preceding integration steps.

Further, it will be useful to develop a special sensitivity model for operative planning and control, to model the annual plan. Likewise, SensiMods are the ideal tool for operative control and for several levels of controlling. All of these models will also include CPCs.

The SensiMod is equally valuable for organizational and management development. Finally, every executive can set up his or her own SensiMod, enabling him/her to model and control his/her area of responsibility and ultimately to shape his/her career and life successfully.

Operations Room: Implementation With Real-Time Control

Creating the Best Conditions for Implementation

From the many positive effects of Syntegration, the following are particularly important for implementation:

1. Participants are able to determine the truly greatest challenge and the twelve sub-issues they consider crucial.
2. Through equitable cooperation, collective consensus is achieved at the level of the greatest common factor, not at the lowest level of the smallest acceptable compromise, as often happens with conventional methods.
3. All participants are able to contribute with all their knowledge, without limits and restraints.
4. For every sub-issue a jointly developed, well-defined catalog of measures becomes available, as opposed to vague declarations of intent.
5. There is a clear change of mood.
6. In addition, there is positive social energy and readiness to act by virtually everybody.

Even with these excellent conditions present, some of the "horsepower" might get lost in the days and weeks after the Syntegration process, since there are only a few companies which have the implementation management in place to ensure that all potential results of Syntegration are really accomplished. Ordinary project management, which most companies today master quite well, is not enough here. That is why we chose new approaches to implementation, in order to ensure that the revolution leading from the Old to the New World would go smoothly and become effective. To understand the Operations Room and its special function, it is necessary to be familiar with the way the Syntegration measures are specifically prepared for this purpose.

New Approaches to Implementation: Systemic Interconnectedness of Measures

The greatest challenges to conventional project management result from three specifics of the measures developed in Syntegration: while they are among the greatest advantages of Syntegration, they can easily be lost if they are forced into the straight-jacket of conventional project management.

1. Most of the resulting 40 to 60 measures have no organizational "home"—they are *cross-functional* measures. They do not fit in the usual organization chart boxes but belong in the organizational sphere beyond the assignment of responsibilities and competencies. That is why implementation is often particularly successful if primary responsibility is located at the top of the organization, which is only logical in view of the enormous significance of the key challenge.
2. The measures *themselves* form a system, for they are almost always interconnected to the extent that their implementation is mutually conditional. It is important, therefore, to be prepared from the start to make changes at *several* points *at the same time*, once you start initiating fundamental change at *one* point.
3. Quite possibly, the overall organization will respond to certain measures in an extreme way. As a result, things may temporarily get out of balance (or possibly even drift towards the negative side) if measures are implemented sequentially and in isolation and if actions undertaken do not take account of existing interdependencies. The effect would be comparable to that of an unbalanced diet, or an unbalanced exercise regimen for athletes.

Using Sensitivity Modeling to Create Systemic Balance

This is where the second function of the SensiMod comes into play—which is why we use sensitivity modeling not only, as shown before, to model the *factual* level of the business but also to model *implementation measures* and their *interdependencies*. The action packages developed in the individual sub-projects are assessed with regard to their *effect and control relevance*. As a result, not the single measures but the most effective *combinations* of measures developed through Syntegration are initiated and controlled in such a way that their dynamic balance is maintained in the process.

Figure 105 is a screenshot from a project carried out for a multinational group. Syntegration results were ultimately three times the targeted profit improvement, which had already been ambitious, and generated a four-digit ROI for the project investment. On the left-hand side of graph we can see the cybernetic cross-linkage model for the 20 key action packages generated. On the right we can see the risk map for these measure packages, making immediately clear which of the measures are *critical*, which are particularly active, which have a *buffer* effect and which are potentially *passive*.

Measures here included the restructuring of international sourcing, product line policy, price strategy, dealing with complexity, and special training measures for selected key people to eliminate bottlenecks, for

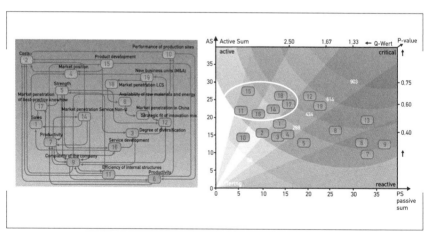

Figure 105: Sensitivity Model and Risk Map of measures for optimal implementation

which we managed to find good solutions thanks to the simultaneous application of EKS. The example shows quite nicely the simultaneous and synergetic impact of the different tools. The action steps within the active sphere of the system, marked by ellipses, were tightly interconnected and thus in the focus of implementation.

Implementation With Syntegration Roll-Out at Country Level

For some of the measures developed, it appeared advisable to have a simultaneous multiple roll-out of Syntegration approaches for individual organizations at national level. Figure 106 shows the road map for implementation with six further SuperSyntegration processes, one of them an abbreviated version—the so-called Octahedron Syntegration—at the level of the top management steering board. The other five full versions, were carried out at a national level and were linked to a Real-Time Control

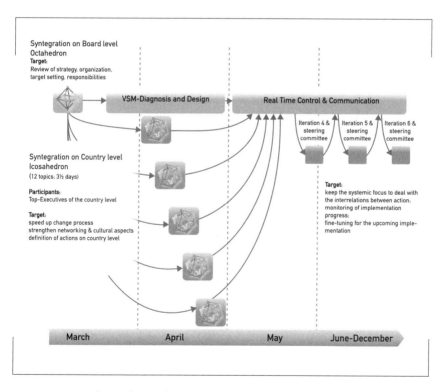

Figure 106: Road map for implementation

and Communication System (RTCCS) for which we developed our Operations Room solution, briefly described after this section. The details of the implementation road map are not that important for the purposes of this chapter. They will be the subject of the fourth volume of my book series, dealing with the structure and process questions of corporate management.

In the next chapter, however, I will describe the increase of implementation power that can be achieved by the multiplicative roll-out of Syntegration.

Real-Time Control From the Operations Room

For the effective steering of usually large and interconnected projects, one crucial element is still missing: a control center permitting an integrated, balanced and dynamic control of implementation while being constantly up-to-date with current financial results. To meet this requirement, we developed the *Operations Room*. It incorporates the *real-time control principle* for corporate management following the laws of nature. Without this principle, organizations would not be able to live or function reliably.[63]

The functioning of an Operations Room will be described in detail in volume 4, as mentioned above. At this point, my focus is on the purpose that a control center of this kind needs to fulfill in order to support the implementation of Syntegration results.

The Operations Room is a physical center where the current state of implementation of the entire system is visualized (with the aid of special IT intelligence) for top managers and in particular for the project's control committee. It provides the perfect *Decision Supporting Environment (DSE)*—an environment in which an interactive simulation of "If-Then" deliberations can be transformed into system-adequate decisions. All executive assistant systems are integrated and put into effect in one place.

This tool permits the steering of all implementation teams at all levels, as required by the given situation, and enters the relevant information directly into the interconnected model, thus providing preparation for the

---

63 Sebastian Hetzler developed the Operations Room during his many years of working for Malik Institute, in the context of a special project. He afterwards wrote his doctoral thesis on the subject at the St. Gallen University. A revised version was published as a book: Hetzler, Sebastian: *Real-Time-Control für das Meistern von Komplexität. Managing Change durch kontinuierlich richtiges Entscheiden*, Frankfurt/New York, 2010.

next decisions. The *State of the System* is present at all times. From here, the "State of the System" messages required for high-performance control are passed on with the appropriate level of confidentiality via the Company's Communication Systems to all relevant recipients, from the Board of Directors to the people responsible for implementation.

It is also the place where the so-called *closure* of the system, which is required for effective communication, is achieved by "Confirmation Messages". This is a cybernetic principle which is indispensable for high-performance functioning.

The Pearl Harbor disaster, during which Japanese aircraft attacked and almost completely destroyed the U.S. Pacific Fleet within a matter of minutes, was possible because these communication principles of system closure had neither been adhered to by the Pearl Harbor command nor controlled by the responsible operations center in San Francisco. It was not the Japanese fighter planes but the lack of feedback from their own system that ultimately destroyed the U.S. fleet, for the Japanese attack could have easily been held off in open waters by the US aircraft carriers.

The Japanese plan of attack was fully known to the Americans, as shortly before they had managed to crack the Japanese radio code, which constituted a success for cybernetic information theory. Like almost all major achievements by the cybernetics pioneers of that time, it had to be kept secret for a long time, as the corresponding research had almost ex-

Figure 107: One version of our Operations Room

clusively been conducted for the U.S. Armed Forces. Only in the late 1940s and afterwards, these groundbreaking insights became public and could also be used for civilian purposes.

The Pearl Harbor disaster caused the then Chief of Staff, General George C. Marshall, to initiate a rapid and complete reorganization of command and communication systems according to cybernetic principles, which was a main reason why the U.S. mission during the Second World War could be steered with utmost precision. Ultimately, the United States victory was owed not only to firepower and superiority in both human resources and materials, but to their cybernetic high-precision control intelligence. Today, the U.S. no longer manages to steer its—technically still by far superior—military machine. Its technical superiority is still there, but its cybernetic control intelligence is in disarray.

As shown in picture 107, files, and paper in general, are neither required nor desirable in the Operations Room. The environment is intended to *support thinking and decision-making*, rather than causing people to leaf through papers and notes. In any case, all information is captured directly in the executives' laptop computers.

It is a new dimension of steering complex, dynamically interconnected systems—one of the top challenges to CEOs and top teams which are increasingly gaining importance and will be key to survival when turbulences hit.

Today, almost anyone can picture real-time control based on his or her own experience (although usually with other applications). Now, GPS has even been incorporated in smartphones, and it is getting increasingly smaller, faster, more reliable and functioning at almost any place in the world. It has changed part of our way of living and revolutionized the way we used to solve problems. Previous applications have shown that this also takes management to a new, higher dimension of functioning, with yet unknown consequences for the way societies operate, and for people's lives.

Chapter 4

How Even Giants Learn to Dance: HyperSyntegration

This chapter illustrates the revolutionary change potential of the Syntegration. With these solutions, for the first time in history the size of an organization is no longer an obstacle. For the first time, even "elephant organizations" are able to move light-footedly, in the full knowledge that this light-footedness presupposes concentration and power. This is true for both business organizations and public institutions.

After this chapter, readers will understand why—based on my long-standing forecasts of economic disaster—I trust we can master imminent economic and societal disasters with new methods for the very first time in history, even turn them around into positive developments, and why, among other things, I speak of a New World.

Please allow me the following mind game: If you can syntegrate 40 individuals for finding intelligent solutions for complex challenges and at the same time mobilize their social energy, can this also be done with even more people? Why not with 80 or 100? Why not unleash 400 or even 4,000 people's intelligence and energy potential?

After several hundred successful applications of Syntegration this idea was in the air and challenged our creativity. Indeed, we did come up with solutions, which is how the *Multiple SuperSyntegration*® approach was developed for *exponential enhancement* of the power of management and change. We refer to this format as HyperSyntegration.

Even the workings of a single Syntegration stretch the imagination of most people, unless they have gained firsthand experience. It is even more difficult to imagine the impact that Syntegration can have when it is a rolled out across a truly large organization and allowed to unfold its enormous potential.

The "Mother"-SuperSyntegration: First Generation of Change

Figure 108 shows the performance parameters of a single Syntegration process and the icosahedron symbol. Let me remind you of the "magic SuperSyntegration formula": 1 key question, 12 sub-issues, 40 top executives, 60 ready-to-implement measures, 3,5 days. Add to this the completed SensiMod, EKS, VSM, and IMS®. In the lower half of the graph, we see the icon of integrated SuperSyntegration with its cyber tools.

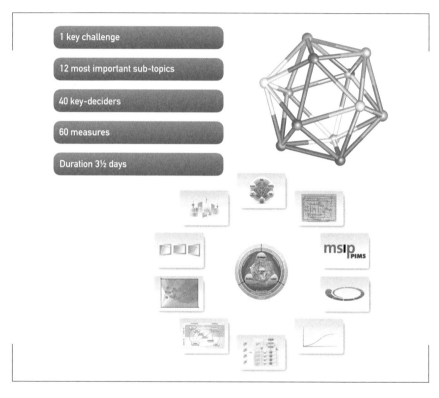

Figure 108: The "Mother"-MSS Malik SuperSyntegration

Parallel Applications for Larger Numbers of People

The first and most obvious expansion of the concept is the *simultaneous* execution of two or more mother-Syntegrations in parallel on the same organizational level, preferably at the same venue. This can be on the same key question or on different ones, according to the challenges individual Syntegration groups have to solve.

This works perfectly and has an enormous integration effect, for instance if a higher number of new top executives has to be familiarized with the company and with each other, as in a post-merger integration or in major restructuring efforts, when a number of people are faced with new tasks, new colleagues and new people reporting to them. Among others, a large, globalized logistics company used Syntegration to prepare for the Great Transformation.

From Syntegration to HyperSyntegration: Second Generation of Change

Just as there are parent and daughter companies, we can also speak of parent and daughter Syntegrations. There are even more powerful applications of Syntegration and I am refering to their multiplicative roll-outs.

These multiplications create a real powerhouse of change. To repeat this once again, the performance parameters are: 12 syntegrative core processes, 12 key questions derived from the Mother-Syntegration, resulting in 144 participants and a total of 480 people involved, creating 720 measures. All of that can basically be done within three days, because the Syntegration processes can be carried out simultaneously. Of course, it is always possible to stretch the overall process to seven or fourteen days if personnel constraints or scheduling conflicts require it. Even then it runs at the "speed of light" compared to any other, conventional change management approaches.

Power Process for Integrated Strategic Corporate Development
As mentioned before, the roll-out of the SuperSyntegration process can just as well be extended by *organizational units* instead of themes, which is even more frequently the case. With this version, instead of twelve issues you syntegrate basically *any* number of business corporate units, such as business divisions or country organizations, all within few days. Again, the corporate development power of the cyber-tools is taken to yet another, higher dimension.

Take, for example, twelve corporate divisions: this means that the cyber-tools are applied twelve times, so each division will get its very own application and results.

Figure 109: Simultaneous vertical and lateral MSS application

This offers unprecedented opportunities for integrated corporate development, as all corporate divisions are now able to implement, in a *coordinated* fashion ensuring group-wide *cohesion* and *compatibility*, their own individual but fully compatible *IMS management systems.* Also they can implement their coordinated *strategy concepts* as well as their *MG navigation systems* and *Strategy Maps*, introduce their individual *"nervous systems"* in line with the Viable System Model®, and conduct their own bionic *system diagnoses* using the specific S-Curves for their markets and technologies. Moreover, they can carry out their own PIMS applications and benchmarking, and pursue their individual, but strategically and methodically coordinated start-up strategies. They could also install their own Real-Time Operations Rooms, which communicates with the corporate and all other divisions' control centers, and finally set up their own *management education and development programs* that are coordinated and compatible with all other divisions.

The result is no less than a company-wide universe of shared language and shared knowledge and also control and regulation systems that are orchestrated, coordinated and coherent. A new reality of shared information and coordinated activity is created, comparable to an organism or even a whole social compound of organisms.

Moving Mass at the "Speed of Light"

Allow me to continue giving my phantasy free reign. What is the "mass" that can be moved in a coordinated manner with this change approach? If we assume that the minimum critical mass of executives required to get an organization to move is about 1 percent of the overall staff, and if we further assume we are dealing with 30 corporate divisions, then 1,200 individuals could be *simultaneously* syntegrated, which means that a corporation with a head count of 120,000 could be brought into a *coordinated change flow*.

The result would be 30 key issues for the overall group, addressed in 360 sub-issues, and 7,200 measure packages if you limit the number of measures to 20 per package. In addition, the social energy fields of 1,200 executives would be activated in the consensus mode. All of this can be accomplished within one week, if required. It will be more realistic, how-ever, to assume an overall duration of three to six weeks, which, in practical terms, is definitely close to the speed of light compared to conventional methods.

So, as I said at the outset, even the largest organizations worldwide will finally have the means to combine size and controllability, basically without limits. Strategic methodology without time or space limits—that was the subheading of Part VI of this book.

The mere existence of this socio-technological possibility leads to an entirely new definition of key issues and global strategies. Key issues such as world market leadership or world technological leadership will obtain a new dimension of significance, as multinational groups can now use their size as an asset. Free of the sluggishness of today's organizations and their conventional management systems, they can act at unprecedented speed, redefining the competitive logic on global markets. Quite obviously, this also means that the fastest will have unprecedented chances at gaining a unique position in several world markets at a time, and with maximum probability.

Equally obvious is the enormous significance of this methodological revolution for public organizations, which are often much larger than the largest businesses. For instance, the two major churches in Germany employ a total of 1.3 million people, plus several hundreds of thousands of volunteers which makes them the largest employers in Germany. The churches' and most other public organizations' need for reform is immense, and the only way to achieve it at the speed and breadth required is with new methods.

Knowing about the power of HyperSyntegration, we can also dream of non-bureaucratic administrative authorities, of harmonic collaboration among a dozen different ministries, and of functional coalition governments. And we may let our minds wander further to the EU and its 27 member states, as well as its sub-sub-sub-systems with their vertical and horizontal cross-linkages ...

The Universe of Exponential HyperSyntegration for Global Megachange

But there is even more to this approach. Let us cast a brief glance at figure 110. The principle is clear; everything else is mathematics and imagination. According to the same principle of reinforcement, we could now easily come close to the implementation of urgently needed global gover-

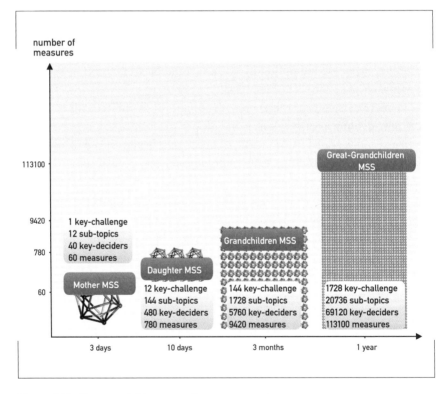

Figure 110: Exponential increase of management impact

nance organizations to effectively coordinate nation states without taking away their sovereignty, e.g. for an effective regulation of world financial systems, a reform of the UN and its numerous sub-organizations, and generally for new organizations ensuring a harmonic, peaceful and globally viable development of mankind. Organizations which came into existence more than half a century ago, and were at that time counted among the most important social innovations, today have to be reconsidered if they are not to become the greatest obstacles to continued progress.

I had asked you to allow me to let my imagination run free. Let me add, though, that those who know these solutions see immediately also the new ways to end crises quickly and even to use them as an impetus for progress into the New World. In the introduction to this volume on strategy, I said that I understood this to involve, among other things, the ethical mission to ensure the news about these innovative and highly effective solutions is spread. After all, these solutions help ensure that evolutions can occur quickly and without violence—thus bringing the much-needed liberation from 20th-century ways of thinking, obsolete management concepts, long outdated organization forms, and sluggish social problem-solving processes.

Appendix

Concept and Logic of the Series "Management: Mastering Complexity"

Management, in my definition, is the function of society which enables its organizations and systems to work properly and reliably. The responsibility for proper functioning lies with the executives in the organizations. With my management theory and my wholistic management systems, I have provided conceptual access to this function of society, as well as means to learn and teach it.

These are the components of my wholistic management systems:

a. The scientific theory of functioning,
b. The necessary models, tools, and other aids for its application in practice,
c. The systems-methodological approaches, processes and tools for practical application, and
d. The application formats, including education and enabling programs as well as consulting services for both organizations and individuals.

As such, the Malik Management Systems are systems of thinking, knowledge and action, reliably enabling executives to be effective in their profession at all levels of management.

The Malik Management Systems are universally valid. They work in any type of organization—in private-sector businesses and organizations in other sectors of society, at all levels of management, in all cultures, and in all settings.

The Whole and Its Parts

The six-volume book series entitled *Management: Mastering Complexity* has a modular and interlinked structure. It corresponds to the heart of my systems: the wholistic, systems-cybernetic *Malik General Management Model* as shown in the following graph.

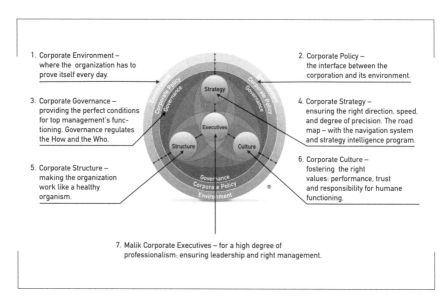

1. Corporate Environment – where the organization has to prove itself every day.

2. Corporate Policy – the interface between the corporation and its environment.

3. Corporate Governance – providing the perfect conditions for top management's functioning. Governance regulates the How and the Who.

4. Corporate Strategy – ensuring the right direction, speed, and degree of precision. The road map – with the navigation system and strategy intelligence program.

5. Corporate Structure – making the organization work like a healthy organism.

6. Corporate Culture – fostering the right values: performance, trust and responsibility for humane functioning.

7. Malik Corporate Executives – for a high degree of professionalism: ensuring leadership and right management.

Figure 111: The Malik General Management Model

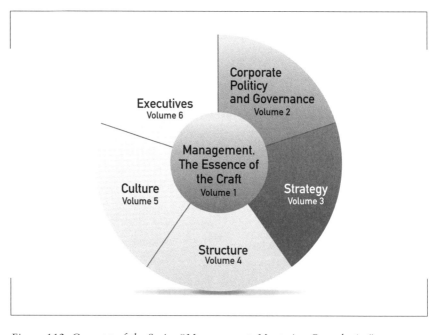

Figure 112: Concept of the Series "Management: Mastering Complexity"

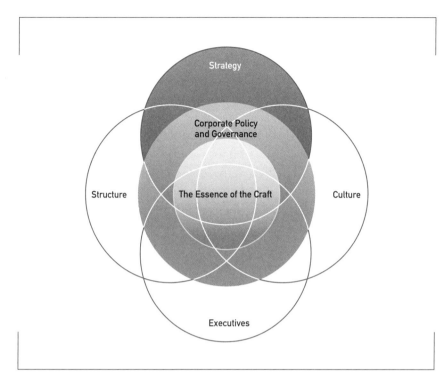

Figure 113: Systemic relationships among the six volumes of the book series

Figure 111 illustrates in a somewhat simplified form the concept of the book series. Its centerpiece is Volume 1: *Management. The Essence of the Craft.* Around it, we can see the remaining five volumes in their sequence of publication as currently planned.

Figure 112 shows the systemic relationships and interfaces between the topics of the individual volumes in detail. Together, the six volumes form an entity. Its parts are distinguishable, but together they describe an inseparably interconnected system for the effective general management of complex societal institutions.

The first volume, *Management. The Essence of the Craft,* describes the overall concept of the book series. Each sub-component is introduced in a chapter of that volume.

The remaining five volumes then describe each sub-system of the General Management System in detail. Volume 2 deals with *corporate policy and governance*, Volume 3 with strategy; Volume 4 focuses on structure; Volume 5 addresses culture and Volume 6 the subject of executives.

Each volume deals with one self-contained topic, always in the context of all other system components and thus linkable in any direction—just as you would expect in an interconnected system.

Each of the volumes can be read independently of the others, and in random succession. However, readers of an individual volume may find it useful to consult the basic volume *Management. The Essence of the Craft*, as this will enable them to put the individual subject matter in context.

A key concept for this series of books is my Basic Model of Right and Good Management, frequently referred to as "Management Wheel" due to its shape. The statements I make in that book are an essential prerequisite for correctly understanding the contents of the series *Management: Mastering Complexity*.

Scientific Foundations

Ultimately, all my books and scientific papers are based on *Strategy of the Management of Complexe Systems*[64], a significantly expanded version of my professorial thesis, which I submitted in 1978 to obtian the academic teaching license from St. Gallen University. I published a revised and amended version in 1984 as a book. It immediately met with considerable attention in the expert community and has become a classic on the topic of systems, currently in its 10th edition.

This book, in turn, is based on *Systemmethodik Teil 1 und Teil 2* "Systems Methodology Part 1 and Part 2",[65] the PhD thesis jointly written by Peter Gomez, Karl-Heinz Oeller, and myself. Both these publications are outcomes of two Swiss national research projects, financed by the Swiss National Science Foundation. They comprise the theoretical principles of cybernetics and system sciences, which represent the cornerstones of all my thinking with regard to management topics.

---

64 Malik, Fredmund: *Strategy for Managing Complex Systems. A Contribution to Management Cybernetics for Evolutionary Systems.* 2016. (first published in German in 1984).

65 Malik, Fredmund; Gomez, Peter; Oeller, Karl-Heinz, *Systemmethodik – Grundlagen einer Methodik zur Erforschung und Gestaltung komplexer soziotechnischer Systeme.* Bern, Stuttgart 1974.

When Language Reaches Its Limits

When you try to depict complex systems and the way they work, you will soon reach the limits of language, and often of conceptual comprehension. This also affects the contents and design of the volumes of this series. While complex systems are relatively quick and easy to demonstrate, and even easier to experience in certain aspects, they are almost impossible to describe. It is like trying to put a classical symphony in words.

The means of language, and hence also the book as a means of communication, are hardly suitable for describing, comprehending and communicating the complexity of interconnected systems. This is one reason why geographic and nautical maps were invented. With complex systems, the old maxim "easier said than done" is quickly reversed into "easier shown and done than said."

What are possibilities do we have, then, despite the limitations of language and books, to make complex systems half-way comprehensible and transparent? Three things are useful: Redundancy, graphical depictions, and browser technology.

Redundancy

One effective way to depict complex systems is by using linguistic redundancy. As the six volumes describe one system with numerous subsystems, repetitions are not only inevitable but intended.[66]

One reason why redundancy is inevitable is that the subject matters described are distinguishable but also inseparable, which is an important but seldom mentioned aspect of systemic thinking. They form an entity and must therefore be understood in terms of the interrelations between them.

Secondly, redundancy is intended because it is an indispensable tool to ensure certainty of communication and understanding. Thus, according to communication theory, redundancy is by no means superfluous but even essential. Not always are these two kinds of redundancy clearly distinguished. Functional redundancy facilitates readers' orientation and com-

---

66 Occasionally, critics find this to be objectionable. However, as I always specify the passages that expert readers are free to skip, I consider such criticism to be irrelevant.

prehension; so redundancy is not simply to be understood as repetition here, but as dealing with the same subject matters from different perspectives. This is necessary, among other things, because the interrelations between subsystems are mutual but usually not symmetrical. For instance, the relation between strategy and structure is not the same kind as between structure and strategy.

Illustrations

As I said before, descriptions and explanations of complex systems come up against the limits of what language is capable of. Language is linear, so it is basically unsuitable for describing non-linearity and simultaneity. Also, it is not complex enough to reflect the actual complexity of systems.

In order to describe the non-linearity and complexity of systems, and unless one wishes to resort to mathematics, the only device that the medium book has to offer besides textual redundancy is illustrations. But even illustrations are by no means sufficient when it comes to describing complex systems: first, because we only have a two-dimensional surface—the book page—for depicting multi-dimensional systems; second, because the illustrations in a book are static whereas systems are dynamic by nature.

For representing the systemically constitutive phenomena of complex systems, such as their being embedded, interlaced and dynamic, the medium book is basically outdated. More adequate means of depiction include hypertext, hyperlinks, and the entire browser technology which is making ever more rapid advances. In particular the topics of the second and third volume of the series require the use of system models and corresponding illustration to explain complex systems, for which the mentioned modern technologies would be suited much better.

Browser Technology

The dynamics of a cybernetic system are best explored in dialog-like interaction. To be able to overcome the limitations of the medium book, interested readers are advised to visit the website www.malik-management.

com. It allows you to explore the *Malik Management System*, understand how it works, and use it in practice. As such, the website offers the easiest possible access to the management of complex systems.

The Malik Management Systems
And Their Users

Terms Used and Identities

The official and probably clearest name for my overall system is *Malik Management System*. It corresponds with *Malik Institute*, the name of the organization I established in 1984, as a spin-off of St. Gallen University, for the purpose of developing, disseminating and using these management systems.

When you study and describe complex systems, initially you never know what the outcomes will be. Usually they emerge carrying working titles, and it often takes a while until the final name or brand is decided on.

The same is true of the names for my overall system and its subsystems. There are many names for them. Most of them are improvisations stemming from different phases of development, different projects, publications, training sessions, and programs. Examples include *Integrated Management System, Right and Good Management, Managerial Effectiveness, Effective Management, General Management Model, Standard Model, "Management Wheel", Malik Model, Malik on Management, and more.*

Experienced users are aware that the actual identity of systems is never determined by their designations but by the systems themselves, their contents and variations. Since the beginning, for reasons of diligence and credibility I have been trying to make these contents and variations transparent in my publications, as far as it was possible at all to render clear and manageable descriptions.

The Beginnings

The first development efforts concerning my management systems date back to the early 1970s. I was on two major national research programs, working closely with Prof. Dr. Hans Ulrich, the pioneer of Systems-Orientierted Management Theory at St. Gallen University. He was my academic mentor and head of research. With great foresight—almost vision—Ulrich established in St. Gallen what he called *systems-oriented management theory*: it was the first scientifically-based study course in general management at a German-speaking university.

For the practical application of his system-oriented management theory, Ulrich also developed the first-generation St. Gallen Management Model. The project received moral and financial support from the Society for the Promotion of Business-Economics Research at the Institute of Business Economics, University of St. Gallen, which Hans Ulrich presided. The project manager for the project "St. Gallen Management Model" was my collage and friend Prof. Dr. Walter Krieg. So, both national research projects mentioned were tightly linked together and focused on the same practical-methodological application.

Even before that time, I had familiarized myself with General Cybernetics and related fields. My diploma thesis had been dedicated to "Cybernetic Concepts and Management Models." Strong influences in the following years were my contacts with the great thinkers of the cybernetics of complex systems and my studies of the underlying philosophical principles. The former included the cyberneticists Heinz von Foerster, Gordon Pask, Stafford Beer, and Frederic Vester; the logician and mathematician Francesco Varela, the physicist and inventor of synergetics and laser technology, Hermann Haken, the philosopher Gotthardt Günther and the communication scientist Paul Watzlawick, as well as the evolution theoreticist Rupert Riedl and the strategy pioner Aloys Gälweiler, with whom I maintained a close collaboration.

A factor of my considerable impact was my early studying of the works of two epistemologists and philosophers on science, Karl Popper und Hans Albert, the economist of social thinker Friedrich von Hayek, the art historian Ernst Gombrich, and the physicist Cesare Marchetti, as well as my personal contacts with these and other scientists at the legendary Alpbach International College Weeks from the 1960s until well into the 1980s

I attach particular significance to my long-time professional friendship with Peter F. Drucker, dating back to the 1980s, which originated from a joint project (the turnaround of the nationalized industrial sector in Austria) and lasted until his death in 2005.

Development History

As explained above, the development efforts related to my management systems date back more than 40 years. Based on cybernetics and systems knowledge, the epochal change from the industrial era to the era of complexity was already visible back then. But it was equally obvious that the general awareness of complexity-driven problems and opportunities would be long in coming, due to the complexity in both society and the markets. So, securing the expensive independent research and development in my organization required plenty of staying power and has been a difficult balancing act over the years.

From the very beginning, we had to combine both: serving our clients to the best of our capabilities, and developing a general management system that was truly independent in terms of time, cultures, industries, and functional areas. On the one hand, this required addressing all those current tasks, questions and issues that were entering into public awareness at any given point. On the other hand, it has been and still is imperative to think and work ahead as far and as broadly as possible. Another key requirement has been for us to keep moving between several levels of language: that of our clients and that represented by the technical terminology of the complexity sciences.

Now the time has come also for the sophisticated cybernetic basics of the entire development, which emerged first and provided a key condition for the functioning of my management system, to be disseminated.

We now have the technical prerequisites for its practical application, provided by high-performance computer technology. Also, many practitioners today have gained sufficient experience with complexity to take an interest in systems-cybernetic solutions. Furthermore, an increasing number of people with sophisticated university degrees in natural sciences, information sciences and technical fields are arriving at the top management levels. More and more often it is possible simply to use the terminology of the complexity sciences, rather than having to take a detour via everyday language.

So, after several decades I finally have the confirmation that it was really important back then to pursue the daring strategy of fully dedicating myself to the challenges of management in the age of complexity.

Applications and Effects

The *Malik Management Systems* were designed for man's living circumstances in the hybrid systems world of the age of complexity. Systems like these for management and self-management have to be the new techniques of civilization and culture, which in this still-young world have additionally become necessary. Without them, existing and potential resources cannot be recognized, let alone translated into results. For results, we need those kinds of information and knowledge that I have organized as navigation systems, models, basic rules and principles, and tools.

Our world is complex and we are facing many highly complex challenges, but that does not mean the solutions to them have to be complicated as well. On the contrary, they can be rather simple, provided they have the potential to generate the complexity required. It is due to years of sustained efforts that the *Malik Management System* meets these requirements. Anyone will surely understand that there can be brief, clear, and simple kinds of information which nevertheless trigger precisely those kinds of actions in a system that are needed at the moment. One example is the fire siren: It triggers all the activities required to ensure safety, as everyone can hear it and everyone knows what the sound means and how to act.

Thanks to the modular structure of my management system, this requirement of relatively simple but highly effective information is met by the signal effect that can support and maintain a system, as well as configure, activate and vitalize it as needed.

The modules of the *Malik Management System* are designed for top effectiveness, efficiency, and viability, based on the forces of information-driven connections working inside them. As a result, there is an unlimited number of possible *combinations, configurations*, and *application*. Depending on the configuration and combination, it is a management system for entire organizations and their subsystems or for self-management of the individual, embedded in his or her respective environment.

Hence the *Malik Management System* offers a system-logical basis for any conceivable purpose, any size and kind of organization in any development phase, any work area and any order of magnitude. Capable of evolution and compatible with natural laws as well as with the workings of the human brain, it ensures that efforts are focused on what is essential and right. As such, my management systems are for complex institutions what the operating system is for a computer. More precisely: they represent an operating system capable of evolving further.

The Malik Management System grows with an organization or person. It also interacts with them. Both develop alongside each other in an evolutionary process, with the brain acting as the interface between them.

Autonomy for Management and Managers

Provided that certan rules are observed, any person or organization can use the *Malik Management Systems* as a basis to configure their *"Our/ My Own Management System"*, just as you can configure your computer hardware and software according to your personal requirements. This is a key requirement, as in the age of complexity managers are required to have a kind of intellectual autonomy, which they can only achieve and maintain (without losing too much time) if they take advantage of comprehensive general management systems that reach down to the capillaries of their organizations. These systems have to be valid across the organization, but also capable of being adapted to their individual needs.

Consequently, one of the key requirements for my management systems was to create a basis for management which would not be subject to a specific period, region, or even fashion, but simply meet the principles that are universally valid and permanent. Just as engineers create systems that follow the physical laws of nature, I built a set of systems that follow the natural laws of information, communication, systems, and complexity. Their key foundation is the science of cybernetics, which provides laws governing the nature of complex systems.

Hence the systemic structure of the *Malik Management System* is based on applied cybernetics, and the system as such is applied cybernetics. They follow the cybernetic principle, *Design a system so as to ensure that from the smallest possible number of modules you will derive the largest possible number of applications.* This principle guarantees autonomy for the user. It is up to the user to what extent he or she will capture such a system intellectually—irrespective of who has developed it.

Modularity and Interfaces

The *Malik Management Systems have a modular* structure. The modules are compatible with each other and with the user's world, so they can be freely combined. Their user interfaces or user templates are all the

- cybernetic *management models* that provide the necessary overview of crucial active elements and connections,
- *tools* to generate and apply the required information,
- *methods* used to solve one's tasks,
- *concepts* helping to reflect things, and
- *application rules* enabling any system to achieve top performance.

The Malik Management Systems can be used in a range of different ways: jointly, as individual models, formally adapted to individual needs, and in several languages. They are accessible through books, articles and essays, seminars, training programs, DVDs, CDs, MP3s, management e-learning courses, and—as far as reasonable and systemically validated—through digital tools and software.

Above all, however, the *Malik Management Systems* have to be a program for the brain: a good manager has to be able to realize and respond to current events faster than a computer can be fed with current data and generate solutions. Due to their evolutionary design, the modules can also be used in any combination or configuration of IT components that appears reasonable and useful. For the transfer of knowledge ad information, and of complex problem solutions from one brain to another, there are experts available in my organization whom I have personally trained.

Management Systems for Self-Thinkers

Anyone striving for organizational solutions that provide a maximum of effectiveness and efficiency is ultimately seeking to become superfluous. Correspondingly, the purpose of my management system is to ultimately make managers independent of management consultants. They certainly played an important role in the 20th century, in particular as the discipline of management had just emerged.

But in the 21ˢᵗ century and beyond, the world will need managers who are well aware that (and why) there can be no one-size-fits-all solutions in management, and why nobody can spare them from making their own observations and forming their own independent thoughts. From the very start they will have to master their profession expertly enough to know that in complex conditions, *asking the right questions* is at least as important as finding the answers.

The reason is that under complex circumstances, in many ways we cannot be sure as to whether our answers are actually right. This is precisely what the *Malik Management Systems* have been designed for: preventing control errors and undesirable developments from the very start.

Success Potential Increases with Qualification

One of the typical phenomena in the course of development of my management system was that for quite a while, only the simplest and most plausible-seeming modules were accepted well and even became standard, whereas the underlying cybernetic principles of function, which had existed much earlier and were much more sophisticated, have remained largely unknown to this date.

To take full advantage of the management system, however, it is important to know that its autonomy grows to the same extent that the user learns not only the simple things at the surface but also what is behind them. Everything required for that is available—the management system in everyday user language, the cybernetic models, and cybernetics itself. In particular the latter will help to solve individual management or object-related questions without any unnecessary workarounds.

Users ought to know, however, that applying even one single principle from the entire management system can have enormous systemic effects. Managers' own effectiveness, however, will multiply if they are able to combine all the relevant contents of the system quickly and correctly, all the more so when others can communicate and collaborate with them on that basis.

Self-Motivation for Self-Developers

Managers using the *Malik Management Systems*, in particular those developing their own solutions on this basis, need to know that we live in a time where you get more recognition for what others understand you to do than for what you actually do and accomplish.

In other words, the motivation to capture and treat systems in the way they need by nature will not come from the outside—you need to find it in yourself. Likewise, users and those concerned measure a system's performance and value by what they actually get out of it, not by what the system is actually capable of. By contrast, the developer cares most about the rationale behind his system, the truly demanding part, because he knows that this is what ultimately matters. As a result, good developers get more recognition for achievements they do not value so highly themselves, while those they are proud of are noticed much less, let alone acknowledged. But this should not be a reason to feel hurt or discouraged. Recognition will come from the system itself, because it only works when users let themselves be guided by its "needs", that is, its intrinsic laws.

Responsibility versus Recognition

It is the lot of responsible managers and experts in the age of complexity to have a difficult choice to make: should they do what is *right and good* or should they act so as to *be in great demand and popular with the masses?* Both are increasingly incompatible. This will continue until the knowledge and way of thinking in our society will have adequately adapted to the requirements of the age of complexity.

The true professionals and pioneers will face more problems than ever, created by self- or media-appointed gurus, dilettantes, and show-offs who are out for quick (but only short-term) success, by which they gain lots of attention—causing many negative developments along the way which will be difficult to correct. In the age of complexity, this kind of superficiality is becoming more than dangerous. This is why we need a solid professional basis for management, based on which true professionals are instantly recognizable as such. This is what I work for. This is what my management systems stands for, as does my claim to establish right and good management.

I therefore wish to give one last piece of advice to the self-thinkers and self-developers among my readers: While the maxim "easier said than done" is often true, it does not work for dealing with complex systems and cybernetics. As mentioned before, it is the other way round: easier done than said! It is much easier and, above all, much quicker to show and demonstrate what this is all about than to describe it.

Once you work with the *Malik Management Systems* you will realize that they enable you to resolve a sizeable number of great tasks quickly. But it will take a major effort to describe to others what you have developed, and do so correctly, comprehensively and in a way they will understand. In classical management practice this is not really an issue. But it does become one once you use my systems to develop your own, which you want to be a valuable and reliable help to others.

In the age of complexity, managers and experts will more than ever feel alone with their truly great achievements. They will get less recognition than ever, sometimes none at all. At the same time, they will have people admiring them for trivial things while ignoring their fundamental accomplishments. The much-deserved recognition they will get for their successful brainwork and system development will come from the systems themselves which, due to their solid foundations, can be shaped, steered and regulated in a highly professional manner.

Authors and Credits

To my knowledge, the Malik Management Systems at present are the only comprehensive, wholistic, integrative general management systems worldwide to be based on cybernetics and its regulating principles, explicitly aimed at tackling complexity, and specifically designed for the management of complex systems. What ultimately brought the Malik Management Systems to life were the long-standing, close cooperation and friendships with the best minds of management science, cybernetics / management cybernetics, and system sciences.

In my publications, I naturally refer to numerous authors and thought leaders of management theory, most notably Peter F. Drucker, Hans Ulrich,

Walter Krieg, my former colleagues at the Institute of Business Administration at St. Gallen university, Stafford Beer, and many more for other areas. My gratitude goes to all authors, customers, discussion partners and friends who have given me suggestions, inspirations and insights, and to my staff for their contributions.

What Readers Need to Know in Order to Understand this Book Series

With the book series *Management: Mastering Complexity* I am publicizing my management theory and my management systems for the age of complexity. In retrospect, historians will probably place the beginning of that era and the associated emergence of a new society in the early 21st century, knowing that epochal transformations can hardly be pinned to a fixed date.

It is a fact, though, that as early as in the late 1940s at the legendary Josiah Macy Conference a new science emerged in response to the issue of complexity: the science of cybernetics. The focus of interest for related research is complexity. With this book *Cybernetics and Management*, published in 1959, the British top manager Stafford Beer laid the groundwork for management cybernetics, since the core problem in management is complexity. We later became close cooperation partners. In 1968, my academic teacher and mentor at St. Gallen University, Prof. Hans Ulrich, took the decisive step when writing his *Systems-Oriented Management Theory*. Together with my friend and colleague Walter Krieg, he presented *the St. Gallen Management Model* in 1972. Hence, since my time as a university student my thinking has been challenged and influenced by thought-leaders far ahead of their time. I was privileged enough to work with them, to research and develop things with them, to experiment and discuss with them. My doctoral thesis deals with what can be translated as the Methodology for *the Research and Design of Complex Systems*, and the title of my 1978 professorial thesis translates as *Strategy for Managing Complex Systems*.

Against this historical and scientific background, the purpose of the series *Management: Mastering Complexity* is to enable the men and women of our new society to survey and take advantage of the products of what has been a rather quiet yet enormously fruitful development effort stretching over some 60 years. In this book series, the most essential things about complexity, management, and cybernetics are expressed in clear and comprehensible language. It is intended as a contribution for the viability of the new society, for the functioning of its institutions, and for the safe orientation of people in a world driven by complexity.

The change that the 21st century is bringing will be more dramatic than most people can imagine. The key conditions for fundamental restructuring processes are already being met. Seemingly paradox, its main cause is the enormous success that has been achieved worldwide by the Western-type management practiced so far. This conventional management practice has been so successful that it is no longer able to understand and control the systems it has generated because they have become too complex. The complex systems of the 21st century cannot be managed using 20th-century thinking—precisely because this is what generated them.

Success Programming Its Own Failure

Never ever has a period of success been here for good. It is inherent in every success that it will systematically overtake itself because it generates the conditions for its own failure. This is one of the many paradoxes of complex systems.

Only few people are capable of recognizing previous accomplishments as a cause of current problems. Only few are capable of understanding that new solutions are required because the previously successful methods, owing to their very success, tend to lose impact or even become counter-productive, and to further exacerbate the difficulties they bring with them.

Whenever difficulties arise in a period of success, most people try addressing them by doing "more of the same". This well-known, well-researched human behavior in complex situations is typical—and it is wrong.

When Thinking Fails to Grow With Practice

History shows us that periods like those keep demanding new ways of thinking, new methods and systems. Continuing on the same track was hardly ever possible; in most cases, radically new concepts were called for.

Today, we are facing the conditions for radical change *on a global scale*. Hence, the challenge of building a creating a new order—the nature of which cannot be predicted in advance—is presenting itself worldwide.

The two success methods of the West are *market* and *management*. Wherever they have been applied so far they caused the free market to unleash their forces, and at the same time the increasingly efficient use of all resources by management.

The impact of free markets continues to be maximized by the elimination of boundaries and of national regulation. The impact of management continues to be maximized by computers and MBA programs. Unless they are fundamentally changed, both of these success methods will hardly survive the conditions they have created. And while a synthesis of both methods can lead to a sweeping success, this very success will also set clear limits for itself, *or rather: its management*. For along with the synthesis of market and management, a process of gigantic complexification was launched, characterized by a progressive intertwining of an ever greater number of systems. This side effect takes the functionality of societies and their institutions to its limits. They become inefficient, and this threatens to overstrain society as a whole.

When entire systems keep getting less and less efficient, clear signals include

- More and more input being required to obtain less and less output
- former liberties leading to excesses, and
- previously decreased regulation returning as an exponentiated degree of bureaucracy.

In other words, the system gets under pressure from its own coercions. What used to be success turns into its opposite and becomes a liability, The overall systems of our society are getting increasingly instable because the market and management-focused success methods practiced so far now generate systemic risks and potential collapses. What used to be healthy growth is turning into cancerous tumors.

Problems Related to Success and System Laws

It is in the nature of problems resulting from success that they cannot be solved with the same methods that led to that success. It is also in their nature that the success methods in practice at any given point in time will turn into a problem and, over time, into the key problem. A main reason for that is that conventional success methods are based on the knowledge of the 20th, in part even the 19th century. This knowledge catered to a world where the key issues +to be dealt with were substance and force or, to put it another way, matter and energy. It was a world made up of simple systems. Those can be *complicated*—which is another seeming paradox—but they are not particularly *complex*.

The subject matter of the age of complexity is another one: as the name says, it is an unprecedented degree of complexity. That is the common denominator of today's societies and their institutions.

As different as commercial enterprises, hospitals, universities, and administrative agencies may be, what they all have in common is that they are complex, dynamic, non-linear, probabilistic, networked systems. Their respective environments—complex systems in themselves—form an interlinked and interwoven, dynamic, non-linear systems ecology. Healthcare, educational, and social systems, utility, energy, transportation, and logistic systems, the media and the information sector, information and communication systems, the global financial system, legal and tax systems—to mention just a few—form a network of complex systems which are essentially intransparent, and absolutely inscrutable to conventional reason.

Complex systems have their own laws, qualities, and behavioral patterns, which are fundamentally different from those of simple systems. Therefore, the management in and of complex system must have a very different focus compared to that of simple systems: it must focus on the natural laws inherent in each complex system. They are what enable us to correctly predict the mode and behavior of a system, at least in its fundamental direction, and influence it accordingly.

For most organizations, functioning in the highly complex systems ecology of the age of complexity requires a radical redesign of the way they are managed, as well as of their strategies, processes, and structures. However, society and its institutions are presently not equipped to comprehend the natural conditions created by rapidly growing complexity.

Old and New Sources of Knowledge and Insight

Many managers instinctively sense that they need new ways and approaches, but few are able to explain why. Their search for suitable solutions amounts to tedious experimentation and groping around, as they still lack the necessary theories, models, and concepts for dealing with the current dimensions of complexity.

Successfully mastering this extent of complexity requires fundamental reorientation, starting with the basic model of management. This fundamental change of direction is comparable to the Copernican transition from the geocentric to the heliocentric view of the universe. On the one hand, it requires radically new concepts of management; on the other hand, it is imperative to take into account the fundamentally new insights about information, systems, and their complexity.

The knowledge required for reorientation cannot be found where people have been looking for it. Neither will it spring from economics nor from the classical natural sciences. That is where the *old* solutions came from—those that are outdated by now. The insights about complex systems, which are going to be indispensable in the future, come from systems, bio-, and neuro-sciences, as well as from evolution theory. In designing man-made organizations and complex systems, we need to use biological systems as a reference because they are astonishingly viable and adaptable. We can and must learn from them.

Using Cybernetics to Understand the New Solutions

It is not enough, however, to simply draw analogies between organisms and organizations: organisms are organizations, but organizations are not organisms. So, insights from the bio- and neuro-sciences cannot (or can only rarely) be transferred directly to societal organizations.

The only place where we can find reliable help is where there are apparent common regularities in both biological and man-made systems. These have been researched and revealed in cyberneticy.

This is how great inventions such as computers and modern medical technology, regulation and control systems in cars and airplanes, modern security systems, and satellite navigation came about. In the entire field of technology, just as in other disciplines, cybernetics and its findings have long been taken advantage of. Wherever cybernetics is used there are demonstrable break-through achievements.

Cybernetics is the science of structuring, controlling, and regulating complex systems by means of information and communication. Its key insights include the laws of self-regulation, self-organization, and self-development—or evolution. Cybernetics is the science that provides the knowledge that is essential for the functioning of society and its institutions in today's complex world, knowledge that is indispensable for well-functioning management.

There is not much that has more significance for man in the age of complexity, who is distinguished from the man of previous ages by his fundamentally different knowledge, his ignorance, and the conditions in which he has to act and make decisions. This is precisely where the insights about the natural laws of cybernetics are enormously useful.

Two Leaps of Evolution

It is beyond doubt that cybernetics works well in technology. The management of complex organizations, however, comprises much more than technical applications. To achieve the same kind of breakthroughs in management as have been achieved in technology, using the insights from cybernetics, two evolutionary leaps will have to be accomplished at once:

- The first is applying cybernetics to much more complex systems than there are in technology: to living and social systems which, by comparison, can be referred to as *hypercomplex*.
- The second is applying cybernetics to the *results* achieved with the first step, or in other words, to system cybernetics *itself*.

Complex systems are generally inscrutable and incalculable. Owing to their complexity, they cannot be analyzed or understood in the classical-scientific sense, and thus cannot be organized or controlled in detail. For hypercomplex systems, as exist in an organized society, this is all the more true.

Cybernetics teaches us how to successfully deal with such systems, master their complexity, and even take advantage of them. This is difficult to imagine as long as you assume that man, and in particular a manager, has complete control over the functioning of systems. It only becomes plausible when you apply one of the most fundamental insights of cybernetics. It says that complex systems *self-organize*, and they do so in accordance with the natural regularities laws of cybernetics. Man has a choice between coming to terms with them or being dominated by them, as he is by any other force of nature.

Hence, the *second* evolutionary leap follows logically from the first: Since we basically cannot know enough to steer, regulate, organize and develop a system, we need to make sure it will do all these things by itself— and do so as intelligently as nature does.

Hence, cybernetic management is the application of cybernetics to management, and the decisive step towards a systematic use of all the "self-concepts" and "self-skills" (as I call them) provided by nature. It is the step from regulating to self-regulating, from organizing to self-organizing, from structuring to self-structuring, from coordinating to self-coordinating, from developing to self-developing—or, in other words, to evolution. It is in this context, and especially in the context of corporate policy, that I also use the term Master Controls.

New Success Levers: Taking Advantage of Complexity

Today's societies and their institutions are systems which keep restructuring themselves in unpredictable ways. They are systems of a particular type. They are characterized by the fact that they *are a result of human action but much more than, and different from, a result of human intent and purpose*, in that these systems are more complex than human being could ever plan and design them to be.

They generate themselves, and that is one of the main reasons why man will not achieve what he wants and expects by relying on conventional means, whereas based on the new insight he can enormously enhance his power and intelligence to achieve much greater goals. Heinz von Foerster has referred to this circumstance in a manner now legendary, when he used the metaphors of "trivial" and "non-trivial machines," and even done the math to go with it.

The two evolutionary leaps mentioned above, in response to the hyper-complexity of our self-originating systems and to the self-capabilities of systems, are comparable in their dimensions and consequences to the historic transition from the flat-earth to the round-earth theory. The practical impact of these evolutionary leaps are enormous.

Not only does cybernetic management take away the fear of complexity, as well its consequence: the need to reduce it. By applying cybernetics to management it also becomes possible to take advantage of the properties of complexity, as well as of its continuously self-generated, often ingenuously simple solutions which ensure that organizations and society as a whole will function better and more autonomously.

All major achievements and advancements result from the increase and better use of complexity, not its reduction, as is commonly suggested. For instance, Ancient Rome drew its superiority from the greater complexity of its traffic routes and from the expertise in orchestrating complex armies. The Gothic builders knew better than the Romanic ones how to deal with complexity. Global business is facilitated by the complexity of modern communication technology, which is exponentially higher than that of the 20th century.

Cybernetic management and the deliberate, systematic use of complexity also helps dissolve most of the contradictions and paradoxes that exist in traditional management thinking. Seemingly incompatible positions can effortlessly be reconciled by using this way of thinking. Systems managed and regulated by cybernetic principles can overcome the paradoxes of simplicity and complexity, freedom and order, variety and unity, decentralized and central structures, community and individuality, free economy and control of excesses, reason and intuition. Reductionist Either-Or thinking is replaced or supplemented by systemic As-Well-As thinking.

Right Management Is Cybernetic Management

Sixty years of research work on complexity and cybernetic phenomena are not that easy to summarize—and even less so when the aim is to present them convincingly to a large audience. One could almost say that only those who have experienced and done this can feel reasonably certain. With such certainty, and looking back onto my 40 years of research, 30 years as head of a business enterprise, and over 20 years as an entrepreneur, I can say this much: Cybernetics, and only cybernetics, shows what right and wrong management is under complex conditions. It shows us what kind of overall management system is required for complex institutions in complex environments in order for them to function, and what subsystems they need to have. It provides insight on what the components of such a management system should be—such as corporate policy, strategy, structure, and culture—and how they should be designed in order to enable an organization to cope with complexity. Cybernetic management shows us how, in the age of complexity, power and money need to be replaced by information and knowledge.

Understanding the regularities of complex systems is the key knowledge of the age of complexity. The key skill will be to use these insights from cybernetics in practice. Together they provide the fundamental prerequisite for managing and mastering complexity in a system-compliant manner. It is in the nature of both, the functionality of societal institutions and the viability of individuals.

Mastering and taking advantage of complexity is the purpose of my management systems. Only based on this purpose can my management models be studied, evaluated and applied correctly. Exactly where they differ from the management theories of the 20th century is described in the different volumes of the book series *Management: Mastering Complexity*. 21st-century managers do not need any other new qualities. They need different skills, another view of the world, different insights, and—based on those—another way of acting.

Glossary

Contrary to advanced, mature sciences and related professions, management has no uniform or common accepted parlance. Instead, there are arbitrary decisions, contradictions, and fashions. Even with regard to individual words such as strategy or organization, there is a lack of clarity and certainty all the way up to the top management bodies. This is a major obstacle to the advance of and learning on management, as it has created an almost unmanageable confusion of terms. I therefore decided to adopt a different approach in this book series.

To ensure some degree of continuity, throughout my six-volume series *Management: Mastering Complexity* I stick to the terminology entailed in the first-generation St. Gallen Management Model, which was created by professors Hans Ulrich and Walter Krieg and which represents the world's first wholistic, systems-oriented management model.[67] Over the years, however, I have greatly expanded that terminology.

In addition, I use the terms coined by Peter F. Drucker, the doyen of 20th-century management theory, wherever appropriate, also in an attempt at providing continuity. With regard to the terminology of cybernetics and system sciences, I use the terms used by Stafford Beer, the originator of management cybernetics, as guidance. In my book *Strategie des Managements komplexer Systeme "Strategy for Managing Complex Systems"* I have refined this system-cybernetic terminology.

*

---

67 When I use the term »St. Gallen Management Model« it refers exclusively to Ulrich Krieg's first-generation model. Later developments have little in common with the original St. Gallen Model, even if they carry the same name, thus suggesting continuity with the first model generation even where there was less and less of it. That is why I decided to go my own way in further developing the model.

Bionics Combination of the words "biology" and "technics." Refers to the interdisciplinary field of research which studies nature's evolutionary solutions to apply their principles for the benefit of humans. So far, bionic findings have mainly been used in the field of technology. However, nature's solution can also be applied to management, e.g. to improve the functioning of organizations.

Complexification Process of increasing complexity, as a result of the natural behavior of systems and their interaction.

Complexity Perhaps the most fundamental characteristic of reality, also referred to as *diversity*. Multiplicity results from possible differences and distinctions. Where these differences come from and what causes them is not that important for verifying complexity as such, but will be important when dealing with complexity in the sense of managing it.

The *consequences* of complexity are inscrutability, non-calculability, non-analyzability, unpredictability, permanent change, dependency on history, but also all the superior qualities found in biological and social systems, such as adaptability, ability to learn, flexibility, responsiveness, the ability to evolve, creativity, and identity. These consequences of complexity make management difficult; at the same time, if dealt with correctly they are what make it successful. The *measure* of complexity is *variety*. The term denominates the number of possible *distinguishable states* a system can have or develop based on its configuration.

Control When I use the term *control* in this book I refer to (self-) steering and (self-) regulation in a system, the purpose being to achieve the appropriate and thus desirable skills and behaviors of that system. Hence, *control* refers to conditions that exist or have been created to enable the mastering and using of complexity, the functioning of systems, and thus a strong resistance to errors. That means that *control* is much more than having a system under control. The system is much more than "under control": it is controlled and regulated in such a way that it will fulfill the intended purpose, eliminate or compensate possible disturbances, and be able to evolve further.

Control and Orientation Variables Terms used in the Malik-Gälweiler Navigation System (MG Navigator). Control variables are the parameters an organization needs to get under control; orientation variables are the pieces of information which indicate whether the organization is under control.

Controlling, Regulating, Steering Different forms of changing complex systems by using the kind of information that, according to cybernetic findings, enable complex systems to function.

Corporation, company, organization, institution Terms I generally use synonymously. Certain variances in meaning relate to the degree of generality, or the special limitation to a segment of society. The most general terms are "institution" and "organization". They refer to all organizations existing in a society, no matter what kind or legal form. The terms "company" and "corporation" essentially belong to the business sector. Whenever no specific hints are provided, it will be clear from the context what I am referring to when using each of these terms.

The terms most frequently used in this book are "organization" and some terms related to the corporate context, such as "corporate policies". The explanations provided will usually be applicable to all kinds of institutions. According to the field of usage, the terms might need some adaptation, such as "educational policy" or "health policy".

In addition to the meaning explained above, in the sense that "an institution is an organization", the term "organization" can also be used in the sense that "an institution has an organization" (or organization structure). It should be clear from the particular context which one of the two meanings it is.

Creative Destruction Term created by the Austrian economist Joseph Schumpeter. It refers to entrepreneurial innovativeness and the resulting large-scale substitution processes where the existing is replaced by the new.

Cyber Tools Methods and approaches to diagnose and shape the cybernetic functionality of organizations.

Cybernetic Management or Management Cybernetics Application of cybernetics to complex systems of society, that is, for the management of any kind of organizations. Management cybernetics is mastering complexity.

Cybernetics   Science of self-regulating, self-controlling and self-organizing complex and autodynamic systems. One of the key terms of cybernetics is the kind of "systemic control" resulting from the self-skills listed above. For his 1948 book *Cybernetics* by which he established modern cybernetcis, the mathematician Prof. Norbert Wiener chose as a subtitle, *Communication and Control in the Animal and the Machine*, thus implying that the same laws of nature applied to both the living and the non-living world. He thus established cybernetics as a cross-disciplinary science. Prof. Stafford Beer, the founder of management cybernetics, subsumed his works as "The Managerial Cybernetics of Organization."

Direttissima   Name I use for the—methodically—fastest way to the right strategy.

Functioning   Most general term I could find to describe the reliable and optimal working of an organization in line with its basic purpose.

General Management   Generic term describing those functions in shaping, steering and developing an organization that can be *generalized* because they are independent of the kind, size, line of business, and legal form of an institution. General management is the sum of all functions that an institution needs in order to function well. The antipole to general management is *special management*, a term that I occasionally use despite of its being rather uncommon. Special management refers, e.g., to the typical functional areas of traditional companies, such as production, marketing, finance, human resources, and the like. This cannot be generalized, though, because each type of institution has different tasks to fulfill and the functional areas common in business enterprises may not be appropriate in many cases.

Also, general management is *not* identical to top management Top management only refers to the general management at the *top* level of an organization; in addition, it also requires special management tasks to be performed. By contrast, general management is required at all levels of a complex organization wherever the same (generalizable) tasks and functions have to be fulfilled.

Great Transformation21   Profound and secular transformation of business and society into the 21st-century society of complexity. What exactly this transformation entails is described in my 1990 book entitled "Krisengefahren in der Weltwirtschaft" ("Risks of Crises in the Global Economy"), and ever since then on a regular basis in my monthly management letters. I explicitly use the term in my 1997 book on corporate governance entitled "Wirksame Unternehmensaufsicht" ("Effective Corporate Governance"), where I dedicated a chapter to the dimensions of the ongoing metamorphosis of business and society, which was already recognizable, and on that basis presented suggestions for right and good governance.

The term "Great Transformation" was first used in 1944 by the Hungaro-Austrian economic sociologist Karl Polanyi, in a similar sense but referring to a completely different era and to different manifestations, in particular the spread of market economics and the nation state. Also, Peter F. Drucker used the term "transformation" in the headline of the introduction to his 1993 book "Post Capitalist Society," where he sketches out, among other things, the great lines of development of capitalism to the knowledge society and from the nation state to the transnational mega-state.

By choosing this term, I am integrating some of its previous meanings to describe the generalized concept of a fundamental transformation process for the 21st century—a process characterized, among other things, by proliferating complexity, the emergency of globally interconnected systems and the dynamics of a self-accelerating change. As a result, we are facing historically new challenges. Mastering them will require radically innovative bionic forms of organization, cybernetic systems for management, governance and leadership, and social technologies of no less than revolutionary effectiveness.

Having or Being a System   Quite frequently, executives demonstrate an aversion to the term "system". Some associate the term with rigidity, schematism, and bureaucracy. The problem resolves itself when we distinguish between the meanings of "*having* systems" and "*being* a system". Any experienced manager will readily accept that companies need systems to function—on the other hand he or she will make sure these systems do not become too bureaucratic More and more managers also understand that organizations comprise many sub-systems that interact with each other, which makes them a system, and that they also from higher-order systems with their environment and its sub-systems.

HyperSyntegration Recursive multiple application of the SuperSyntegration method

Information The term *information* is not to be understood in its everyday meaning here. Instead it refers to the signals, data, and news that indicate differences which trigger further differences or cause changes. Above all, information includes decisions, distinctions, and new insights.

Information is the third basic element of nature besides matter and energy, which has to be considered in order to understand states and events in systems and in particular the way they function. In that sense, it was one of the most important and first discoveries in cybernetics.

Innovation Stage in which the new, by being introduced to the market, starts to become effective in society.

Institution Most general term to be used for all kinds of societal organizations, both in the private and the public sector, as well as for the systems and rules guiding social behavior. In this sense, a business enterprise is both an institution and an organization.

Integrated Management System (IMS) One of the three basic models in my management systems, along with the General Management Model (GMM) and the Managerial Effectiveness Model (MEM).

Invention Stage within the overall transformation process in which innovations are developed—from their first inception to their market launch.

Malik Gälweiler Navigation system/MG Navigator Complete and universally valid system for developing an effective strategy and reliably steering an organization.

Malik ManagementSystem Name (mostly used in plural) for the cybernetic, wholistic management systems I have developed, including all sub-systemes and management models, including as their logic, grafical depictions, and contents, as well as the procedures, methods and tools required for their application.

Management See editorial note preceding each volume of this series. I use the term "management" in three meanings: Firstly, it is a function that has to exist in any kind of organization to ensure that organization can function. This is the so-called functional dimension of management. It is neither linked to specific persons nor to organizational elements. This function is not immediately perceptible to the senses. It is incorporated in certain actions by humans, thereby taking its effects.

Secondly, the term "management" can be understood to be the sum of the legal and/or organizational bodies of an institution. Examples include the executive board of a private company, the executive committee of a public company, a national government, or a university's board of directors. This is the institutional dimension of management. It also includes an expanded board of managers, a group management, a management circle, or a partners conference. When it comes to mandatory and/or higher-level bodies, their responsibilities, rights, obligations, and accountabilities are governed by laws, by-laws, or statutes. Those of other organizational entities are determined by customs and habits.

Thirdly, management can also refer to the members of said management bodies. This is the personal dimension of management. In particular the terms "top management" and "top manager" frequently carry that meaning.

In German, I alternate the words "Führung" and "Management", as both mean the same. In all my publications, I use both these terms synonymously. By contrast, the terms "management" and "leadership" are not synonymous.

Management System Audit MSA Method used to reliably analyze my Integrated Management System (IMS) in an organization.

Master Control(s) Most fundamental regulations that are effective in an entire system, all the way to its peripheral elements, irrespective of their source—be it laws of nature, structural conditions, or man-made regulating decisions in the sense of principles or guidelines. The most important Master Controls are decisions and principles that bring about the cybernetic self-capabilites of a system, which are self-regulation, self-organization, self-direction, and self-control.

Minium-factor Focused Strategy (EKS—from the German term "Engpass-konzentrierte Strategie") Most reliable method to create a unique and unassailable position in the market. The strategy leads to a high-level yet adaptable and dynamic specialization.

Old World and New World Pair of terms relating to the fundamental secular change I refer to as "The Great Transformation21," in which the existing order is replaced by a new order.

Operational and Strategic Describe the levels of reliable navigation of an enterprise or organization

Operations Room Informational, sensory environment in which real-time decisions are made and implemented.

Organization (See Institution)

PIMS Look-Alike Term used in PIMS research to describe the similarity of businesses.

PIMS Par Term used in PIMS research, referring to the potential—as opposed to actual—output of corporate strategy.

Profit Impact of Market Strategy PIMS Largest empirical-quantitative strategic research program so far known worldwide in which the "Laws of the Marketplace" were discovered for both existing and new businesses, or start-ups (see Volume 3, Parts IV and V).

(R)Evolution Combination of "revolution" and "evolution"—a term I use to describe a) the ongoing, profound changes taking place in the course of the Great Transformation21 and b) the innovations in management, leadership, governance, as well as their rules, systems and tools, that are required to cope with these changes.

Right and Good Management Goal for the development, design and application of my management systems. The term refers to the functioning of organizations, the management professions, and the degree of professionalism ("lege artis") in managers' execution of the profession. Consequently, the same criteria also define the responsibility and ethics of managers. The sub-systems and elements, as well as the tools, methods and models have been selected using "right" and "good" as criteria. Opposite terms are "wrong" and "poor." Right and Good Management is independent of cultures.

S-Curves Describe the typical, S-shaped course of healthy growth processes.

Self-Organization In a cybernetic sense and as a management concept, is the ability of complex systems to function and fulfill their purpose without any need for external interventions. The purpose of each system can be system-internal or external. Self-organization depends on the structure of the system and on the information effective in that system.

An important distinction to be made is between the self-organization of complex systems in their entirety, and the self-organization of persons in the sense of personal working methods.

Sensitivitätsmodell (SensiMod) A system-cybernetic procedure used to model the cybernetic regulation loops in complex systems as well as their cause-effect relationships. Its early development was accomplished by Prof. Frederic Vester.

Society of organizations, organized society Society where almost everything people do is done in and through organizations. This one of the most significant yet often overlooked characteristics of modern-day societies. More than anything else, this characteristic determines how a society is structured and functions.

Solution-Invariant Customer Problem One of the key terms and the "Archimedian point" of corporate strategy. It refers to the motive for a purchase, irrespective of existing solutions. For instance, a wrist watch is one of several possible solutions to the solution-invariant problem of indicating the time.

Start-up Business Stage of a strategy where something new, having previously been invented and developed, is about to be marketed. The start-up phase marks the beginning of the actual innovation, which must always be defined based on market success and which requires a very specific strategy.

Strategy   Includes doing the right things, even when we do not know what the future will bring, as well as the necessary rules. Strategy determines the path of development for an institution. The right strategy lays out the principles and guidelines that will guide an organization's activities in the long run. These principles and guidelines are changed as newly arising circumstances require.

Substitution   Replacing something that exists with something new (see "Creative Destruction"). Examples include the replacement of analog photography by digital imaging, of terrestrial by mobile telephony, or of manual labor by machines.

Sustainability   Refers to the attempt to determine time horizons for thoughts, decisions and actions.

Syntegration   High-performance social methodology which helps to master complex challenges and problems by simultaneously using the knowledge of a large number of people. The Syntegration methodology comprises a self-coordinating cybernetic communication proves and the synchronous application of cyber-tools. The registered trademark is Malik SuperSyntegration.

System   Coherent entity consisting of different parts connected by mechanical, energetic, or information links, with characteristics and functions that differ from those of its individual parts. Systems are never only objects, organizations, or organisms in themselves, but always in *conjunction* with the relevant environment.

System, Model, Concept   A *system* is the section of the world that is, or should be, interesting to us from the perspective of a certain purpose and the functionality defined by that purpose.

A *model* is the depiction or image of what we know about the configuration of systems—including the blank spots of our ignorance, the "white spaces on the map".

A *concept* is what we want to observe and do based on the model of a system.

Systemics, Content, Form   Three *dimensions* are important in my management theory: Systemics, content, and form The first two are constitutive, the third can be varied.

Systemics refers to the logical structure or architecture of a management system or management model. Their systemics must be the structural logic of a functioning system, and thus of a cybernetic system, because the cybernetics of a system defines its function and vice versa.

When the systemics are right, it depends on the *content whether management is right*. Terms are not identical to their contents. A mere congruence of terms does not necessarily mean that contents are identical as well.

The *form* in the sense of graphic depiction can be varied, as long as this will not change the systemics or logic.

System Methodology   Set of methods and technologies for investigating, designing, steering, and developing complex socio-technical and productive systems. In a national research project supported by the Swiss National Fund, system methodology was first developed by Peter Gomez, Fredmund Malik, and Karl-Heinz Oeller. See *Systemmethodik.. Grundlagen einer Methodik zur Erforschung und Gestaltung komplexer soziotechnischer Systeme*. Berne: Paul Haupt, 1975

Terms   Refers to the usual differentiation by short-, mid- and long-term. Defining management dimensions in this way, however, is misleading and therefore extremely risky. Instead, the correct distinction is between "operative" and "strategic." That is the only way to arrive at the right timing, never the other way round. There are long-term decisions which are largely operative and short-term decisions that have an enormous strategic impact.

Time Constants and Dead Time   Key terms within the Malik-Gälweiler Navigation System. They refer to the time elapsing between the point when the need for action is first identified and the point when strategic measures become effective, specifically generating new profit potential.

Top management   Refers to three things: organs, persons, and functions of the company's top level. Their definition can differ in detail, depending on the relevant legal system and the company's internal rules and regulations. As has been mentioned before, top management is not identical to general management Theoretically, the opposite term would be "bottom management", possibly also "layer management" if it refers to different levels between the bottom and the top—in any case, terms that are not in common use.

The meaning of other terms not explained here should be obvious from the context.

Universally valid   Right and good management is universal, invariant, and independent of culture.

Termin protected by trademark and copyright

This work including all of its parts is protected by copyright.
All mentioned modules, expressions, models, illustrations etc. are also subject to copyright protection.

Any exploitation, use or application etc. outside the narrow limits of copyright law without prior written consent of the publisher and/or the author is inadmissible.

This applies in particular also to any duplication, dissemination, reproduction, translation, microfilming, storage and processing in electronic systems, as well as for any form of commercial distribution. Registered trademarks of Malik are:

Ecopolocy®
Engpasskonzentrierte Strategie® (EKS®)
Ganzheitliche ManagementSysteme®
Integriertes ManagementSystem® (IMS)
Malik Führungsrad®
Malik Gälweiler Navigationssystem® (MG Navigator®)
Malik General Management Modell® (GMM)
Malik HyperSyntegration®
Malik Management®
Malik ManagementSystem®
Malik Sensitivitätsmodell®
Malik StrategyMap®
Malik SuperSyntegration® (MSS®)
Malik Syntegration®
Malik Viable System Model® (VSM®)
Management System Audit® (MSA®)
Managerial Effectiveness Modell® (MEM®)
MSIP-Malik Strategy Intelligence Programs®
PIMS® Profit Impact of Market Strategies
Real Time Operations Room® (RTO®)
Total Immersion Exploration® (TIEx®)

About the Author

Like hardly anyone else, Fredmund Malik has succeeded in establishing professional management in both scientific theory and practical application. His understanding of management as a key societal function, a concept largely unaffected by the zeitgeist over several decades, has been and still is influencing generations of managers. Malik is a pioneer of breakthrough management systems whose capabilities revolutionize the functioning of organizations in business and society as a whole.

After graduating from high school and working in the industrial sector for several years, Malik studied economics and social sciences, with a focus on corporate management, as well as economic philosophy and logic at the universities of Innsbruck, Austria, and St. Gallen, Switzerland.

In the course of his involvement in two research projects for the Swiss National Funds for Fundamental Research, Malik in 1975 obtained his doctorate *summa cum laude* a St. Gallen University (the title of his thesis translates *as System methodology—Basic principles of a method for studying and shaping complex socio-technical systems)*, and in 1978 received his professorship *("Strategy for Managing Complex Systems")*. He was awarded with the academic Venia Legendi for corporate management. From the 1960s until well into the 1980s, Malik maintained an intense exchange with the pioneers of epistemology, natural and social sciences at the legendary Alpbach International College Weeks (now "European Forum Alpbach") as well as regular contacts with leading representatives of the international scientific community, politics, business, and culture.

Malik held his academic teaching assignments at St. Gallen University from 1974 to 2004, where he was a member to the Board of Directors at the Business Economics Institute from 1974 to 2004. He also was a visiting lecturer at the Universities of Innsbruck (1981 to 1982) and Vienna, Austria (1992 to 1997). As early as in 1977—at the time of his teaching assignment in St. Gallen—, Malik was appointed Director of the Management Centre St. Gallen. The Centre was established as a bridge organization linking science to practice, its purpose being to develop and disseminate the St. Gallen Management Model and System-Oriented Management Theory. Malik himself made substantial contributions to this breakthrough management theory, and in 1984 transformed the foundation into an independent enterprise focusing on practical application. Ever since then, Malik has headed the Centre as a Chairman and CEO. It is now a leading knowledge institution in the field of systems-cybernetic management systems, with offices in Zurich, Vienna, Berlin, London, Toronto, Beijing, and Shanghai.

As a member and/or chairman of various supervisory, foundation, and administrative boards, Malik has profound expertise in the practice of corporate governance, as well as more than 40 years of experience in the global financial markets. It is due to this experience that he was able to realize years ago that the world was heading toward a major financial and debt crisis. It was in the early 1990s that he described in his publications the developments that have meanwhile taken place. He was the first to realize that the main causes of the crisis had to be sought in Anglo-Saxon Neoliberalism, and that the related business education with its one-dimensional shareholder value thinking and its predominantly financial management priorities would lead to the historically unprecedented misallocation of economic and social resources from the real economy to the financial sector.

As a consequence of these insights, he developed innovative management tools, first and foremost the revolutionary Syntegration method for mastering mega-change in large systems. Based on the modern complexity sciences, Malik was the first to develop a theory for the systems-cybernetic functioning of organizations, comprising both socially responsible leadership and effective governance. His wholistic management systems, derived from that theory for practical application, enable entire organizations to function reliably and at the same time ensure the effectiveness of the people working in these organizations.

An best-selling author who has won numerous awards, Malik is one of the most distinguished thought leaders in management today. His book *Managing, Performing, Living* was rated one of the 100 best business books of all times. Peter F. Drucker, the doyen of management, says about Malik: *"Fredmund Malik has become the leading analyst of, and expert on, management in Europe … and a powerful force in shaping it as a consultant. He is a commanding figure—in theory as well as in the practice of management."* The US magazine *Business Week* called Malik *"one of the most influential business thinkers in Europe."*

Fredmund Malik lives in St. Gallen, Switzerland. He is married and has two grown-up children. His interests are philosophy and history, in particular economic history and the history of science, as well as music and art. His sporting passion is alpinism, which he practices at the highest levels of difficulty.

Selected affiliations

- Swiss Management Association
- Austrian Society for General Systems Research and Cybernetics
- Deutsche Gesellschaft für Kybernetik e.V. German Society of Cybernetics
- American Society of Cybernetics

- Europäische Akademie der Wissenschaften und Künste European Academy of the Sciences and Arts
- Schweizerische Gesellschaft für Statistik und Volkswirtschaft Swiss Society for Statistics and Economy
- Vereinigung Schweizerischer Betriebswirtschafter Association of Swiss Business Economists
- Gesellschaft für Wirtschafts- und Sozialkybernetik Society for Economic and Social Cybernetics
- Verband der Hochschullehrer für Betriebswirtschaft e.V. Association of Business Economics Lecturers

Selected awards

- 2011 "Special Professor of System Cybernetic Management" at the Beijing Capital University of Economics and Business, China, and the Inner Mongolian University of Agriculture
- 2010 Heinz von Foerster Award for organizational cybernetics from the German Cybernetics Society
- 2009 Honorary Cross of the Republic of Austria for Sciences and Arts, for the development of his wholistic management systems.
- 1984 Honorary Consul of the Republic of Austria
- 1975 Doctorate (Dr. oec) *summa cum laude* at St. Gallen University
- Amititia Award for best doctoral theses of the academic year 1974/75

Malik Management Zentrum St. Gallen AG
Geltenwilenstr. 16
CH-9001 St. Gallen
Switzerland
info@malik-mzsg.ch

Bibliography

Ashby, W. Ross: *An Introduction to Cybernetics*, London, 1956.

Bavelas, Alex: *Communication Patterns in Problem Solving Groups*, 1952.

Beer, Stafford: *Beyond Dispute. The Invention of Team Syntegrity*, Chichester, 1994.

Beer, Stafford: Brain of the Firm. *The Managerial Cybernetics of Organization*, Chichester 1994, first published in 1972.

– *Platform for Change*, London 1975.

– *The Heart of Enterprise*, London, 1979, first published in 1979.

Bresch, Carsten: *Zwischenstufe Leben—Evolution ohne Ziel?*, Munich, 1977.

Buzzell, Robert D./Gale, Bradley T.: The PIMS Principles. Linking Strategy to Performance, London 1987.

Casti, John L.: *Mood Matters. From Rising Skirt Lengths to the Collapse of World Powers*, New York, 2010.

Ceccarelli, Piercarlo/Ferri, Andrea/Martelli, Carlo: *La crescita sostenibile nei mer cati maturi* ['*Sustainable Growth in Mature Markets*'], Milan, 2008.

Ceccarelli, Piercarlo/Roberts, Keith: *I Nuovi Principi PIMS*, Milan, 2002.

Chussil, Mark/Roberts, Keith: "The meaning and value of customer value" in: *Malik Online Blatt*, 2008.

Dörner, Dietrich: *The Logic of Failure. Recognizing and Avoiding Error in Complex Situations*. New York, 1989, 1997.

Drucker, Peter: *Managing for Results*, Oxford 1999.

Drucker, Peter F.: *Post-capitalist society*, New York 1993

Farschtschian, Pedram: *Private Equity für die Herausforderungen der neuen Zeit. Strategische Innovation für das Funktionieren von Private Equity im 21. Jahrhundert*, Frankfurt/New York. 2010.

Frankl, Viktor: *Man's Search for Meaning*, Washington, 1984.

Gale, Bradley T.: *Managing Customer Value*, London, 1994.

Gälweiler, Aloys: *Strategische Unternehmensführung*. Edited by Markus Schwaniger, 3rd edition, Frankfurt, 2005, first published in 1987.

Hetzler, Sebastian: *Real-Time-Control für das Meistern von Komplexität. Managing Change durch kontinuierlich richtiges Entscheiden*, Frankfurt/New York, 2010.

Klauser, Marius: *Lenke, was dein Unternehmen lenkt. Management-Prozess-Architektur (MPA) als Quantensprung in der Unternehmens- und Mitarbeiterführung*, Frankfurt/New York, 2010.

Klingaman, William: *Der Crash. Chronik und Psychogramm einer Epoche, die im Börsenkrach von 1929 zusammenbrach*, Bern 1990.

Krieg, Walter/Galler, Klaus/Stadelmann, Peter (eds.): *Right and good management. vom System zur Praxis*, Bern/Stuttgart/Vienna, 2005.

Malik, Constantin: *Ahead of Change. How Crowd Psychology and Cybernetics Transform the Way We Govern*, Frankfurt/New York, 2010.

Malik, Fredmund (Ed.): *Bionik im Management*, 3tf International Bionics Congress, DVD, Malik Management Centre St. Gallen, 2008.

– *Der Quantensprung im Top-Management, 1. Internationaler Bionik Kongress*, DVD, Malik Management Zentrum St. Gallen 2006.

– *Die neue Corporate Governance* DVD; Malik Management Centre St. Gallen, 2002.

– *Die richtige Corporate Governance*. Mit wirksamer Unternehmensaufsicht Komplexität meistern, revised and amended new new edition of Die Neue Corporate Governance, Frankfurt/New York 2008.

– *Faszination Bionik:* Die Intelligenz der Schöpfung, Malik Management Centre St. Gallen, 2006.

– »Konservatismus und effektives Management. Wege aus der Orientierungskrise«, in: Peter F. Drucker, Peter Paschek (eds.): *Kardinaltugenden effektiver Führung*, Frankfurt am Main 2004.

– *Managing, Performing, Living*. Effective Management for a New Era, Frankfurt/New York, 2006.

– *Management. The Essence of the Craft*. (Volume 1 of the series "Management: Mastering Complexity", revised and amended new edition, Frankfurt, 2005.

– *Management-Systeme*, in the series "Die Orientierung", Nr. 78, Schweiz. Volksbank, Bern (ed.), 1981.

– *Strategie der Evolution*, 2nd International Bionics Congress, DVD, Malik Management Centra St. Gallen, 2007.

– *Strategy for Managing Complex Systems*, revised and considerably amended habilitation treatise, published in the series "Unternehmung und Unternehmensführung" of the Institute of Business Administration at the University of St. Gallen, Frankfurt/New York 2016, published in 1984.

Malik, Fredmund; Friedrich, Kerstin, and Seiwert, Lothar: *Das große 1×1 der Erfolgsstrategie*; EKS®—*Erfolg durch Spezialisierung*, 13th completely revised and amended new edition, Offenbach, 2009.

Malik, Fredmund/Gomez, Peter/Oeller, Karl-Heinz: *Systemmethodik—Grundlagen einer Methodik zur Erforschung und Gestaltung komplexer, soziotechnischer Systeme*, 2 volumes, Bern/Stuttgart, 1974.

Marchetti, Cesare: *Pervasive long waves: is human society cyc lotymic?* Prepared for the Conference "Offensiv zu Arbeitsplätzen", Cologne: Weltmärkte 2010, September 14–15, 1996.

Mensch, Gerhard: *Das technologische Patt*, Frankfurt, 1977. "Society as a Learning System—Discovery, Invention and Innovation Cycles Revisited", in: *Technological Forecasting and Social Change*, Vol. 18, 1980.

Mieg, Harald A./Töpfer, Klaus (eds.), *Institutional and social Innovation for sustainable urban Development*, London 2013.

Miller, George A.: "The magical number seven, plus or minus two: Some limits on our capacity for processing information", in: *Psychological Review* 63 (2): 81—97, 1956.

Nakicenovic, Nebojsa: *Transportation and Energy Systems in the United States*, Laxenburg (Austria), 1986.

Pelzmann, Linda: "Collective Panic", Malik Letter (02/03).

– "The Triumph of Mass Manufactured Will—Circumstances and Rules", *M.o.M, Malik Management®* 11/2002.

Polanyi, Karl, The Great Transformation, New York 1944

Powers, William T.: *Behavior. The Control of Perception*, Chicago 1973.

Prechter, Robert R. Jr.: *Socionomics. The Science of History and Social Prediction*, Gainesville, 2003.

– *The Wave Principle of Human Social Behaviour and the New Science of Socionomics*, Gainesville, 1999.

Roberts, Keith: "Evidence on start up businesses: take off requires full throttle", in: *Malik Online Blatt*, 2007.

– "Getting the right business metrics", in: *Malik Online Blatt*, 2008. "Good benchmarking versus bad benchmarking", in: *Malik Online Blatt*, 2010.

– "Hard working capital?" In: *Malik Online Blatt*, 2008.

– "Nine basic findings on business strategy" in: *Malik Online Blatt*, 2009.

Roberts, Keith/Ceccarelli, Piercarlo: *I Nuovi Principi PIMS*, Mailand, 2002.

Roberts, Keith/Chussil, Mark: *The meaning and value of customer value*, Malik Online Blatt 2008.

Simon, Hermann: *Hidden Champions. Lessons from 500 of the World's Best Unknown Companies.* New York, 1996.

Stöger, Roman: *Prozessmanagement: Qualität, Produktivität, Konkurrenzfähigkeit*, Stuttgart, 2009.

Vester, Frederic: *The Art of Interconnected Thinking. Tools and Concepts for a New Approach to Tackling Complexity*, Munich, 2007.

von Hayek, Friedrich: "Degrees of Explanation", in: *Studies in Philosophy, Politics and Economics*, Chicago 1967.

Index

Strengths 26, 69 f., 78, 100, 102 f., 131, 163, 185, 204, 320, 323
Structural configuration 181 f., 198
Substitution 26, 30, 34, 70, 118, 137–139, 140, 150, 223, 233, 238, 375, 382
– dynamics 149 f., 151, 156, 307
– effect 139, 151
– time curve 159, 160
Sunk cost 260
SuperSyntegration see Malik SuperSyntegration (MSS)
Supervisory board 56, 62, 80
Supply chain 186, 193, 199
Sustainability/sustainable profit 34, 58, 114 f., 134, 138, 142, 162, 382
Systemics 383, 8 f.

Target group 161, 226, 323 f.
Tautologies 72,
Total Immersion Exploration (TIEx) 307
Traction
– assistance 326
– systems 50
Transparency 68
Treasury 125

Ulrich, Hans 355, 362, 364, 373
Unhealthy growth 164 f.
Unique position 163, 180, 307, 319, 324 f., 341
Upturn 239, 243, 246

U.S. share prices 52
User problem 147, 150, 152, 226 f., 262

Value, sources of 103
Value
– added 167, 178 f., 181, 187 f., 193 f., 197
– creation 48, 95 f., 113
Varela, Francesco 355
Venetian method 123
Vertical integration 187 f.
Vester, Frederic 33, 79, 116, 288, 311, 355, 381
Viability 29, 59, 108, 138, 141, 187, 226. 306, 357, 365, 372
Viable System Model (VSM) 290 f., 307, 311, 333, 338, 340
Vision 72, 177

Waste disposal 275
Watson, Thomas 64
Wholistic Management Systems 10, 28 f., 54, 77, 114, 295, 305, 347, 378, 388

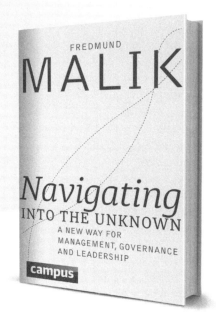

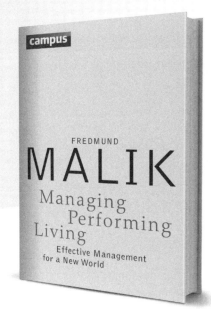